IMAGES
of America

INDIANA TOWNSHIP

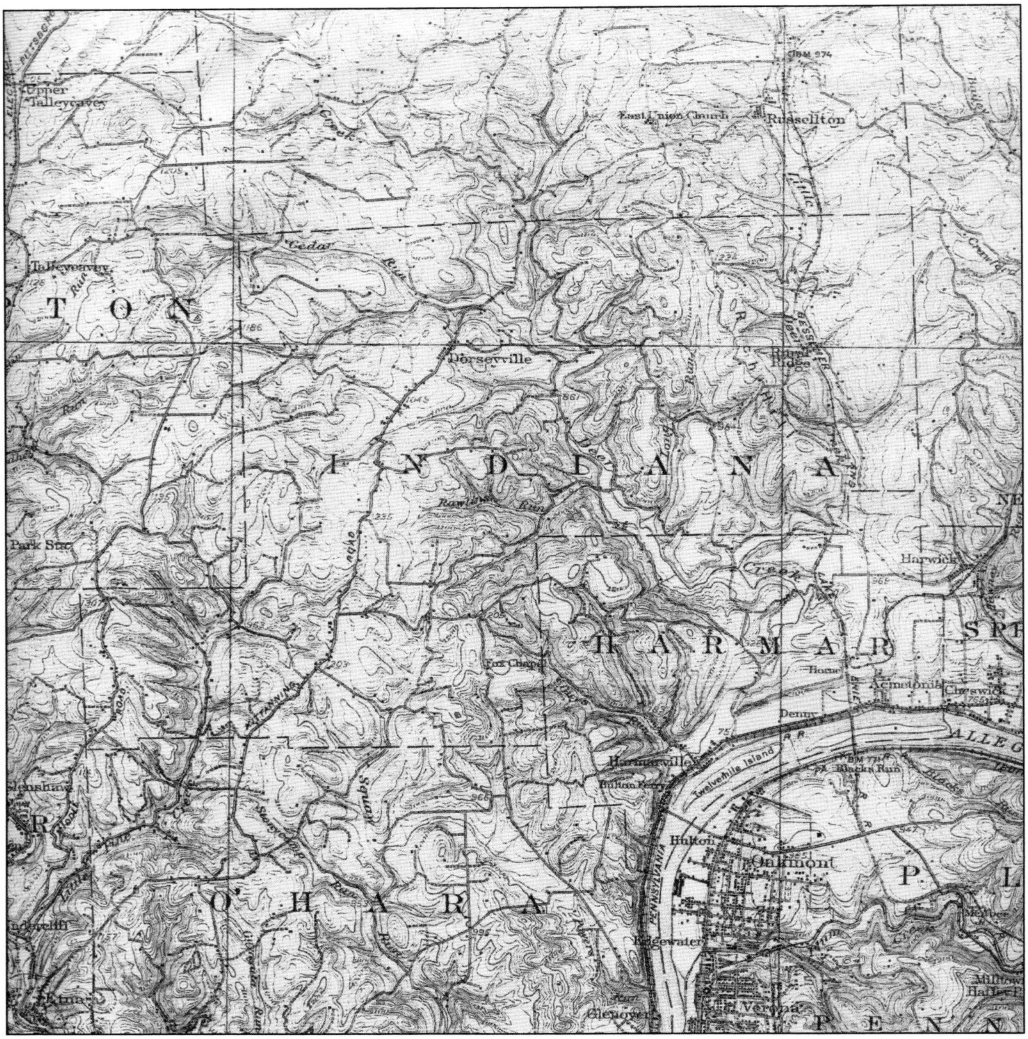

This is a topographic map of Indiana Township and the surrounding areas. Its scale is 1:62,500, and its contour interval is 20 feet. The hills and valleys covering the central and eastern portions of Indiana Township are clearly visible. This landscape made it somewhat difficult to travel from one end to the other in the early days of the township. (Courtesy of the US Department of the Interior.)

On the Cover: The caption written on the back of this photograph simply states, "Janet and Roy at the Saw Mill. Fosters." Some people think the Roy may be Roy Miersch; the little girl next to him may be his sister. The background gives a good picture of Indiana Township's landscape and what pioneers faced when settling the area. (Courtesy of Dorothy Preston Bauer via John F. Bauer III.)

IMAGES
of America

INDIANA TOWNSHIP

Erica Alderdice Birkner
Foreword by Joseph Stephenson

ARCADIA
PUBLISHING

ISBN 978-0-7385-9254-1

Published by Arcadia Publishing
Charleston, South Carolina

Printed in the United States of America

Library of Congress Control Number: 2011945125

For all general information, please contact Arcadia Publishing:
Telephone 843-853-2070
Fax 843-853-0044
E-mail sales@arcadiapublishing.com
For customer service and orders:
Toll-Free 1-888-313-2665

Visit us on the Internet at www.arcadiapublishing.com

To the people of Indiana Township—without their generosity and effort in bringing forth photographs and stories, this book would not have been possible.

Contents

FOREWORD

My name is Joseph. I was born in Dorseyville in 1942 and am the fourth generation to occupy the house in Dorseyville that was built by my great-grandfather in the 1870s. My great-grandfather, William McIntyre, was born in Scotland and was taken to Northern Ireland as a small child when the entire McIntyre clan was transported from their homelands. At the age of 19, William immigrated to America, passing through old Allegheny en route to the gold fields in the West as a farrier. He remained in California through the end of the Civil War, making his way back east to Old Allegheny City in 1869. He married his childhood sweetheart and moved to Dorseyville, where he built a large blacksmith shop with space in the back for his partner to build farm wagons to serve the vast farming community surrounding the village of Dorseyville. He then built a two-story house with a detached two-story summer kitchen. On the nearly two acres of property behind his business and home, he grew all the fruits and vegetables used in his home. I was the first male heir born from William McIntyre. One of William's ancestors was Duncan McIntyre, who composed 90 percent of the music played on bagpipes to this day. My second son is a bagpiper, too, and can play most of the music composed by Duncan so long ago.

I consider myself a historian and have two degrees in architecture, two minor degrees in history, and two minor degrees in literature, all from the Carnegie Institute of Technology. The day after I received my master's degrees, the school ceased to exist, but the buildings still remain. I received my high school diploma from Aspinwall High School, which ceased to exist the following day. I received my elementary school diploma from Dorseyville Elementary School, which also ceased to exist the following day. Do you see a pattern in this record? I did not pursue any doctorate degrees.

I am chairman of the Indiana Township Historic Commission. There are six of us appointed to the commission by the supervisors. All of us have had a lot of fun composing this book and hope you enjoy it as you go through it.

—Joseph Stephenson
Local historian
Fourth-generation Dorseyville resident

ACKNOWLEDGMENTS

Since the inception of the Indiana Township Historic Commission in 1986, many projects have been thought up and carried out. It is indeed a daunting task to keep track of all of the changes and brainstorming projects that will keep the community interested and involved with their 206-year-old township. The people of the commission and dozens upon dozens of dedicated residents of the township have contributed many hours, stories, and photographs to help document these changes and keep people involved with the history of their beloved township. Unless otherwise noted, all images appearing in this book came from the historic commission's files.

I wish to thank my editors at Arcadia Publishing. The Indiana Township Historic Commission is a very small organization with little to no budget, and we did as much as we could as fast as we could. Erin Vosgien contacted our commission about this project and supplied us with much of the start-up material. Darcy Mahan took over for Erin and answered many questions for me and was very kind and helpful. Abby Henry was equally as helpful and pleasant to work with.

I also need to thank Tawnya Panizzi, staff writer at the *Herald*; her taking an interest in this project and running stories in the paper were instrumental in getting the word out to people about this book. Along these lines, I need to thank Dan Anderson (township manager), Holly Sammartino, Carolyn Kustra, Marian Gentile, Candy Wygonik, and Jacque Rouggie of Indiana Township, who ran articles in the newsletters and put up with my questions and requests for copies and computer printouts and provided me with some much-needed information to complete the proposal process.

Many photographs are included thanks to Mary Yelich of Rural Ridge. She has spent years collecting and preserving the memories of this coal-mining town. She is the local historian of Rural Ridge and has a vast collection of photographs, newspaper clippings, and other memorabilia. Our own Karen Sue Haley is also a local historian, but for her own hometown of Indianola. Along with Yelich, Haley submitted many photographs and stories for this publication. Haley also greatly assisted in the editing process. Most of the captions for photographs of Indianola were written by her. Her knowledge of and passion for Indianola was instrumental throughout the editing portion of this project. Joseph Stephenson, his friend Ron Wobb (a lifelong resident of Indiana Township), and Charles Hart also contributed to the editing process.

Members of the Indiana Township Historic Commission are: Joseph Stephenson, chairman; Richard Johnson, vice chairman; Charles Hart, secretary; Marnie Applegate, treasurer; Karen Sue Haley; and myself, Erica Alderdice Birkner.

INTRODUCTION

The following information was taken from the introductions of previous volumes of Indiana Township's history books and a 2005 newsletter write-up from former historic commission chairman Thomas Prager. The boundaries of Pennsylvania in its present state were not determined until after the Revolutionary War. The land on which Pennsylvania was established was obtained by treaty and purchase from Native Americans between the years 1682 and 1792. Land in Western Pennsylvania was set apart for the redemption of certificates of depreciation given, in lieu of money, to the officers and soldiers of Pennsylvania as payment for service in the Revolutionary War. Present-day Indiana Township was in District 4 of those "Depreciation Lands" and was surveyed by James Cunningham.

Indiana was the fourth township formed in the county north of the Ohio and Allegheny Rivers. Its organization was preceded by that of Pine and Deer in 1796 and Ohio in 1803, all of which were originally included in Pitt Township. On December 26, 1805, the court approved the formation of Indiana Township. The original township area was much larger than the present area and extended south to the Allegheny River. Parts of the original Indiana Township were taken to form East Deer (1836), Hampton (1847), Shaler (1860), and O'Hara and Harmar (1875). In addition, land was annexed to Fox Chapel Borough in the 1900s.

The township was primarily rural from its earliest days, but there have been a number of industrial waves that have swept through. The first wave was the oil boom, which began soon after Drake's Well was first discovered in Titusville in about 1859. This was succeeded by coal mining, which began in the early 1900s and continued through the immediate post–World War II era. There were at least four major deep mines: Harmar; Rural Ridge; Indianola, which was the largest mine; and Indiana Township Historic Commission chairman Joseph Stephenson thinks that Harrison and Quinette (also known as the Thomas mine) was the fourth mine, but it also could have been the Harwick mine. Timbering was also serious business, as the land had to be cleared of the dense tree cover before farming could begin.

The present Indiana Township is an irregular strip of land about five and a half miles long by two and a half miles wide that stretches east to west from the eastern side of Little Deer Creek valley to the eastern ridge of Little Pine Creek valley. It is bounded on the north by West Deer Township and on the east by Frazer Township. To the south are Harmer Township, Fox Chapel Borough, and O'Hara Township, and bordering the tail of the township to the west are Shaler and Hampton Townships.

The terrain of the township changes dramatically as one moves from east to west. In the east, streams broaden as they approach the Allegheny River. West of Deer Creek, the land rises to higher, rolling hills. The southwest corner of the township is pierced by Little Pine Creek.

Two of the earliest recorded settlers in Indiana Township were Jacob Huddle and Henry Strohm, brothers-in-law and native Germans. Native Americans and others surely lived in the area, but without records, we must use our imaginations. Huddle and Strohm arrived in 1798, although their deeds for land transferred from Benjamin Herr are dated August 21, 1805. The first birth occurred in the family of Henry Strohm, a boy named Peter who died at a young age. Ancestors of these two families, the Huddles and Strohms, are still represented in present-day Indiana Township. Other families that resided in the township prior to 1820 included Weaver, Bave, Sweeney, Marshall, Black, McKee, Patterson, McClelland, Quinette, Neff, Edward, Snyder, Brooks, Powell, Stewart, and McWilliams.

The early routes through the township were little more than mud wagon paths. Putting travel in the early 1800s in perspective, it would have taken a full day to travel from Pittsburgh to Dorseyville with a horse and wagon. Saxonburg Boulevard was not paved until 1905, and State Route 910 was a cinder-covered road until the 1930s, when it was improved as part of Pres. Franklin D. Roosevelt's Public Works Administration program.

Several early routes connecting Pittsburgh to towns in the north cross through Indiana Township. Saxonburg Boulevard, which was known as Creek Road (later KDKA Boulevard), was the most important of the early routes and runs basically north and south at the western end of the township; it follows Pine Creek, Blue Run, and Cunningham's Run. Middle Road runs through the southwestern ("tail") section of the township parallel to and west of Saxonburg Boulevard. Dorseyville Road roughly parallels Saxonburg Boulevard to the east and runs from Etna to Dorseyville. State Route 910 winds through Indiana Township from the southeast to the northwest, crossing Saxonburg Boulevard in Dorseyville. Little Deer Creek Road runs north and south about three quarters of a mile from the eastern border of the township; it strings together industrial villages and coal areas, including Rural Ridge.

Thirteen known cemeteries are located in Indiana Township. One of these cemeteries is a pet cemetery, and two of them are geographically outside the township limits, but are legally still considered part of Indiana Township. These are Strohm Cemetery (Fox Chapel Borough) and Henderson Cemetery (Harmar Township).

There were several early populated areas in the township: the village of Dorseyville; the mining villages of Rural Ridge and Indianola; the tail, or Middle Road, area; and the Rich Hill Road area. Dorseyville was an early village developed as a service center at the heart of the rolling hills of farmland making up the western half of Indiana Township. It was named for Elizabeth Bartholomew Dorsey, a landowner from the early 1800s, and her husband, Greenberry Dorsey. It was a rather large village during the middle of the 19th century, with many sustaining businesses including stores, blacksmith shops, churches, and hotels.

The present town of Russellton was named Rural Ridge until about 1907. The name Rural Ridge was then transferred to its present location south of Russellton. Rural Ridge was a coal-mining town with amenities to serve the mine, such as housing for the miners.

Southwest of Rural Ridge, another coal-mining town developed along Deer Creek. The town, named Indianola, is bisected by Route 910. It was near the junction of Deer and Little Deer Creeks and was accessed by a railroad spur leading to the Bessemer & Lake Erie Railroad (B&LE). The major portion of this town was built in the early 1900s and included the mine structures, elementary school, company store, post office, and three churches. On the western side of Route 910, company housing was constructed and rented to the miners. The Inland Collieries Company occupied most of the area on the eastern side of Route 910, including the mine entrance. The only building that remains from the Inland Collieries Company is the hospital near MEDRAD. That building and all the Inland mine property is currently owned by Bayer HealthCare, which acquired Schering AG, the owner of MEDRAD, in 2006. MEDRAD produces cardiovascular medical supplies used in diagnosing heart disease.

The small square "tail" section in the southwestern corner of the township had no central town or village, but did have a post office at the start of the 20th century. The post office was called Montooth and was situated on Middle Road. Along Middle Road, there were several taverns and grocery stores; today, only one tavern remains—the Middle Road Inn.

There are three large estates within Indiana Township: Serenity Hill, the Flaccus Estate, and Hartwood Acres. The Hartwood and Flaccus properties were the site of annual fox hunts for over 50 years, and Hartwood is still home to annual polo matches, a series of summer concerts, and a variety of automobile shows (antique and British). Each Christmas season, Hartwood hosts a "Celebration of Lights" that rivals the one at Oglebay in West Virginia.

Today, there are two major medical facilities in the township, HealthSouth Harmarville Rehabilitation Hospital (a world-class facility) and MEDRAD, which occupies much of the Inland Collieries Company site. The township is also home to two major research facilities—the University of Pittsburgh Applied Research Center (U-PARC) and the PPG Harmar Glass Business and Discovery Center. Both are located in Harmar Township, which was portioned off from Indiana Township in 1875.

The Singing Winds site of the Council of the Three Rivers American Indian center occupies a former Nike site military station on a high hill overlooking Dorseyville. Due to the steel industry being based in Pittsburgh, there were three Nike sites—locations where Nike Ajax missiles were housed in the ground during the Cold War—around the Indiana Township area. Teen Challenge of Western Pennsylvania, a faith-based drug and alcohol rehabilitation center located off of Lefever Hill Road, occupies another former Nike site.

There are many buildings in the township that date back to the 1800s, including the Martin Giesy house (Camp Deer Creek), which is believed to be the oldest house in Allegheny County and dates back to at least the early 1800s. The Silver Star Hotel (Andre's Hotel) also goes back to the 1800s; the original building was a log structure and has been remodeled and added on to several times in the past. The building is now known as the Middle Road Inn. John and Mary Flinn Lawrence constructed Hartwood Acres in the 1920s. In 1969, Allegheny County acquired the estate and created the 629-acre Hartwood Acres Park, located in both Hampton and Indiana Townships, with entrances along Saxonburg Boulevard and Middle Road. The house and horse barn are open to the public at various times throughout the year. Emmerling House, located in Emmerling Park off of State Route 910, was built around 1856. The house was named for Dr. John Emmerling and his wife, Jane Beeson Emmerling, who purchased the property in 1941. The property where the house stands was part of Cunningham's Depreciation Land, District 4, Lot 127; *Indiana Township History Book Volume II* has more information about the Emmerling House and property.

Besides the large mines in Rural Ridge and Indianola, there were quite a few smaller and earlier coal mines in the township. Some of these mines were "slope" mines, meaning that the coal seams were exposed on the hillsides.

After all the changes Indiana Township has seen over its 206-year history, the rural aspect of the town still remains strong. Driving along the winding roads, one can still observe acres of farmland with various animals and crops occupying the fields.

One

Business and Street Scenes

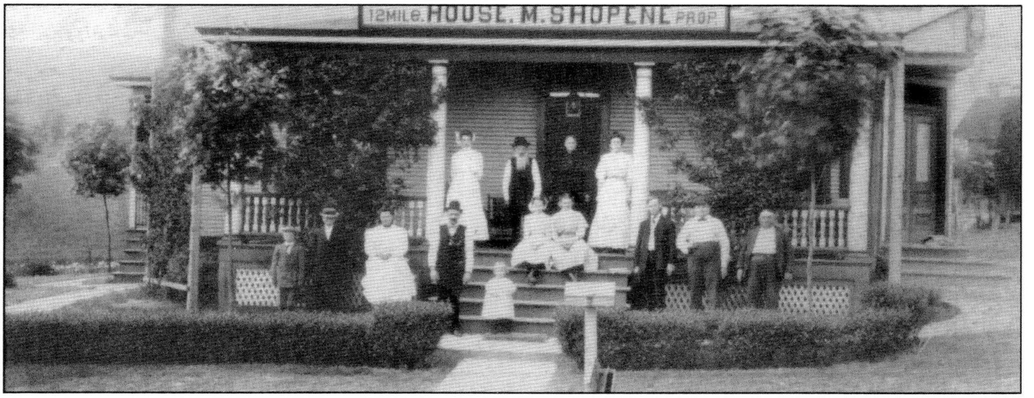

The 12-Mile House, as it was known in the first decade of the 20th century because it was 12 miles from Pittsburgh, was owned and operated by Michael Shopene and his wife, Matilda. Standing in front of it are, from left to right, (first row) Delmar Shopene, John Prager, Matilda Shopene, Michael Shopene (owner), Regina Shopene (child on first step), unidentified, Tony Hankey (bartender), and unidentified; (second row, sitting) Ella Prager and Leona Shopene; (third row) May Prager, George Prager, Anna Martha Klein Prager, and Bertha Prager Carmichael.

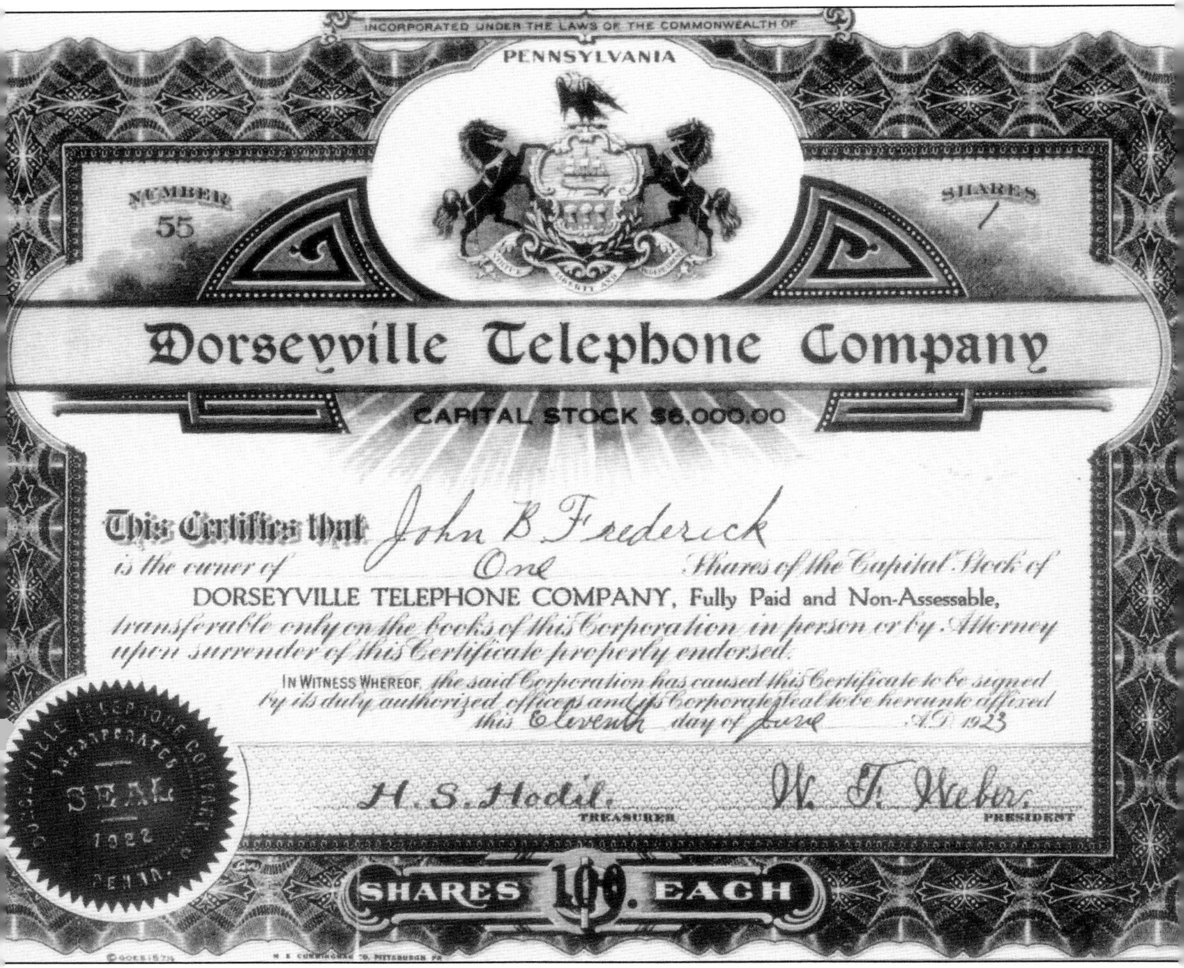

This is a Dorseyville Telephone Company stock certificate. William C. Dietrich, who worked for the Bell Telephone Company, decided to start the Dorseyville Telephone Company. Since he already had experience working as a telephone man, he was able to convince investors to contribute financing to start a local company. The first telephone operator for the Dorseyville telephone system was Mollie Hodil, and C. Elverda Hassinger was a later operator. Hassinger and her brother Logan lived in the family homestead on Middle Road. Logan Hassinger worked in the Glenshaw Post Office for many years. The Dorseyville Telephone Company charter was sent to the governor of Pennsylvania in November 1921, and the company became incorporated on March 8, 1922. During the Depression, Bell Telephone offered to buy the Dorseyville Telephone Company; the stockholders panicked because of the Depression and voted to sell. The telephone switchboard was in the home of Mollie and Harry Hodil, and Freda and Viola Keck helped run the switchboard after Harry died.

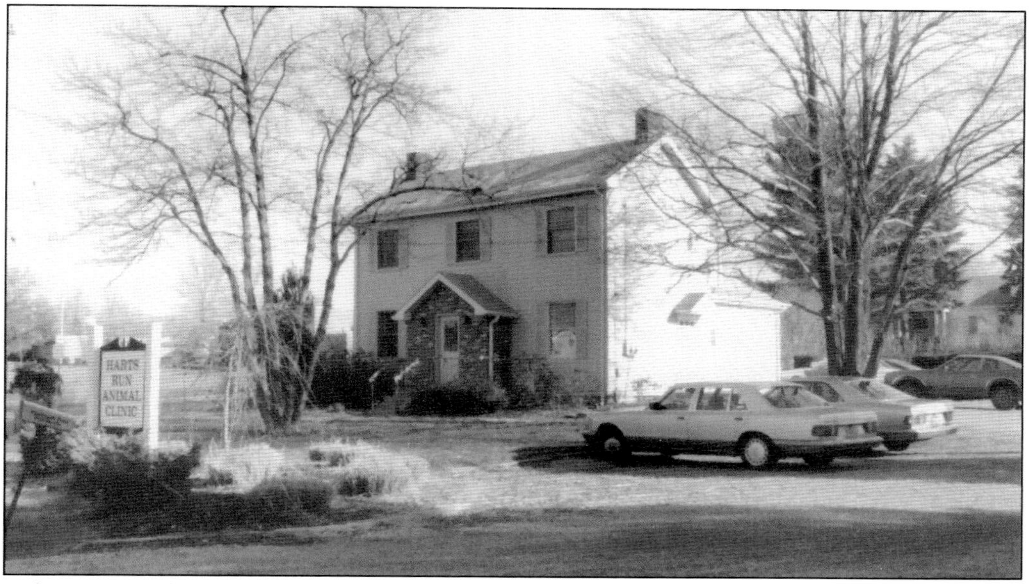

Indiana Township had a number of blacksmith shops in the area. The one pictured above is now Harts Run Veterinary Hospital. The shop was owned by Albert Grabb's father (his name is unknown), who made his home with the James Weber family. The Strohms bought it from Albert Grabb's father, and then Lawrence J. Kelly took over proprietorship with Edward Baumgartle. This business is located at the corner of Harts Run and Dorseyville Roads.

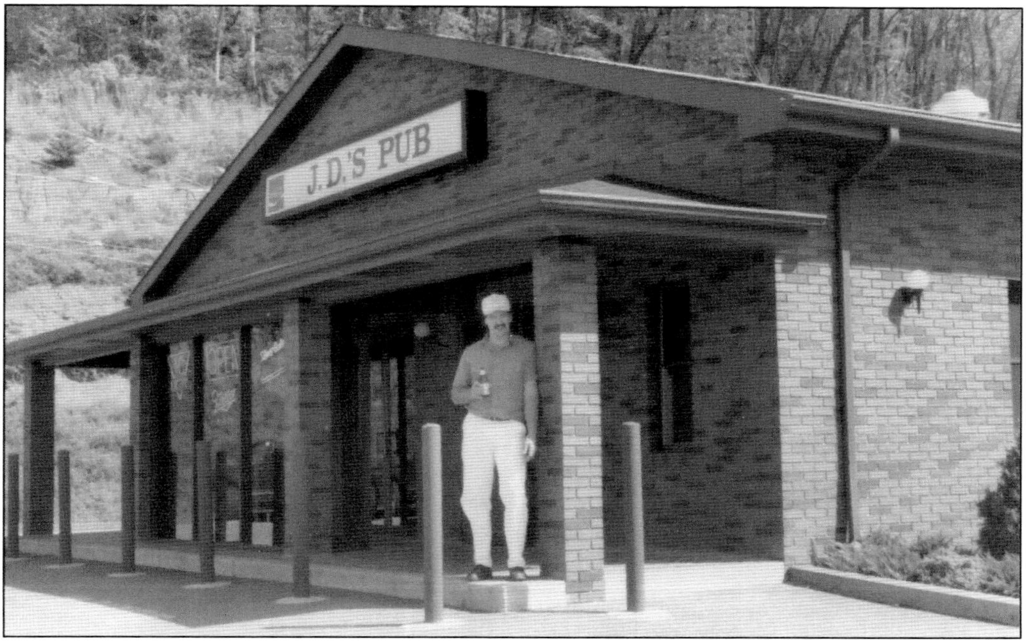

J.D.'s Pub, located at the corner of Harts Run Road and Saxonburg Boulevard, is pictured with owner Joe DeBaldo standing out front. J.D.'s Pub, which was renamed Gator's Grille sometime around 2011, is a very popular restaurant and bar—one of the only ones located in Indiana Township. The establishment has an outdoor cabana complete with bocce ball and sand volleyball courts. Before J.D.'s, Sallade's BBQ occupied this location.

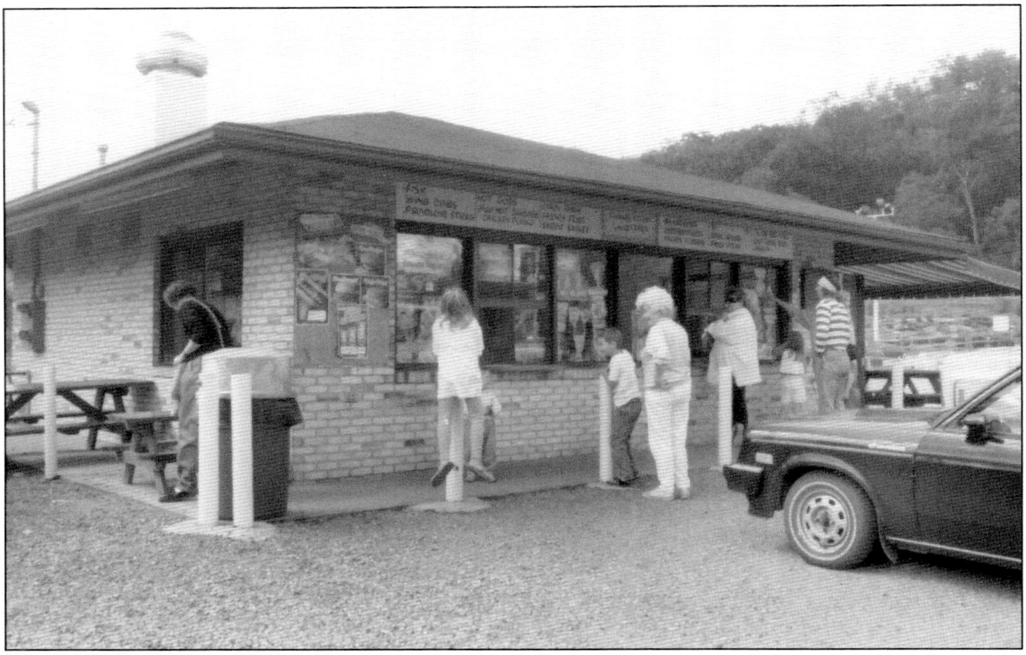

Ice Cream World may seem like a silly name for an establishment, but the food is delicious, and there are plenty of activities to keep little ones occupied. Located at the busy corner of Harts Run Road and Saxonburg Boulevard, it is across from Gator's Grille and DeBaldo's Sales & Service.

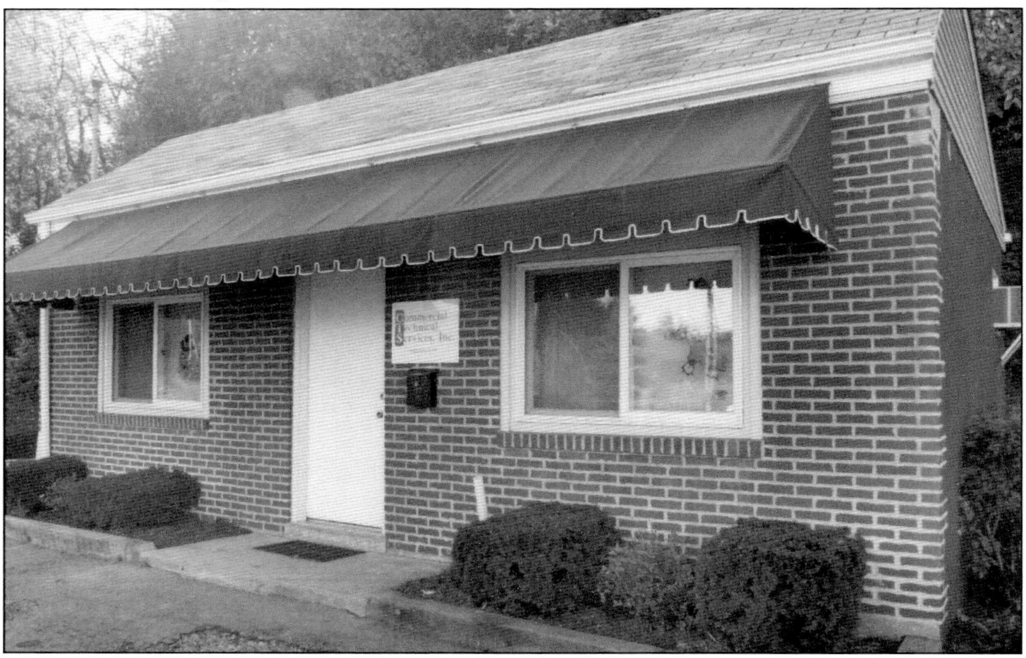

In 1993, Bob and Shari Hiller opened a floral shop called Wildflower Florist in this structure in Indianola, which was the former post office building on State Route 910, near Grieco's restaurant. Many small businesses have failed in this little one-room building, including Commercial Technical Services, Inc. (pictured), Wildflower Florist, and a pizza parlor.

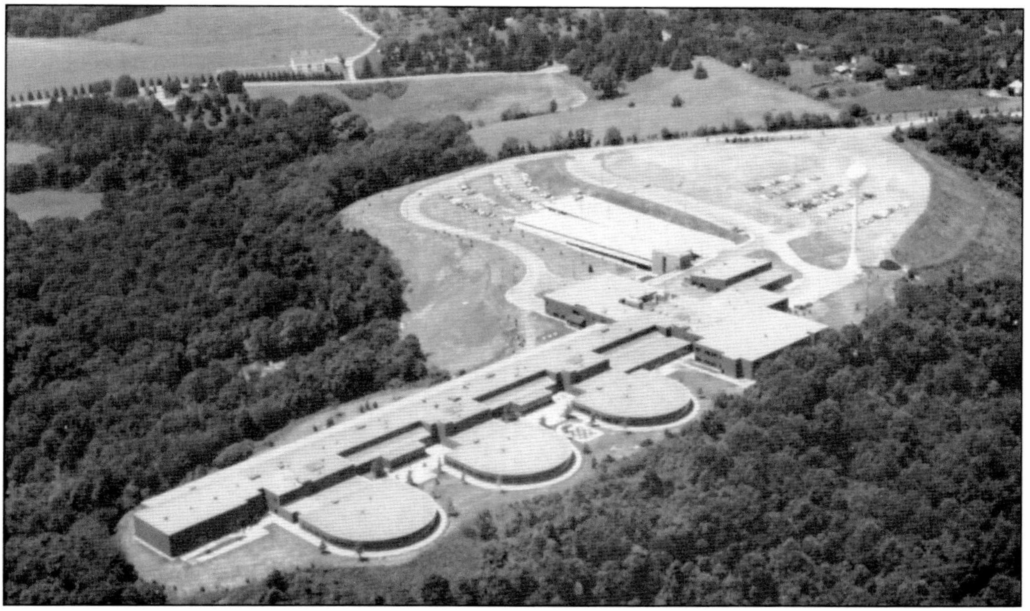

Harmarville Rehabilitation Center opened in 1913 as a convalescent home for women and was operated by a group known as the Federation of Girls' School Societies (now the Federation of Independent School Alumnae). In 1969, this facility relocated to its current 69-acre site in Indiana Township. Today, HealthSouth Harmarville Rehabilitation Hospital has satellite facilities, admits roughly 2,000 patients per year, and employs over 900 people.

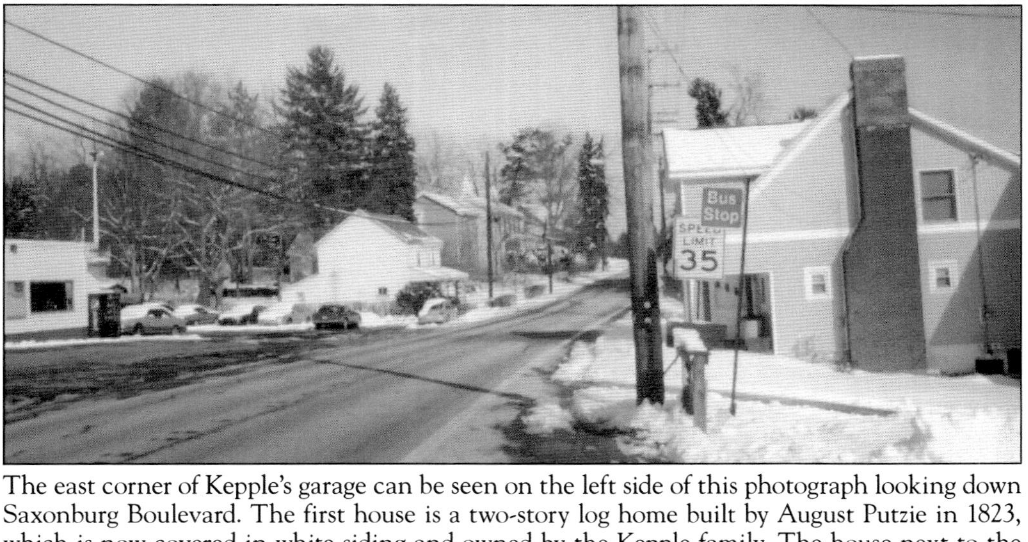

The east corner of Kepple's garage can be seen on the left side of this photograph looking down Saxonburg Boulevard. The first house is a two-story log home built by August Putzie in 1823, which is now covered in white siding and owned by the Kepple family. The house next to the Putzie house is the McIntyre house as it appears today. August Putzie was William McIntyre's partner in the shop and was both a blacksmith and a wagon maker. He provided farm wagons for a broad area of the farms surrounding the village of Dorseyville. The house at right, across Saxonburg Boulevard, is also an original log cabin that is now covered in blue siding. It was built in 1831 and was originally one and a half stories. It has been considerably added on to both vertically and in the back. These three houses are among the oldest still standing in the village of Dorseyville. (Courtesy of Joseph Stephenson.)

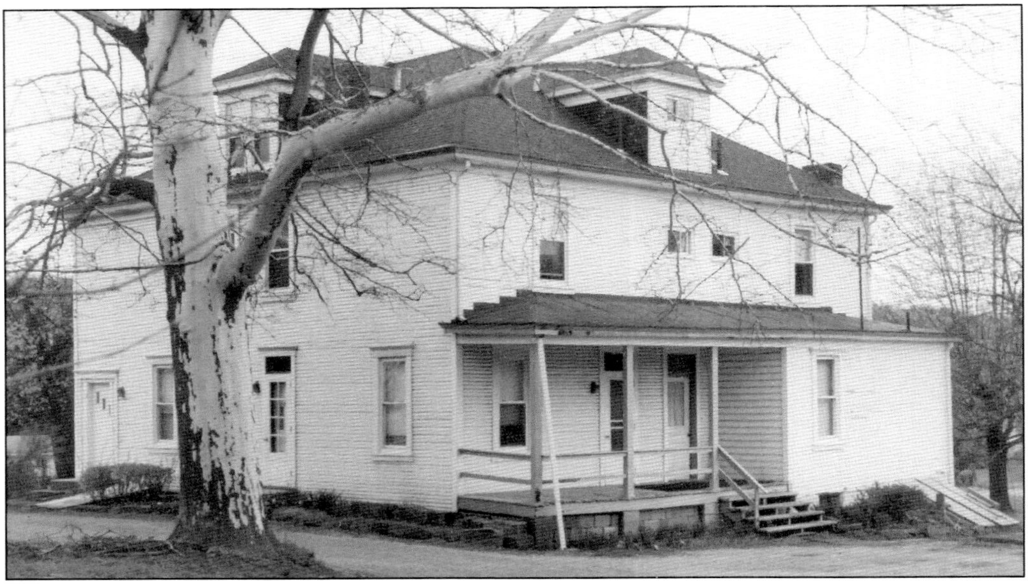

The rear of the old 12-Mile House, located on Saxonburg Boulevard, is pictured as it appears today, after being converted into apartments. In the late 19th and early 20th centuries, the 12-Mile House operated as a roadhouse and contained 16 rooms, a large dining room, and a back room, which hosted private parties and meetings.

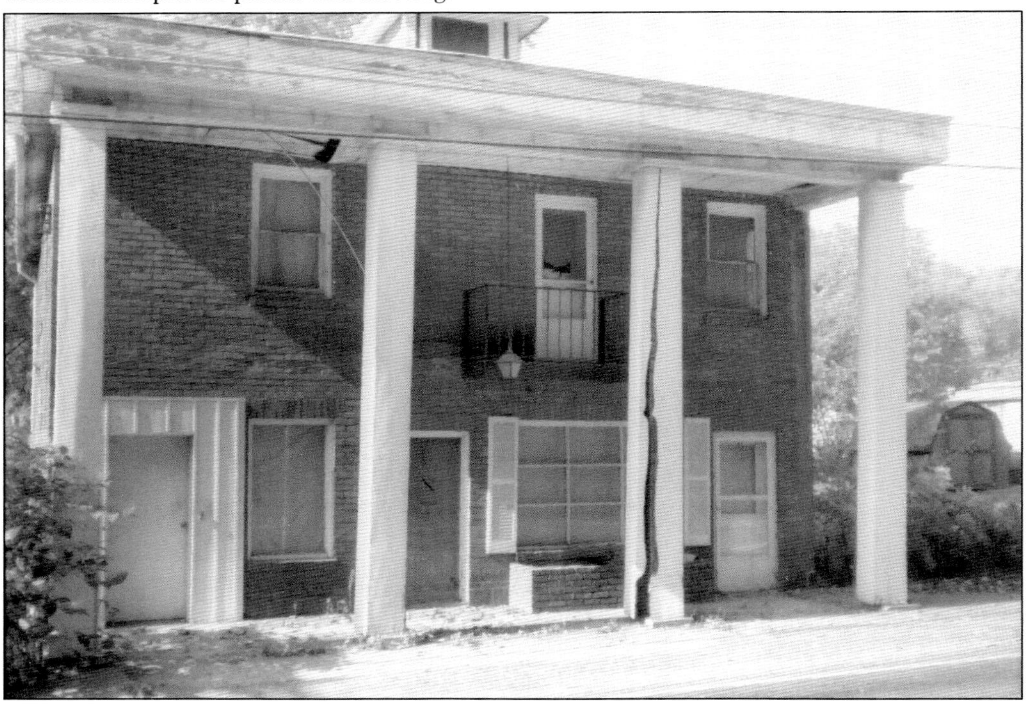

The photograph of this building on Little Deer Creek Road in Rural Ridge was taken in 1989. In 1938, the left side of this building was Rural Ridge's post office, with Sophia Brozek serving as postmaster, while a barbershop was housed on the right. In 1951, Rural Ridge's post office was moved to its current site on Little Deer Creek Road next to Elwood's Pub.

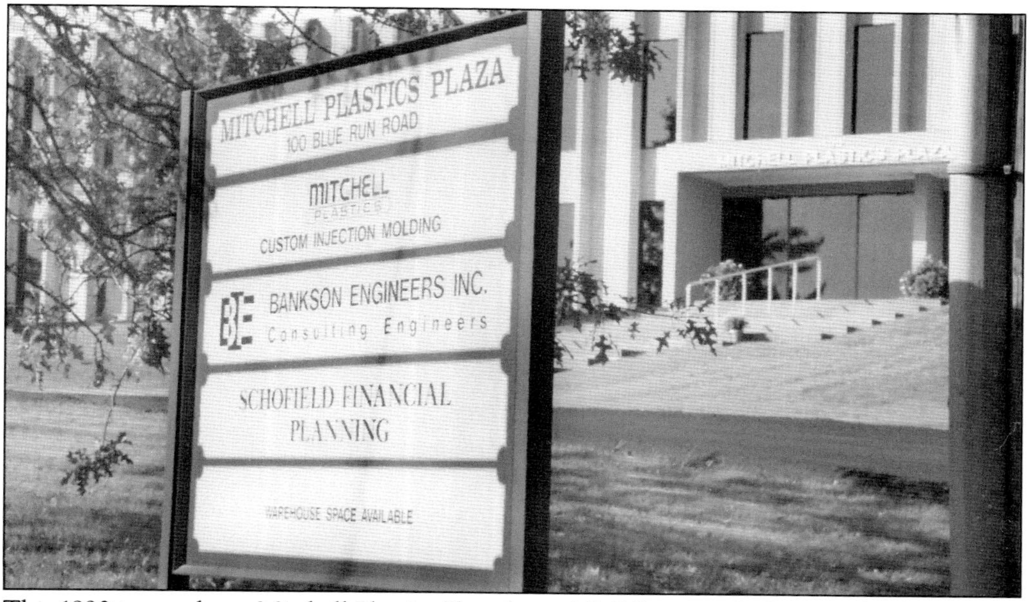

This 1990 image shows Mitchell Plastics Plaza (now A.J. Silberman & Company). The business park's mailing address is in Cheswick (but it is considered to be in Indianola) on Blue Run Road, which connects Indianola Road with State Route 910. This is an example of the kind of business space that Indianola—home to many manufacturing companies and warehouses—has to offer.

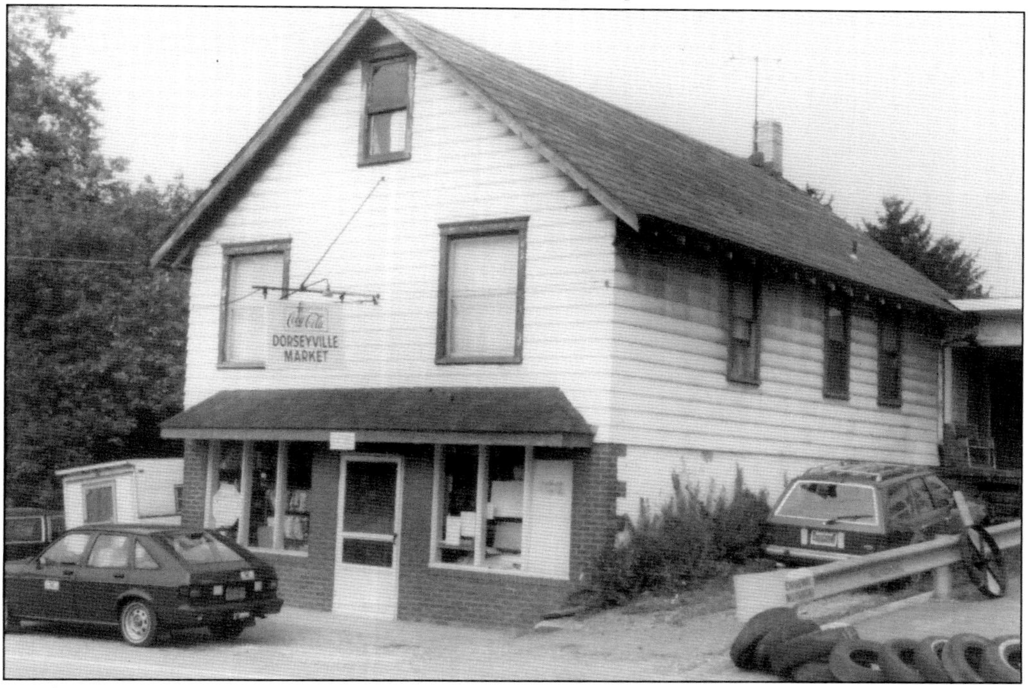

Much grocery shopping was done in little markets—such as this one—scattered throughout the township. This was the Dorseyville Market. A lot of mom-and-pop grocery stores went out of business due to the influx of cheaper megastores. This building still stands and is next to the former Campbell's Auto Service (now Kremer Automotive) on Saxonburg Boulevard.

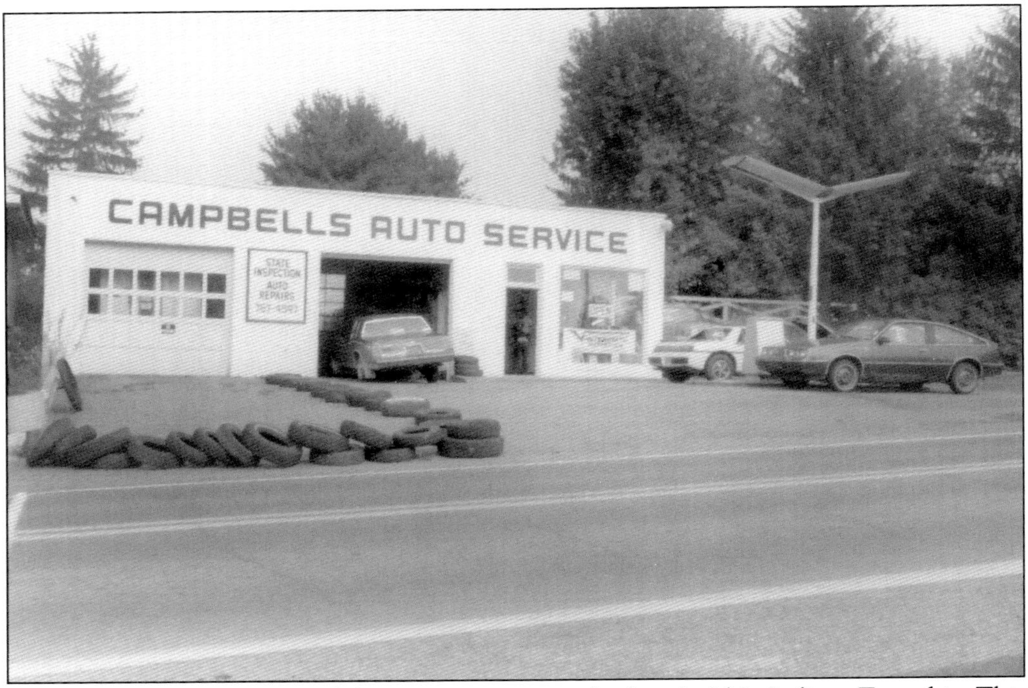

Numerous garages and automobile service stations can be found within Indiana Township. This 1990 image shows Campbell's Auto Service. Many of the present-day automotive centers are located near the former locations of blacksmith shops. This business is now called Kremer Automotive and is a booming automobile service center on Saxonburg Boulevard.

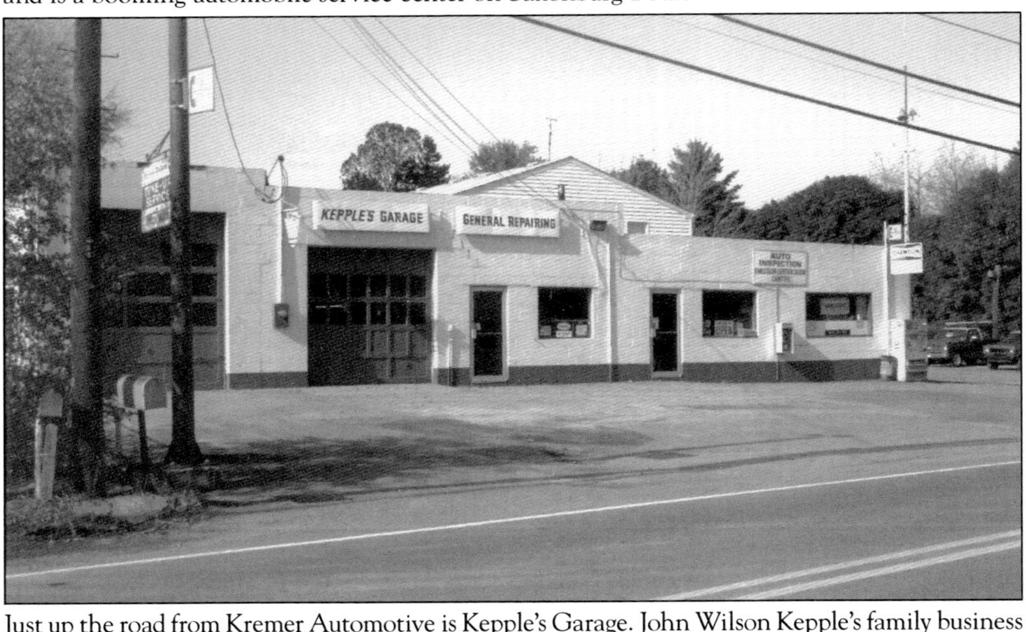

Just up the road from Kremer Automotive is Kepple's Garage. John Wilson Kepple's family business has been operating on Saxonburg Boulevard for over 50 years; Kepple says his garage was built in 1949 and has been family-owned and operated since its opening. Many local residents take their vehicles to this establishment and highly recommend Kepple's service.

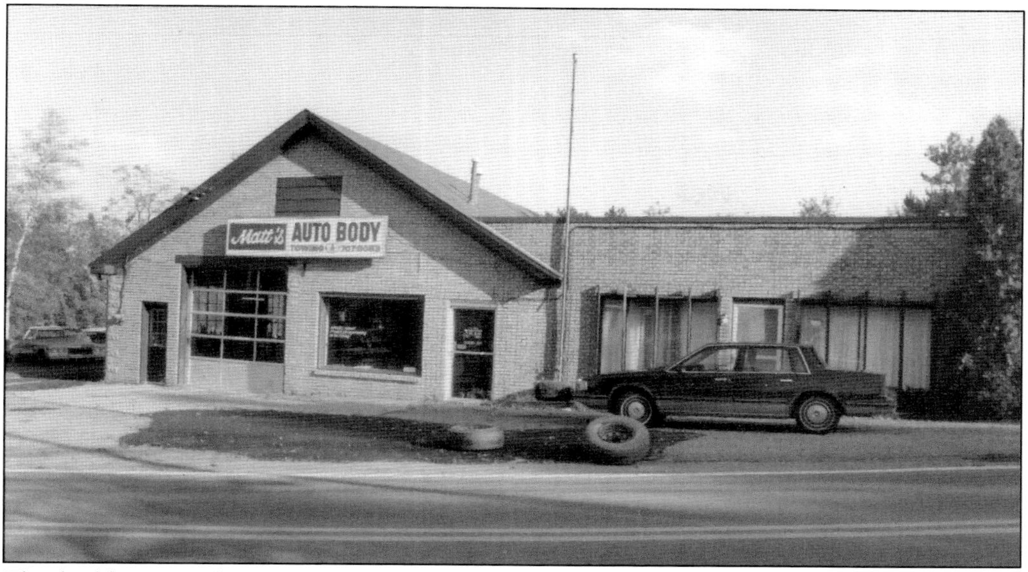

This building once housed Matt's Auto Body, located in a great spot on Saxonburg Boulevard, with Kremer Automotive and Kepple's Garage just across the street. Matt's Auto Body used to get some of the bodywork the garages were not equipped to handle. This photograph was taken in 1990; JSK Flooring now occupies the space, along with two apartments. Matt's Auto Body was originally Schmidt's Store, a restaurant where Tilda (Kepple) Thomas was a cook.

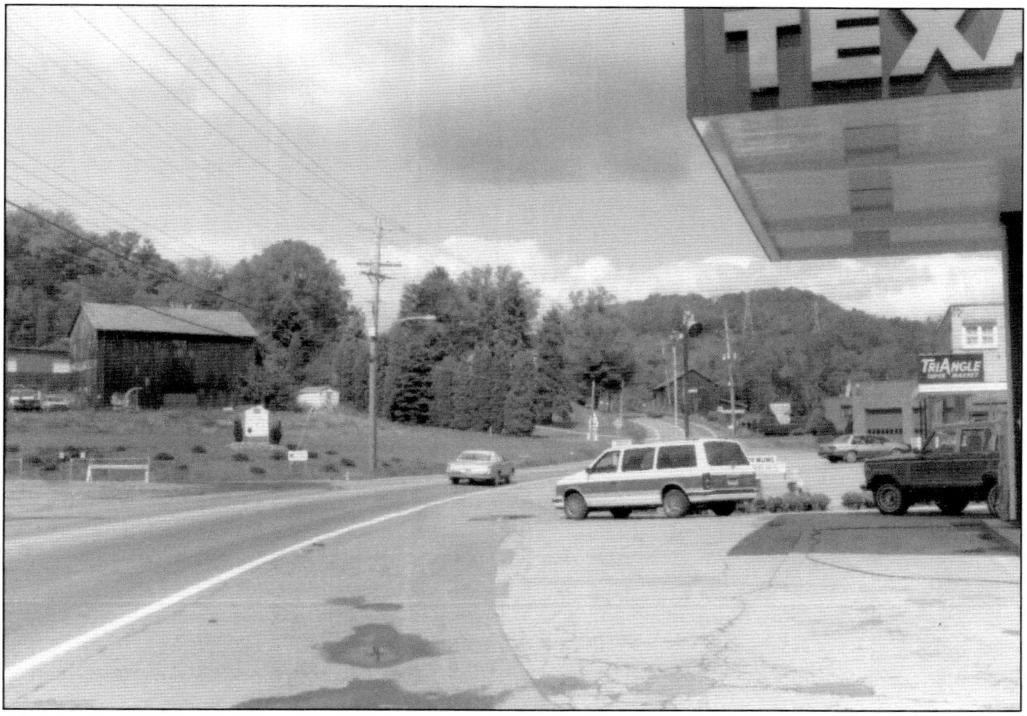

This 1990 image shows Harts Run Road near Saxonburg Boulevard, looking north toward Hampton Township and the old Hodil Farm. The large barn at left may have belonged to John Dietrich, since his family settled most of this area (once known as Dietrich's Crossroads).

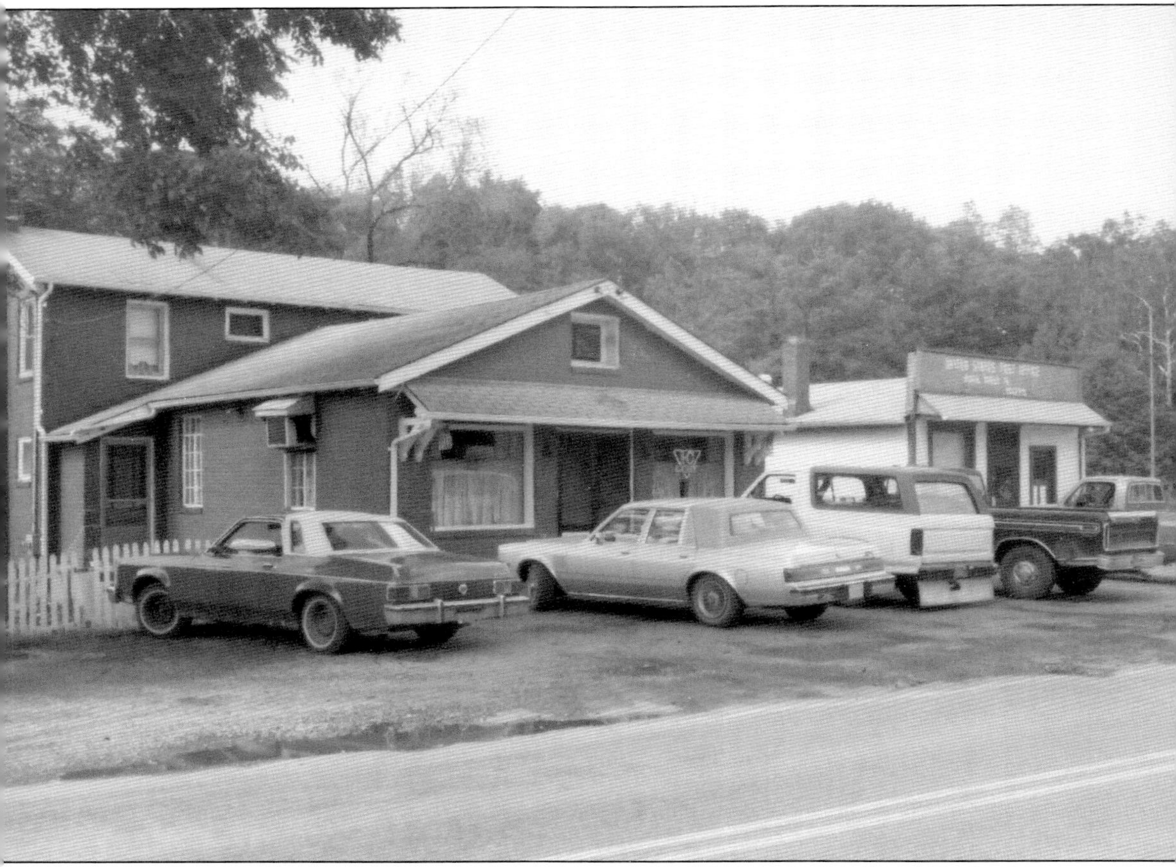

Rural Ridge Tavern, now known as Elwood's Pub, serves the residents of Rural Ridge. The post office is visible in the background. Rural Ridge is a small community located within Indiana Township. Once a booming mecca for the coal-mining industry, the community takes pride in its history and close-knit relationships. People reminisce about the "days of yore" while enjoying a refreshing beverage after a long day of work. Dave and Kathy Crowell are the current owners of this quaint place that has a great atmosphere. They specialize in craft beers and great food and host acoustic musical performances. The Crowells have taken an interest in presenting local history to their patrons, decorating the walls of their restaurant and pub with old photographs of Rural Ridge that depict the successful coal-mining industry and the evolution of local housing.

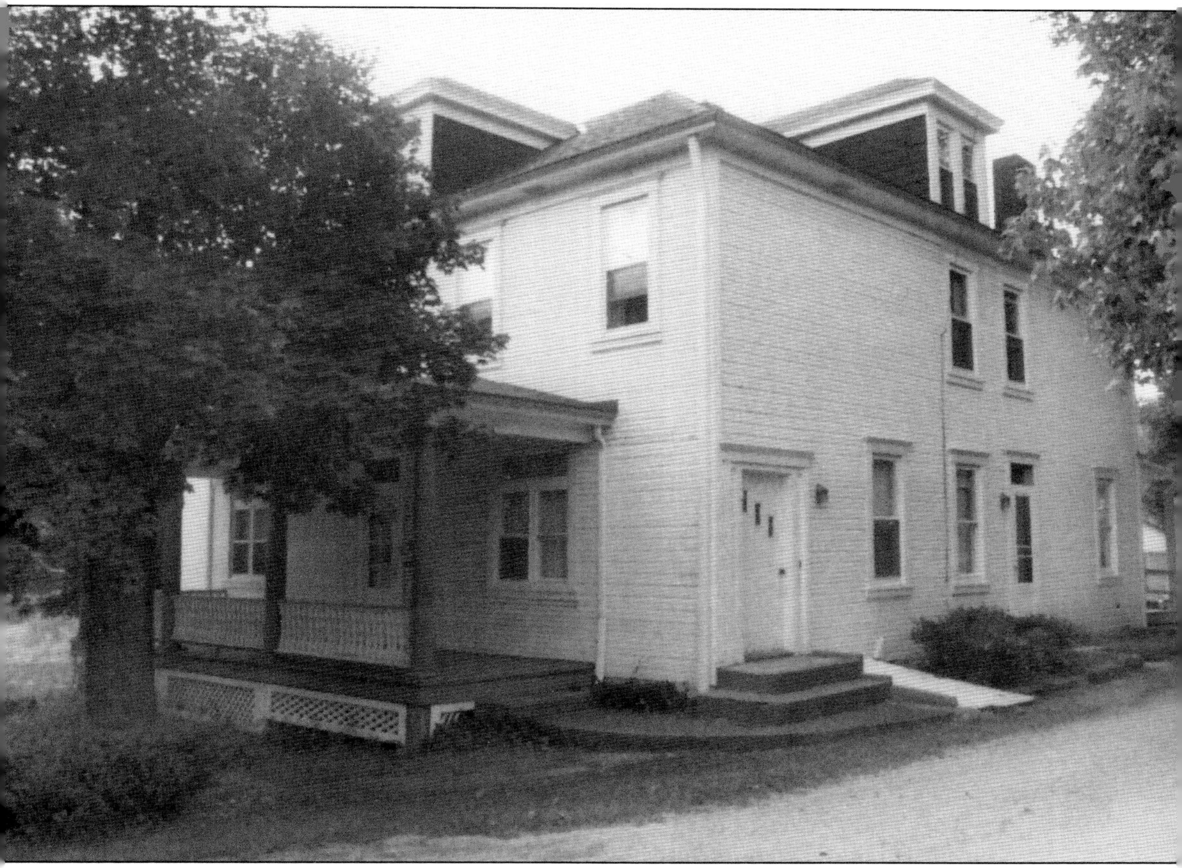

Prohibition, which passed in 1919, spelled the beginning of the end for the 12-Mile House. The Shopenes moved to Aspinwall, but continued to use the once-prosperous roadhouse as a summer home. Michael Shopene's oldest daughter, Regina, and her husband, Eugene Yaley, purchased the property from her father in the early 1940s and began the conversion to apartments while they lived there. Edward and Eleanor Wagner completed the conversion in the mid-1950s, and the above photograph represents the front of the 12-Mile House as it appeared in 1988. The address of the 12-Mile House was formerly 537 Saxonburg Boulevard, but it is now near 3725 Saxonburg Boulevard due to the 9-1-1 address conversion that occurred around 1997. The building had three porches: one facing the road, which was used by customers; a second to the side, which overlooked a generous spring-fed pond; and a third that stretched across the rear of the building and opened off the kitchen. During the winter, ice was cut from the pond and kept in the nearby icehouse for use in the hotel in the summer months.

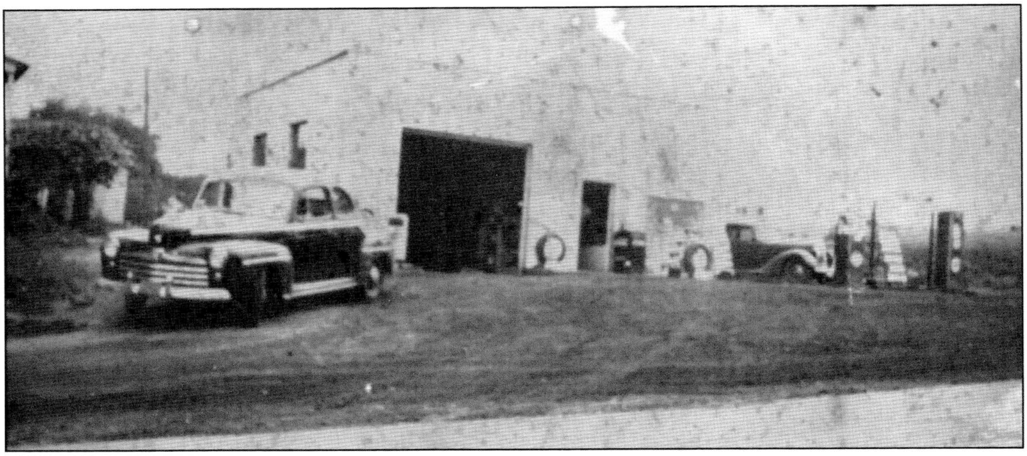

This 1949 photograph of Campbell's garage and gas station—renamed Campbell's Auto Center after they stopped selling gasoline—shows what an automobile garage looked like in the late 1940s. A rather large blacksmith shop owned by Frank Shopene was located next door, behind what was once the Dorseyville Market, offering an interesting contrast of services. These businesses were located on Saxonburg Boulevard in Dorseyville, near State Route 910.

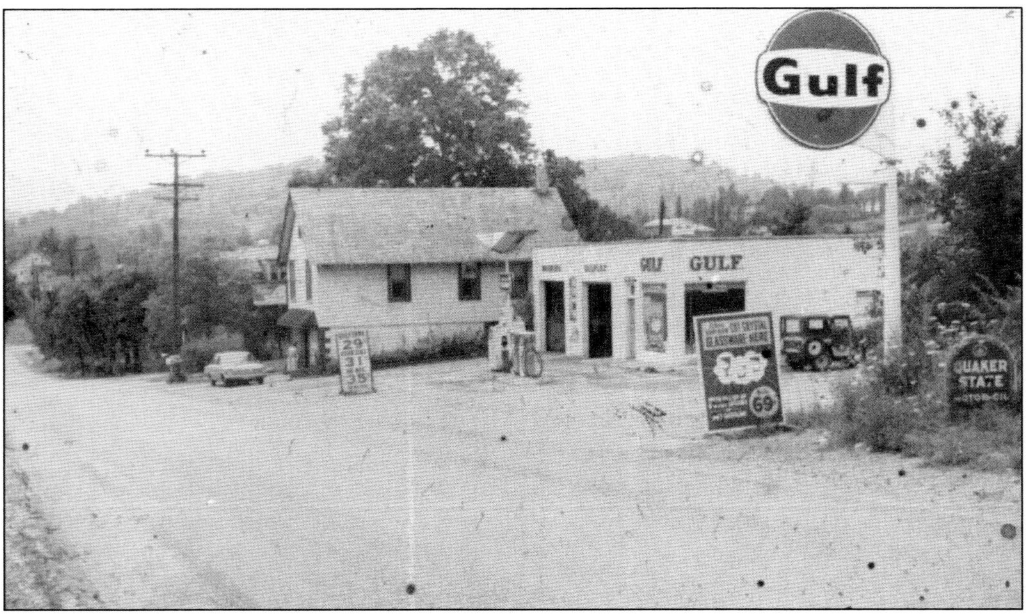

This 1957 view of Campbell's gas station and automotive center shows Saxonburg Boulevard and the Dorseyville Market. The Dorseyville Market has since been remodeled into apartments, and Campbell's is still an automotive business but is now called Kremer Automotive.

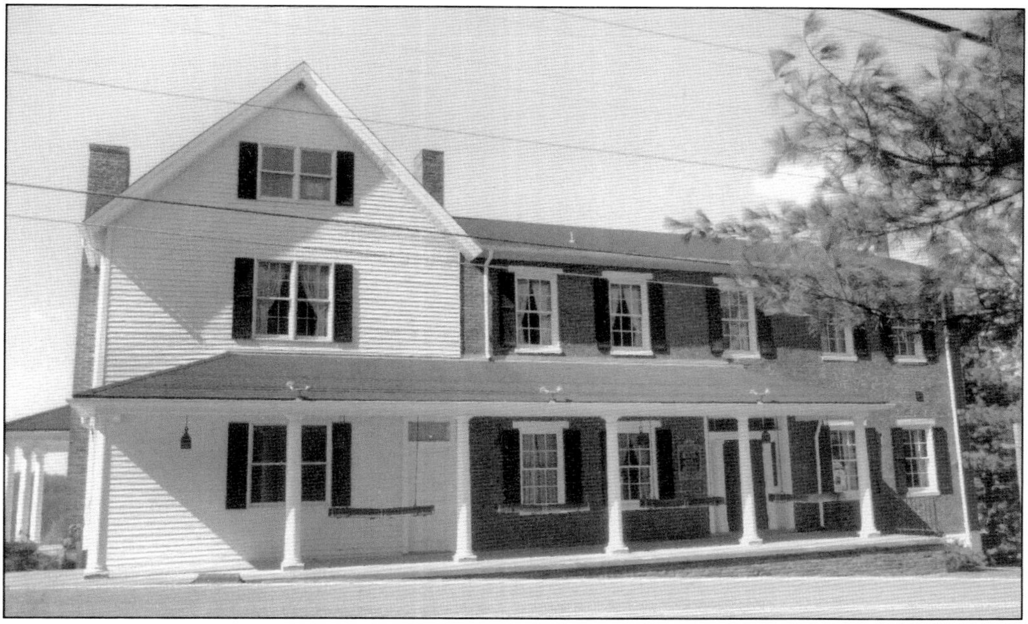

The Cross Keys Hotel, built in 1850 on Dorseyville Road (then Kittanning Pike), served as a popular stopping point between Kittanning and Pittsburgh. Another selling point of stopping here was that the blacksmith shop, owned by J. Hunter, was across the street, which made it convenient for travelers who needed wagon or horse assistance.

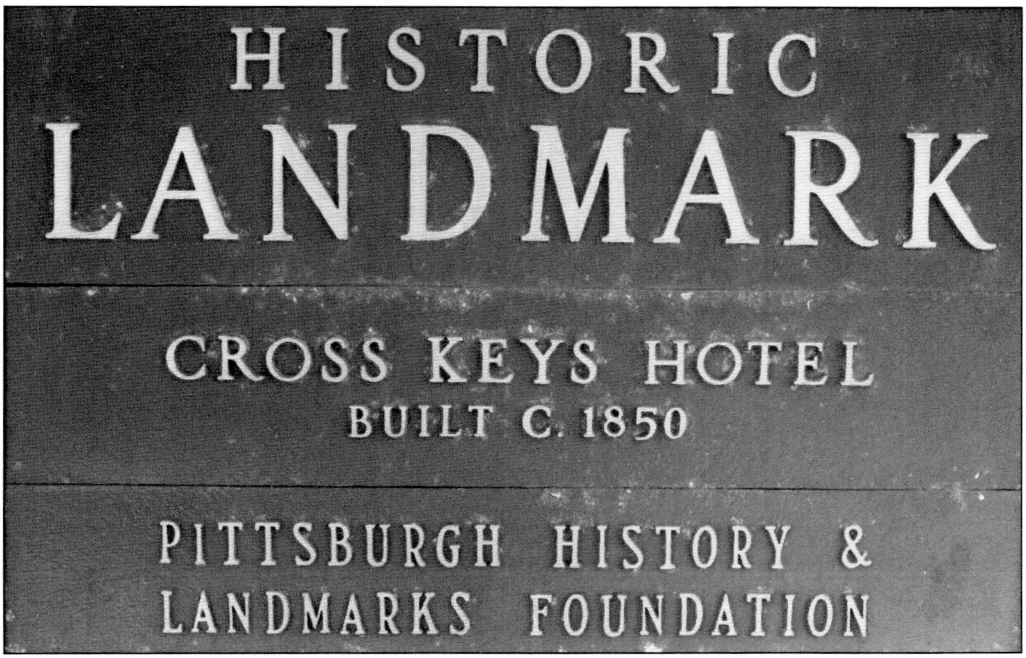

The structure that displays this plaque was known as the G.F. Thomas Tavern from 1850 until 1876, when it became the Cross Keys Hotel. In 1900, the Schmitkinson family took over but kept the name "Cross Keys Hotel." This building was known as the Cross Keys Hotel until early 2012, when it was purchased by new owners; it is now the Andora restaurant.

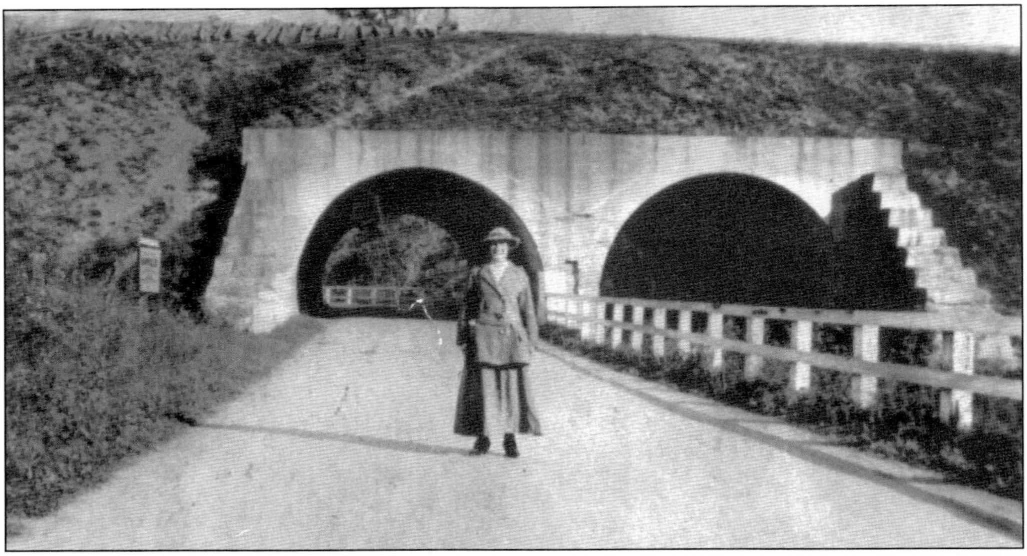

An unidentified woman stands on Little Deer Creek Road in front of the railroad bridge for the Bessemer & Lake Erie (B&LE) Railroad. Even though this photograph was taken in the 1930s, this stretch of road remains much the same. Because of the sharp bend and narrow road, drivers must sound their horns as they come through the tunnel to alert oncoming vehicles of their approach. (Courtesy of Mary Yelich.)

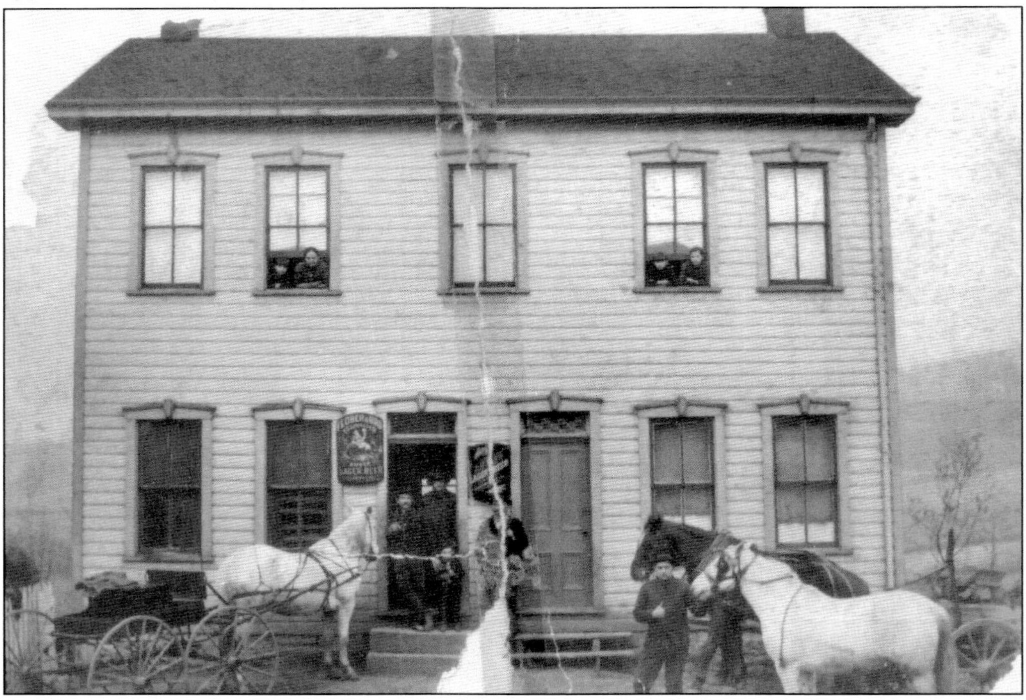

Shopene's Saloon on Saxonburg Boulevard may have been built sometime in the 1850s and was torn down in the early 1900s. This roadhouse served as a waypoint between Kittanning and Pittsburgh and was replaced by a larger structure known as the 12-Mile House, which was located just across the street from the former saloon.

According to an interview with Helen Rekasie, during the 1930s there was a thriving mushroom-growing industry in Rural Ridge. The mushrooms were housed in the Lubatti-Bracco Mushroom House. It was a family-oriented industry where husbands, wives, and children worked together. There were six or seven mushroom houses in Rural Ridge; the owners would take them down to the Strip District in Pittsburgh to sell. (Courtesy of Mary Yelich.)

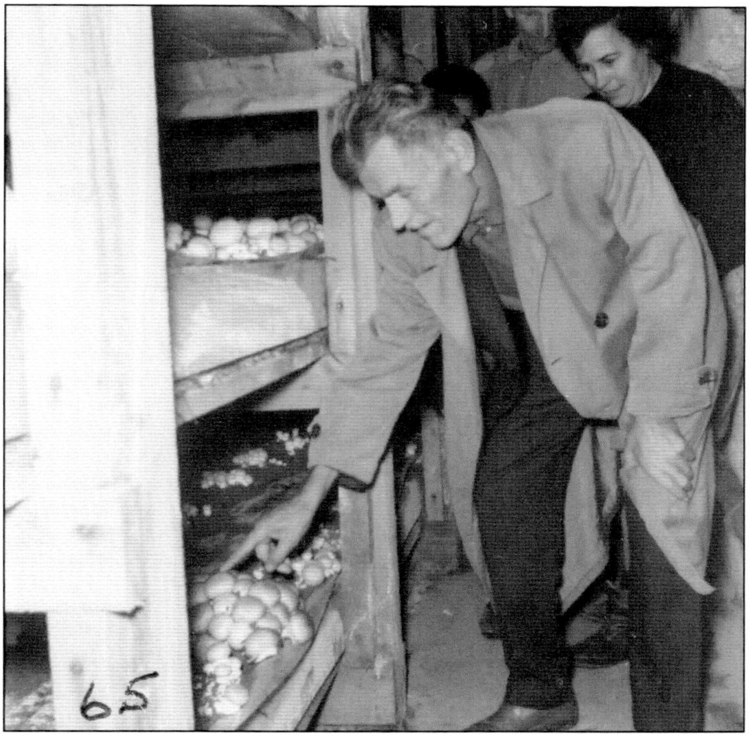

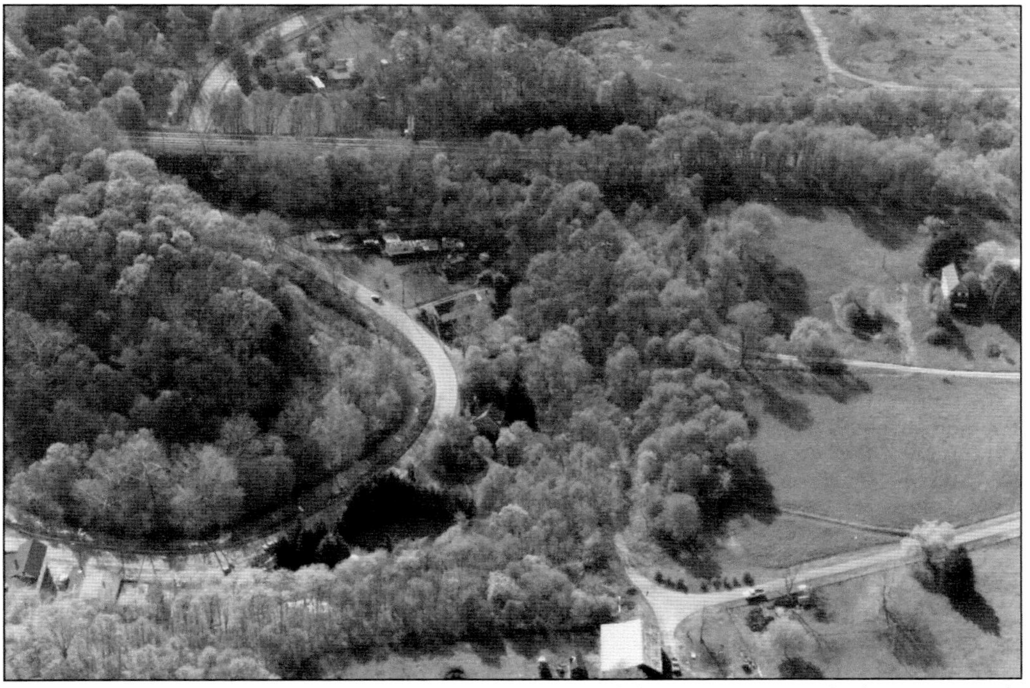

This early 1990s aerial photograph shows the rural nature of the community, with glimpses at Little Deer Creek Road winding through the town, the B&LE Railroad tunnel, and Little Deer Creek. A small part of the tunnel opening is visible under the railroad. (Courtesy of Mary Yelich.)

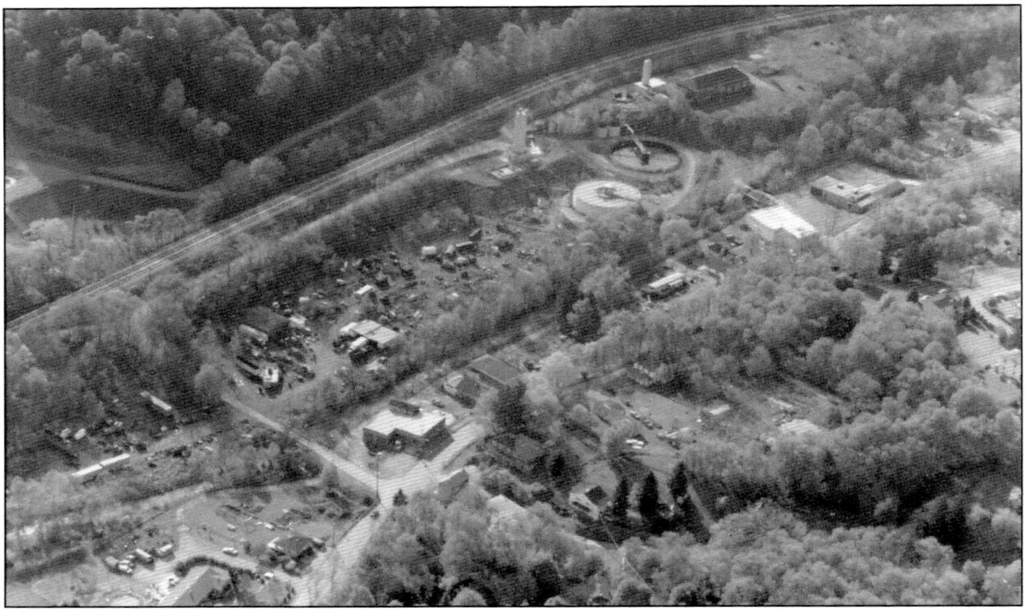

The Duquesne Light Fly Ash Dump is visible in the upper left corner of this image. The Bessemer & Lake Erie (B&LE) Railroad runs diagonally through the photograph. Mine Road, which leads to the Duquesne Light Filtering Plant, is on the left. The Voskamp plan of houses is located in the center. The intersection of Mine Road and Voskamp Drive with Little Deer Creek Road is also visible. (Courtesy of Mary Yelich.)

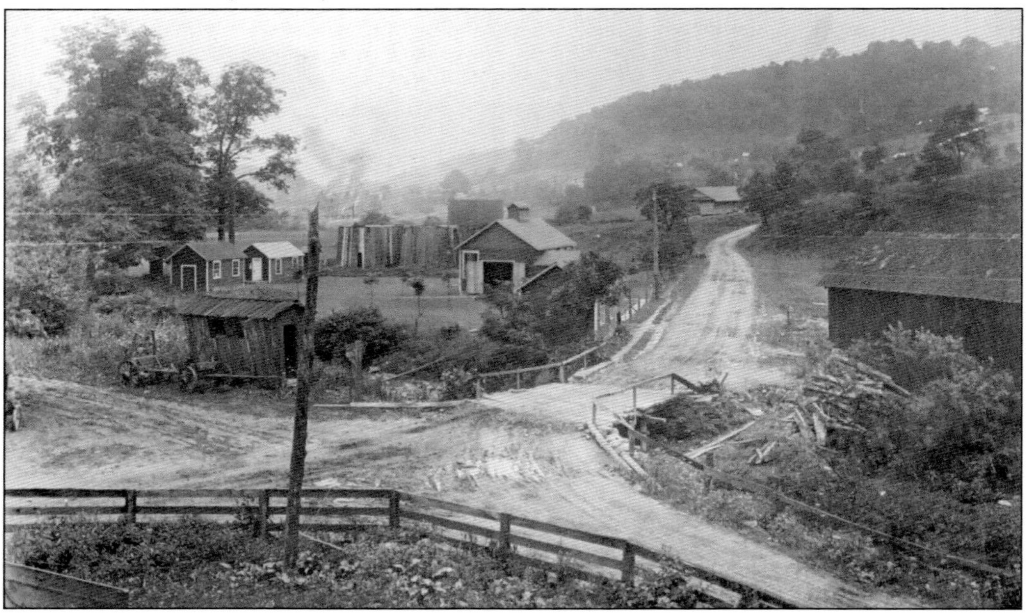

These Indianola crossroads are the intersection of State Route 910, going straight toward Harmarville, and Indianola Road (to the right). The buildings in the center belonged to the Pittsburgh Pipe Line Company; the oil storage tanks are visible in the center background. The building at right is part of the Frederick Crawford farm, and the fenced pasture at the bottom is now Republic Avenue. (Courtesy of Karen Sue Haley.)

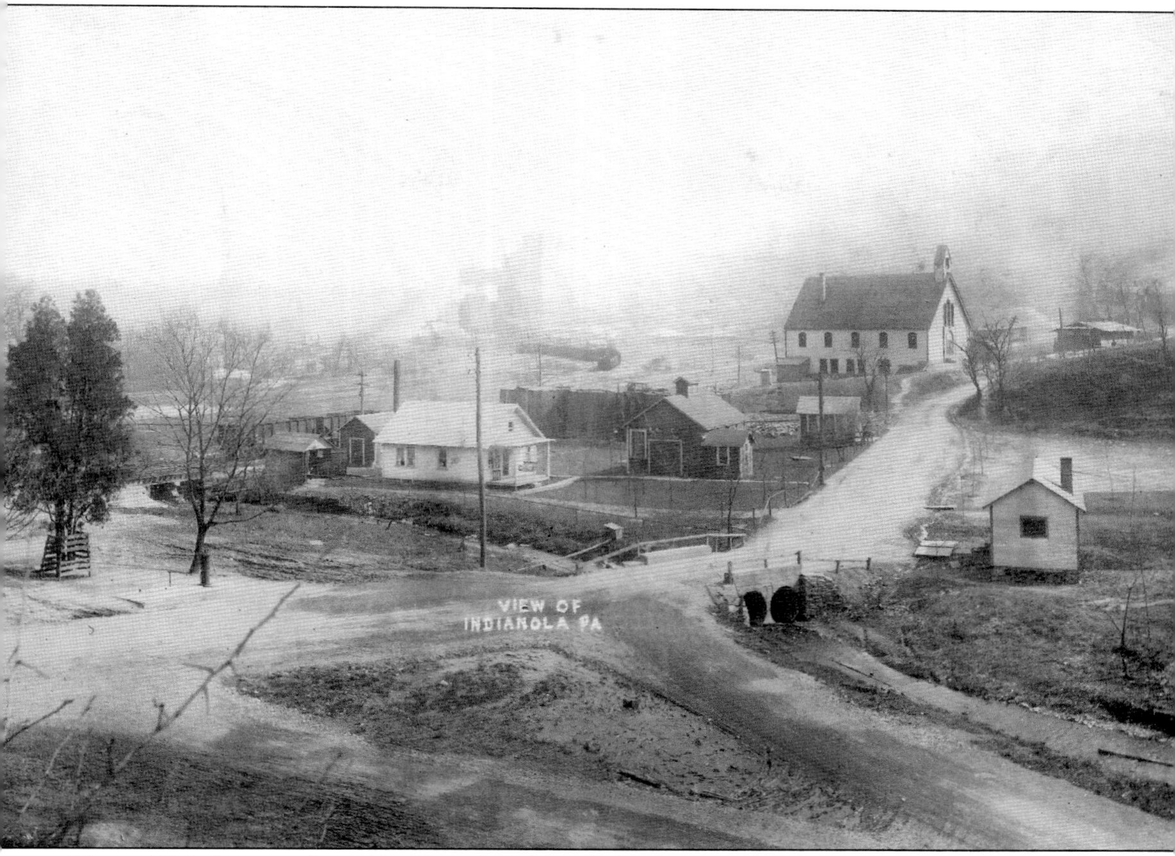

This c. 1920 photograph is of St. Timothy's Church (built in 1920) and the tipple at the Indianola mine, which was erected in 1918. Pittsburgh National Coal and Coke Company sunk a mineshaft in 1903, but it was abandoned before completion after the Harwick mine, located on the former Cheswick & Harwick Railroad in present-day Springdale Township, exploded in 1904. The disaster in Harwick killed 179 miners and was one of the worst mining accidents of its time. Inland Collieries, a subsidiary of Inland Steel Corporation, opened the Indianola mine in 1917. Men were reluctant to enter the mines after the Harwick explosion, also known as "the day the valley wept." The first house in Indianola was finished in 1918. Ellen Walker, wife of mining engineer George William Walker, was expecting twins, so the couple was permitted to move into the first finished company house. Prior to that, Inland Collieries employees lived in tents in the apple orchard on the hill—an area known to the miners as "Peanut Heaven." (Courtesy of Karen Sue Haley.)

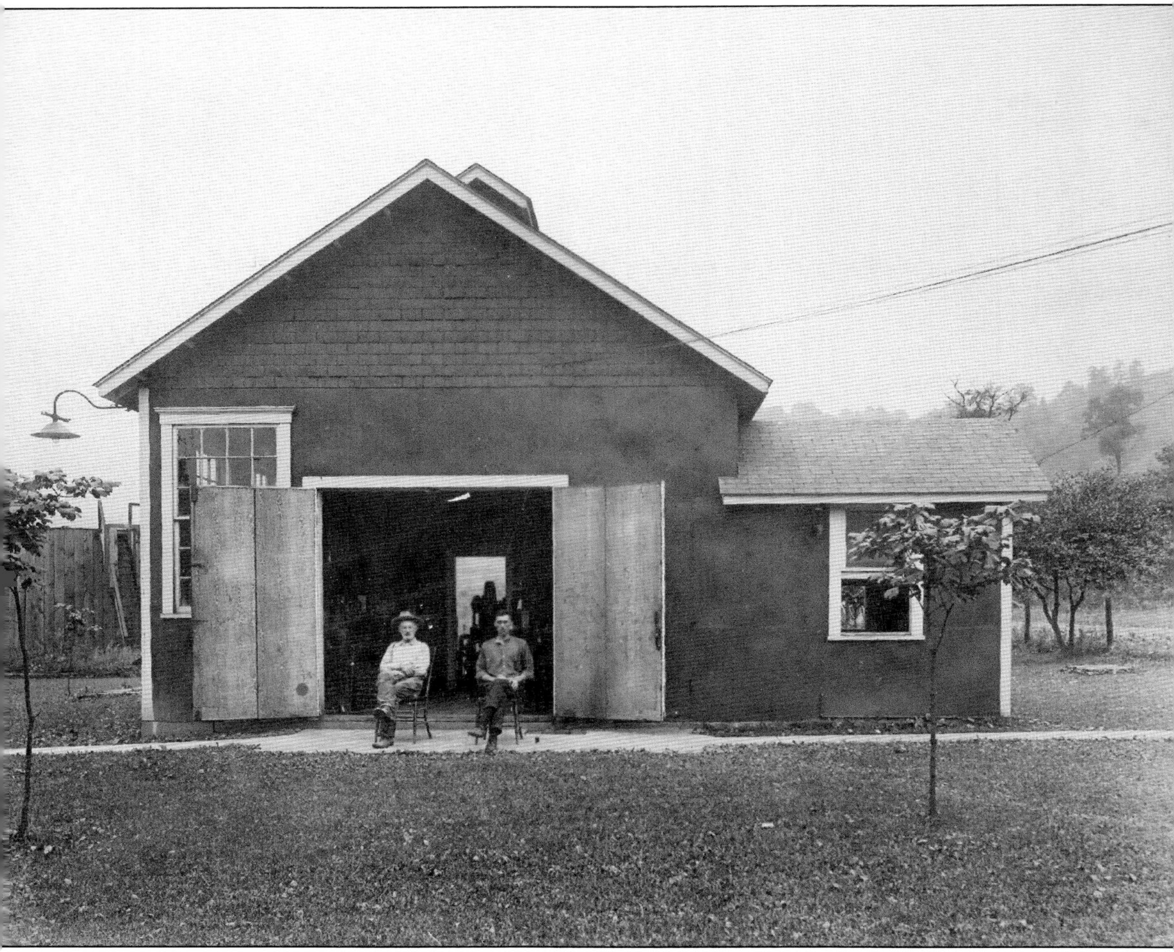

Alfred G. Bartley (left) and his son Owen B. Bartley (Dorothy M. Bartley Shockey-Sharp's father) sit in front of the building that would become Pittsburgh Pipe Line Company's Crawford Station in Indianola. The wooden steps leading up to the lip of the oil barrel are visible in the background at left, behind the house. (Courtesy of Karen Sue Haley.)

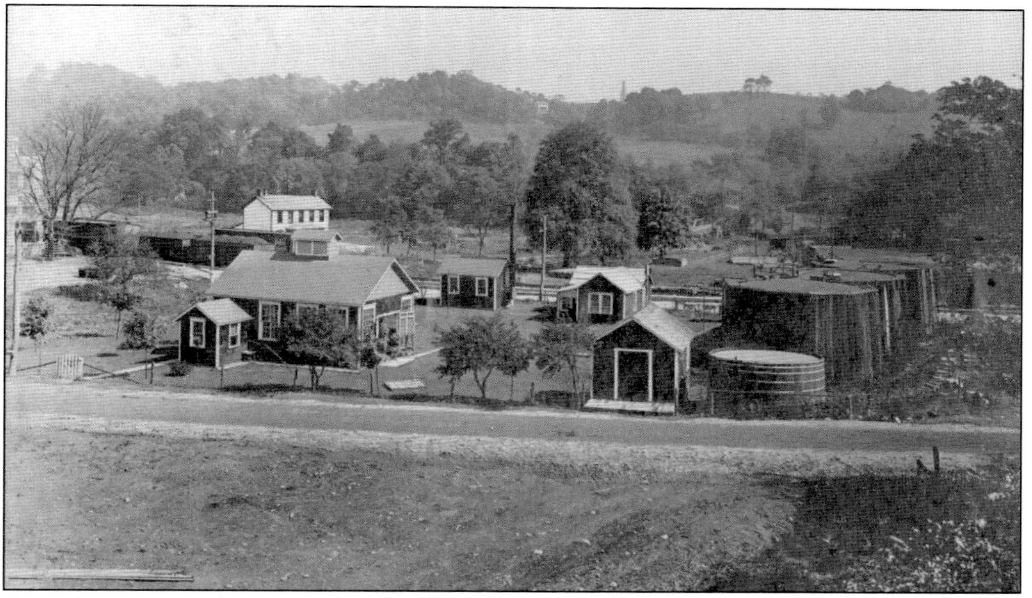

According to Dorothy M. Bartley Shockey-Sharp, "this picture shows the ball field behind the oil tanks. We used to go to the top of the tanks to sit and watch the games." Karen Sue Haley said that the company store is barely visible at the left edge of this image, and the tipple would have been all the way to the right. (Courtesy of Karen Sue Haley.)

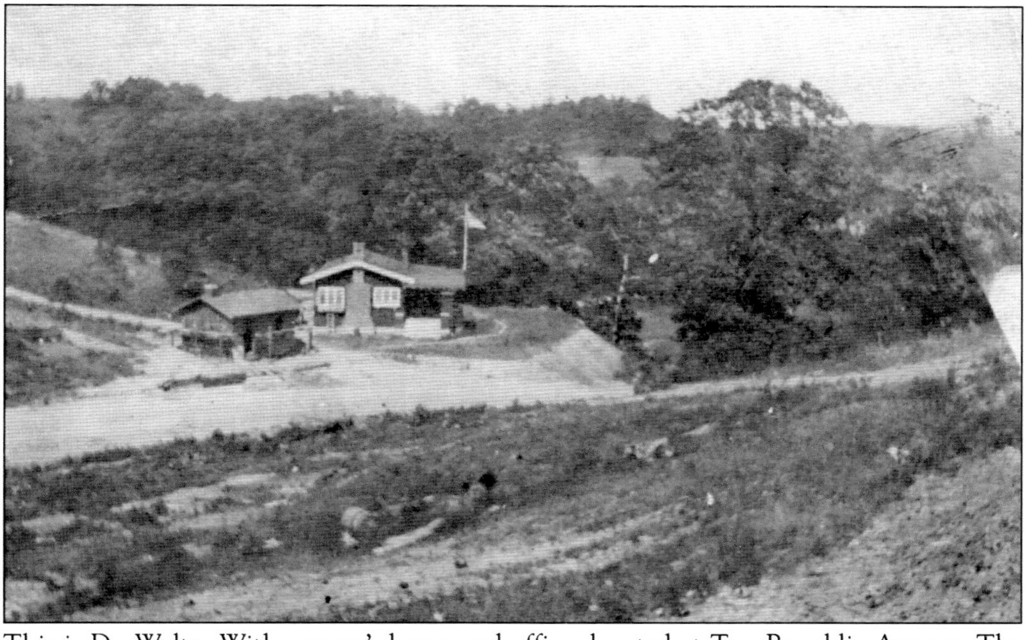

This is Dr. Walter Witherspoon's home and office, located at Two Republic Avenue. The superintendent's house was house number one, and Doctor Witherspoon's house was number two. After Doctor Witherspoon went to Torrence Hospital, the Boy Scouts used his office as their meeting place. Later, the small building used as Witherspoon's office was rolled on logs down Republic Avenue (originally called Disposal Plant Boulevard) for use as the service station next to the gasoline pump at the company store. (Courtesy of Karen Sue Haley.)

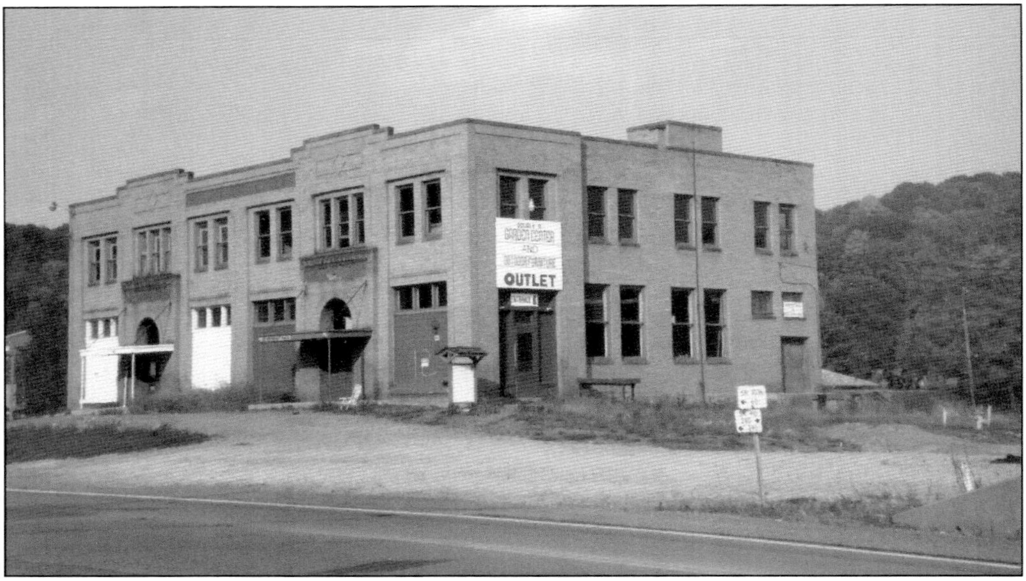

The Indianola company store, built in 1918, is pictured here in 1997. Mine workers were paid in scrip redeemable only at the company store. The company store sold a large variety of items, including furniture, clothing, household goods, meat, produce, and canned goods. There was also an ice-cream shop called "The Dope Stand" in the company store. Indianola residents would send orders to the company store, and clerks would fill them so that all they had to do was come in and pick an order up or have William L. "Willis" Peteet deliver the orders to their homes. (Courtesy of Karen Sue Haley.)

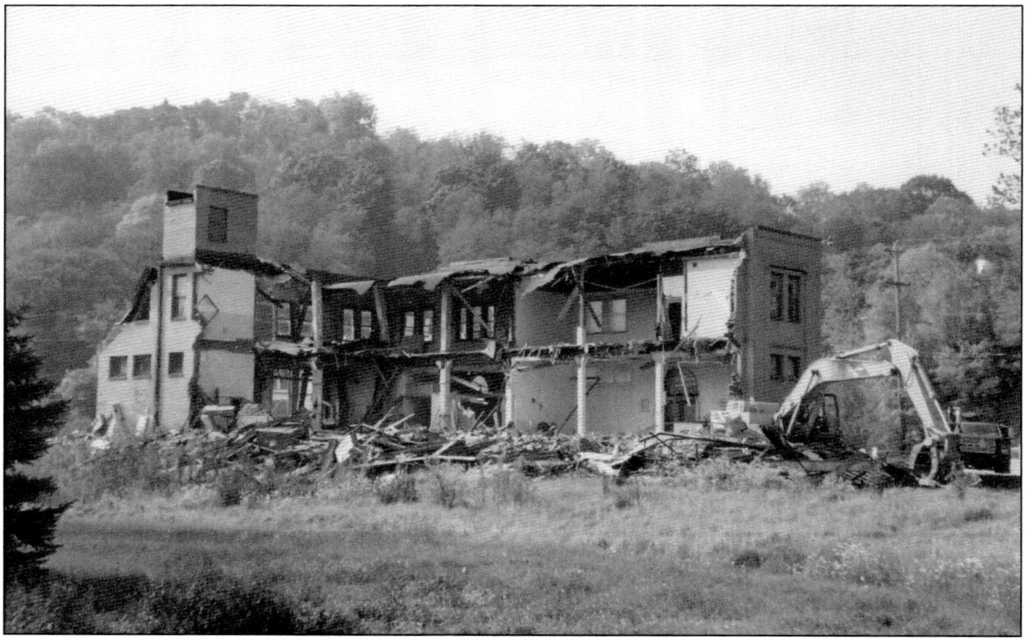

This building housed Deer Creek Mercantile, then the Bessemer Store, and then the Indianola company store. The Indianola company store was not actually owned by the mine, but they worked closely together. MEDRAD tore down the building in 1997. (Courtesy of Karen Sue Haley.)

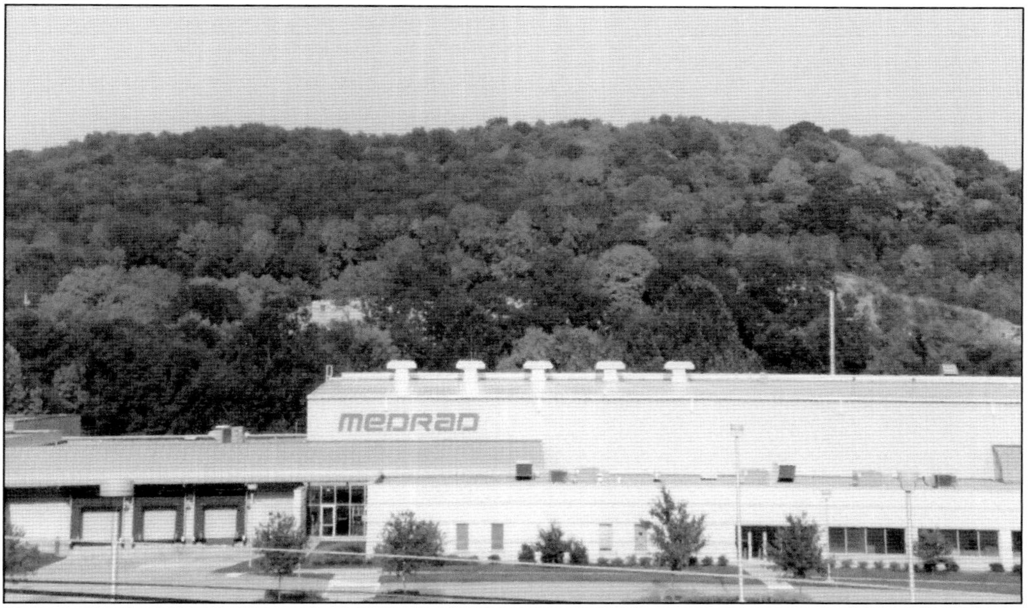

When MEDRAD came to Indianola, many Indianola residents found themselves with new jobs. The company's main source of revenue is making medical supplies used for a certain kind of imaging test. This photograph was taken in 1997. (Courtesy of Karen Sue Haley.)

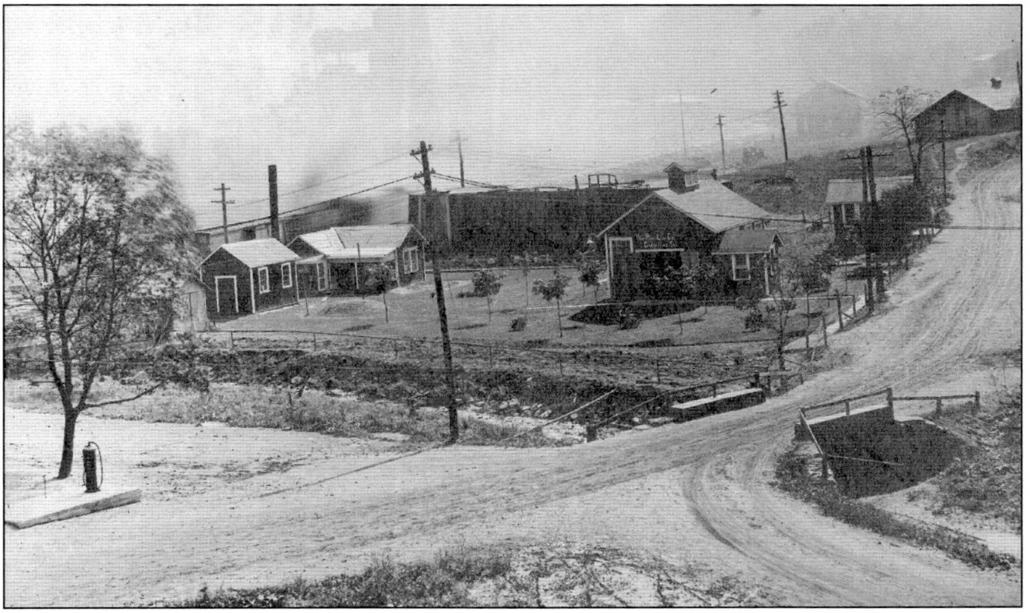

The Pittsburgh Pipe Line Company's Crawford Station is visible in the center of this photograph. This is the location of the current Indianola post office, which now occupies the top floor of the former Indianola Fire Hall. This photograph dates from around 1919, based on the existence of the tipple (built in 1918) and lack of St. Timothy's Church (built in 1920). The small two-window structure at left is a "shanty." Dorothy M. Bartley Shockey-Sharp recalls that her father lived in a shanty before he got married. She also recalls that her parents were the first in Indianola to have the luxuries of electricity and telephone. (Courtesy of Karen Sue Haley.)

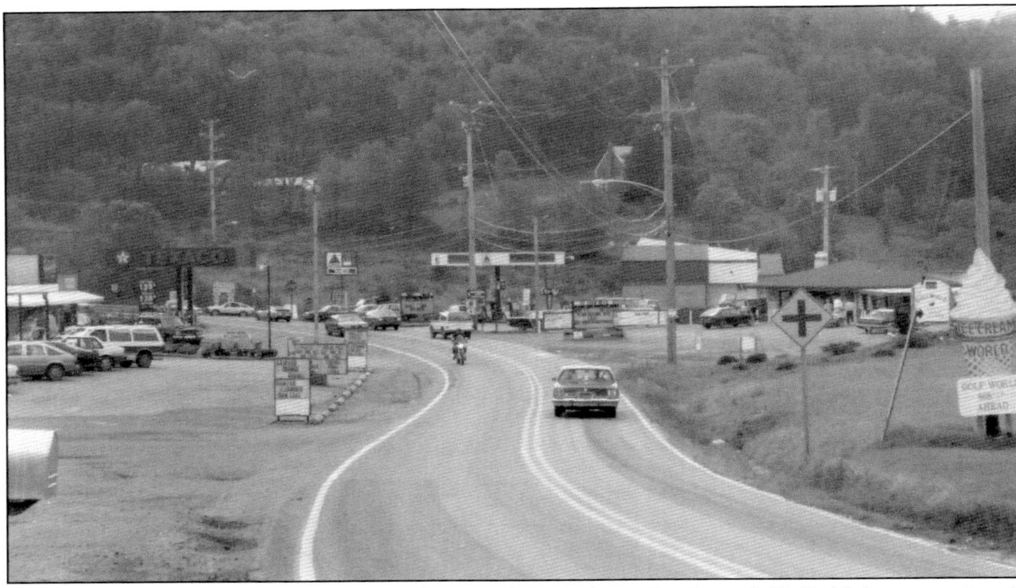

This is Harts Run Road, looking south toward Saxonburg Boulevard. DeBaldo's gas station is on the left, while Ice Cream World is on the right. Ice Cream World also houses Golf World, Caboose World, Arcade World, and Paintball World. Some might consider this area "downtown" Indiana Township.

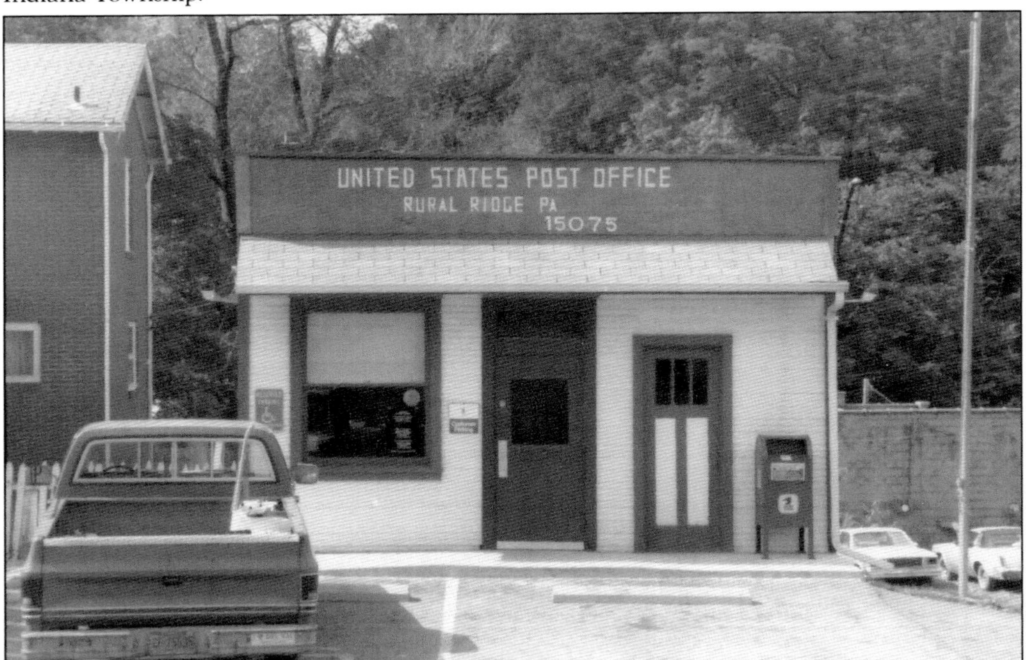

The Rural Ridge Post Office is located on Little Deer Creek Road, which is a major road that travels through many townships and boroughs. The first post office, named Rural Ridge, was founded in 1853 on the property of William Porter; many early post offices were located in people's homes. The building pictured here became a post office in 1951.

Two

Coal Culture

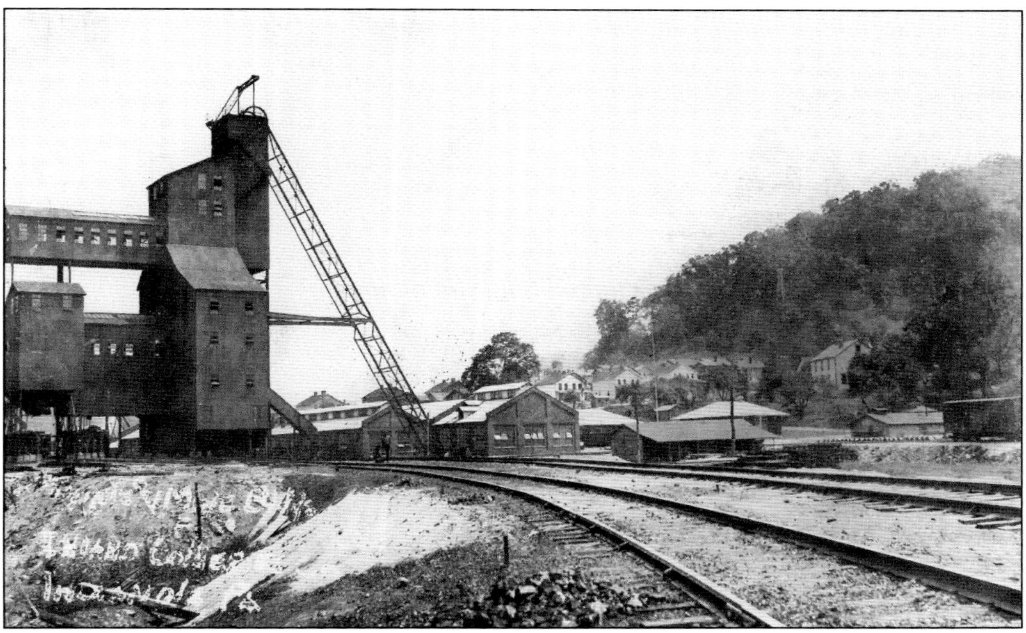

The Indianola mine tipple is pictured perhaps around the mid-1940s. The writing on the photograph appears to read, "Tipple Mine, Inland Collieries, Indianola, PA." The date cannot be deciphered, but could possibly say "1945." This structure is called a tipple because a coal car is carried to the top and then tipped over in order to empty the car of its coal. (Courtesy of Karen Sue Haley.)

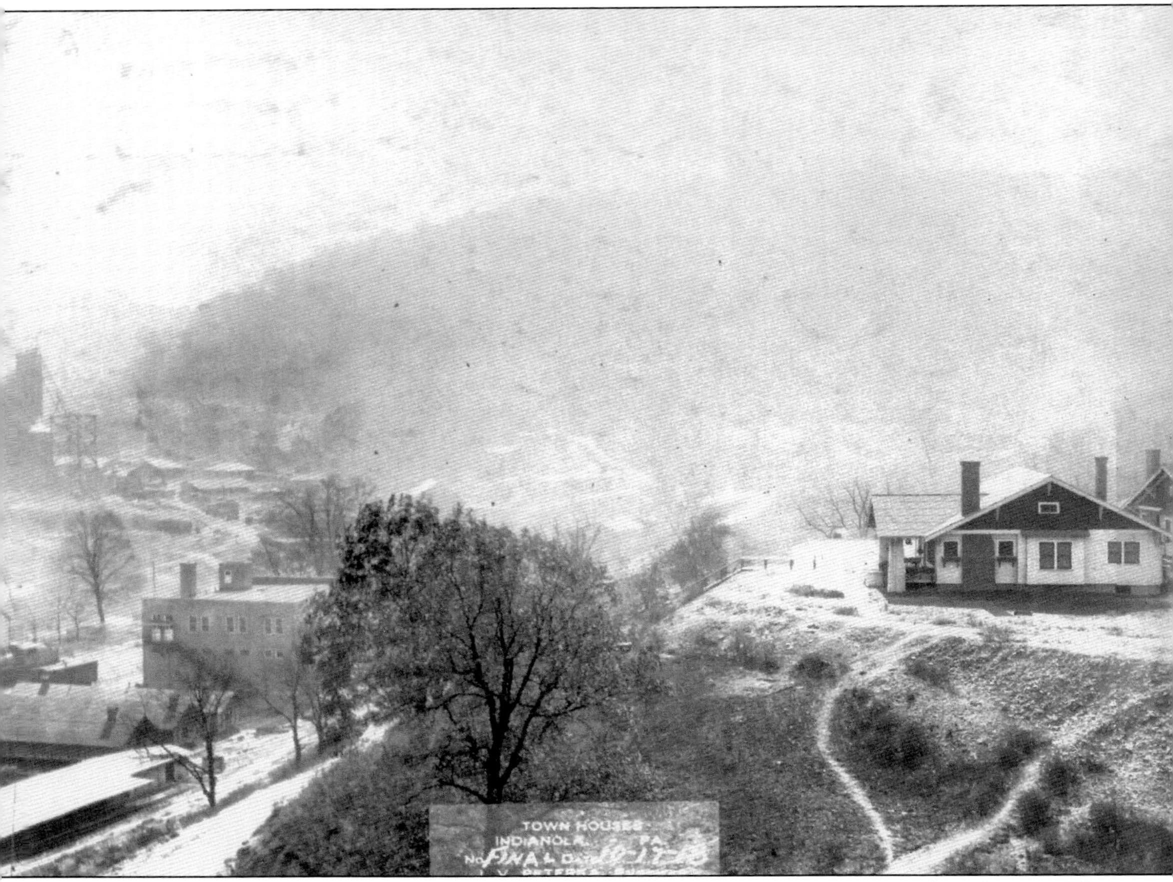

This photograph was taken from the roof of house 80 on Summit Drive on October 17, 1918. The mine tipple is visible at far left center, along with a train on the railroad tracks. The company store is near the lower left corner. The house pictured farthest to the left on the hill is house

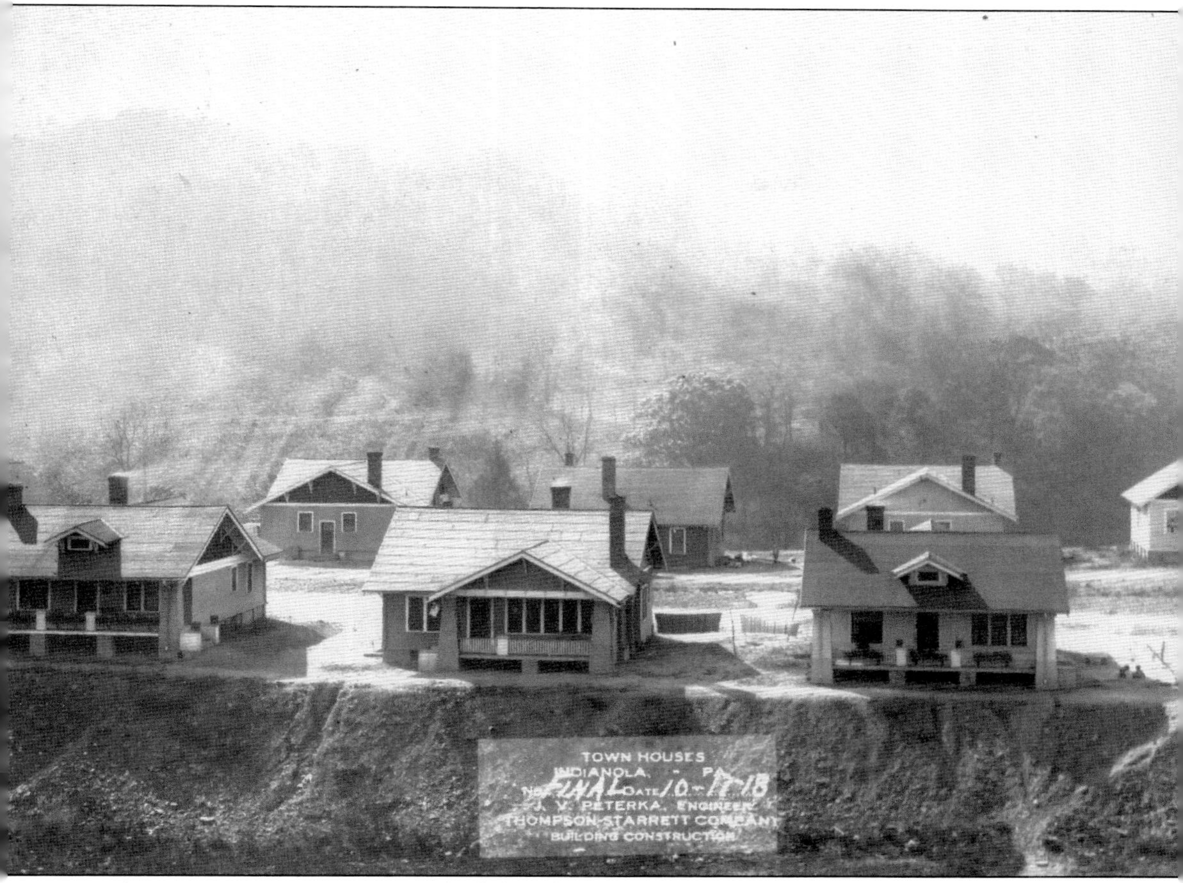

number nine on Crest Drive. To the left of house number nine is the handrail of the wooden steps that connected Crest Drive with Republic Avenue. House number 14 on Crest Drive is on the far right and is only partially visible. (Courtesy of Karen Sue Haley.)

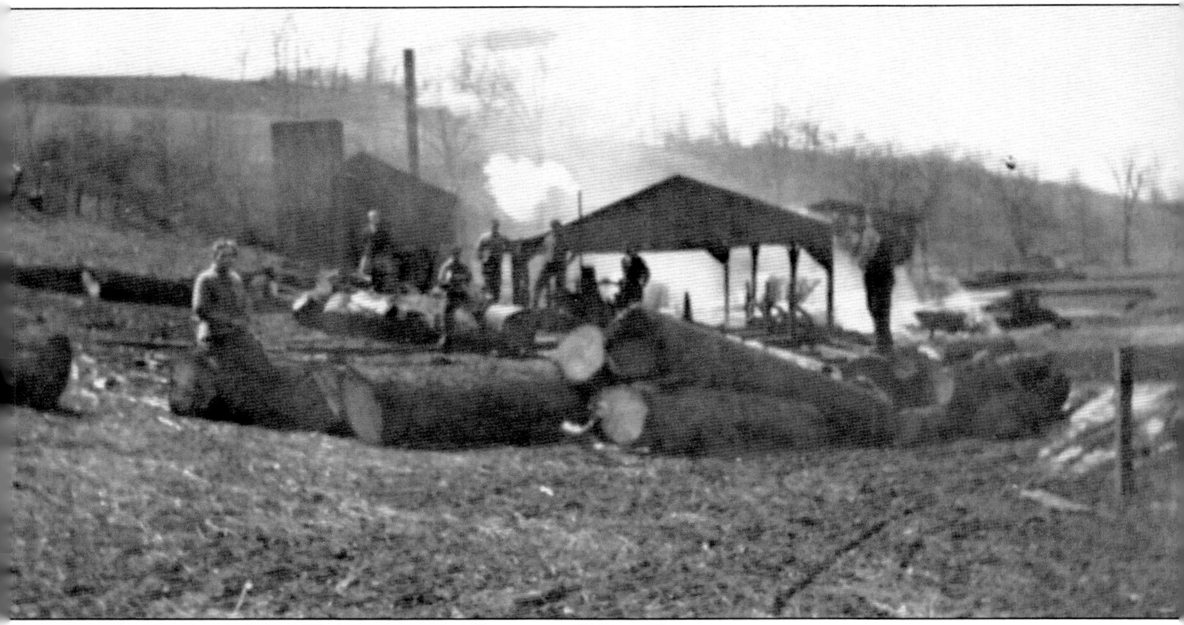

Following the migration of Scotch-Irish immigrants to Dorseyville, the Mink family came to America during a massive influx of Germans around 1820. Peter, Jake, and Henry Mink owned and operated a number of businesses on their property, including a sawmill and coal mine. Pictured here is the Minks' sawmill, with their mine in the background. Peter and Jake sold out to their brother Henry in the early 1930s, and Henry asked his sons Irwin, Clarence, and Howard to take over operations in 1946. The Minks had such an impact on this area that some people still refer to it as Mink's Hill; it is located near the Farm and Garden Center on the corner of Cedar Run Road where State Route 910 crosses over the present-day Pennsylvania Turnpike.

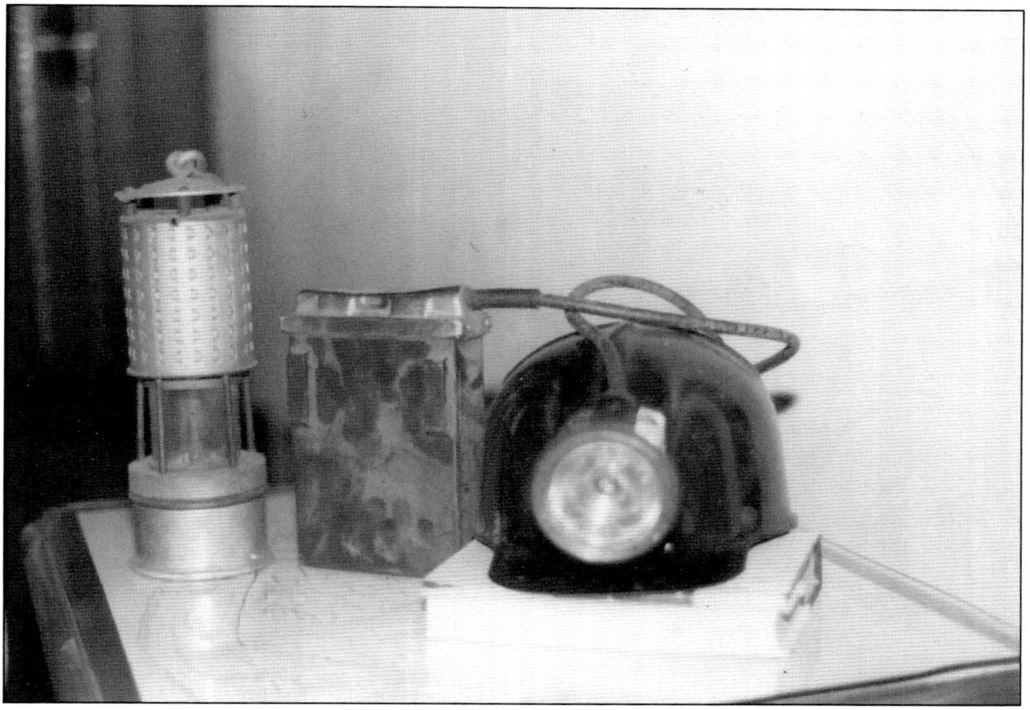

Michael Hertz maintained equipment for the mine until 1935, when he had to spend two years in the hospital after being crushed against a wall by a seven-ton machine. Pictured is some mine safety equipment—an old helmet and lantern. Hertz and his wife, Sylvia, have quite a collection of antique relics.

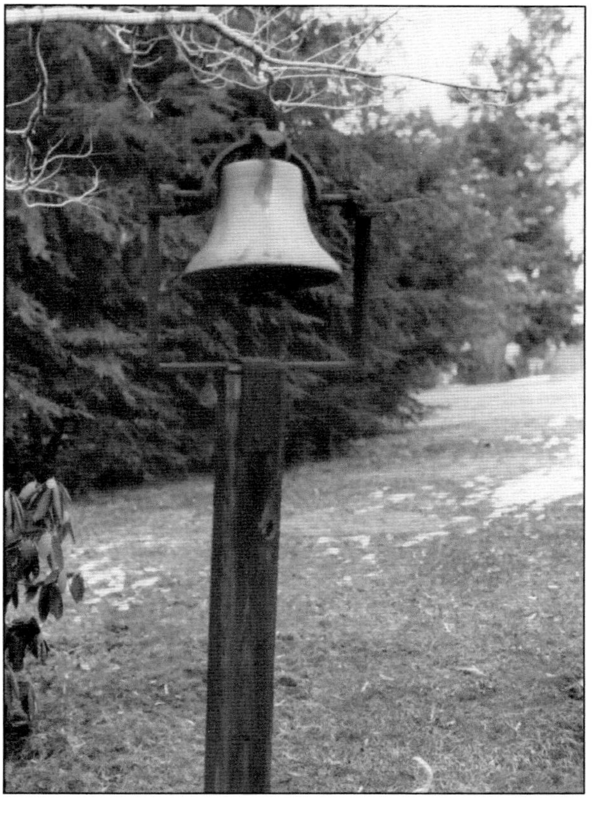

Michael and Sylvia Hertz own many antiques, including this old railroad engine bell. It is assumedly from the Bessemer & Lake Erie Railroad (founded in 1897 by Andrew Carnegie), which runs through Indiana Township, but no one knows the bell's definite history.

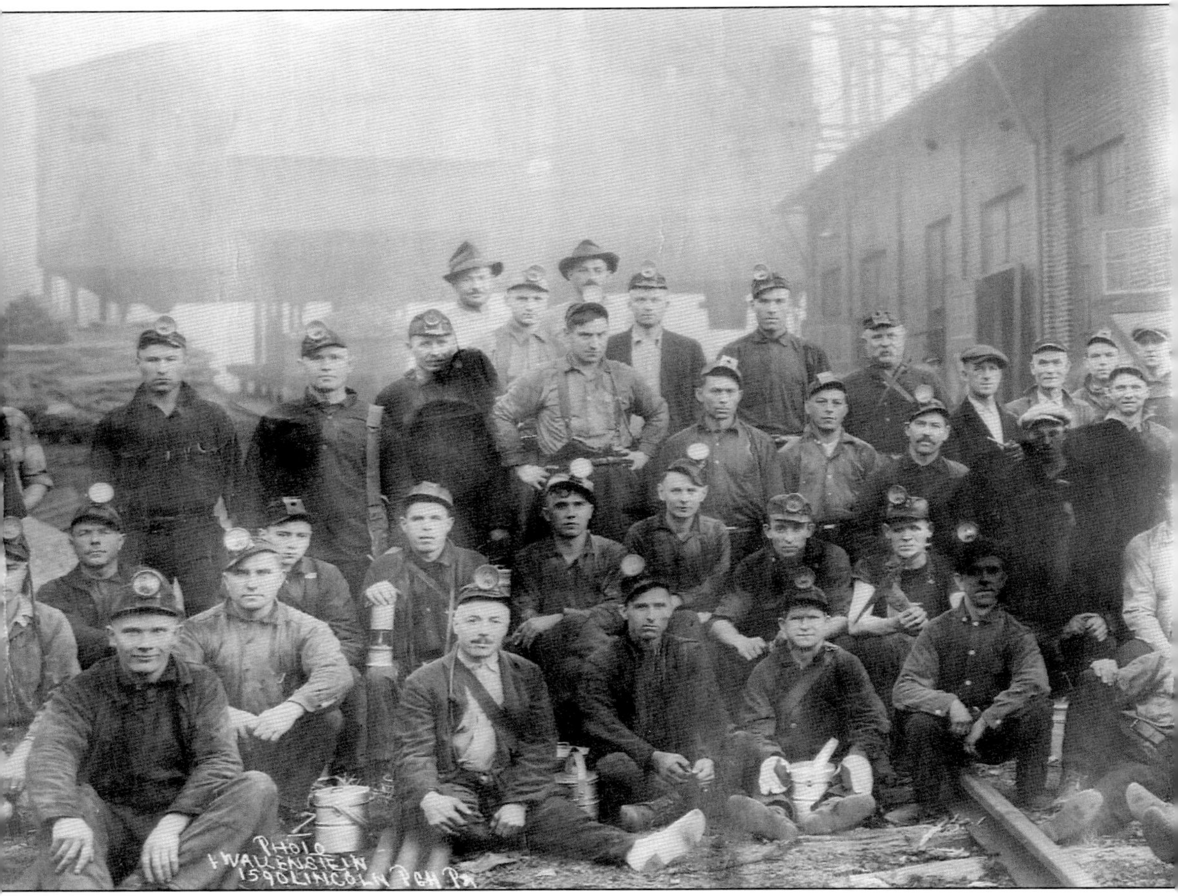

This August 21, 1923, photograph shows miners in front of Rural Ridge Mine (also known as the Monarch Mine), which was owned by the Monarch Fuel Company. Their helmets indicate that they were still using carbide lamps instead of battery-operated lamps that affixed to their

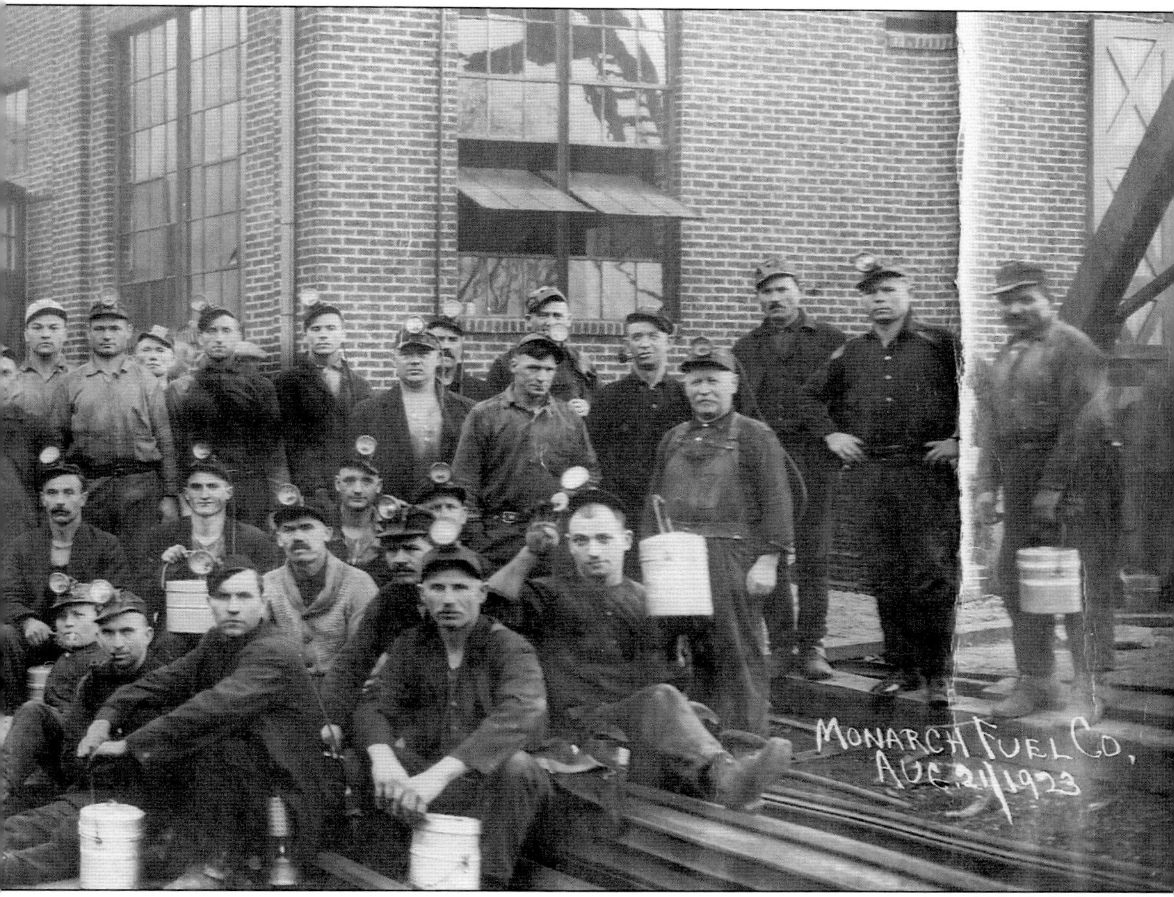

belts. Saxman and Sons Company originally owned the Rural Ridge Mine, starting in the early 1920s. Monarch Fuel Company took over after Saxman and Sons, and Duquesne Light bought the property from Monarch Fuel in the 1940s. (Courtesy of Mary Yelich.)

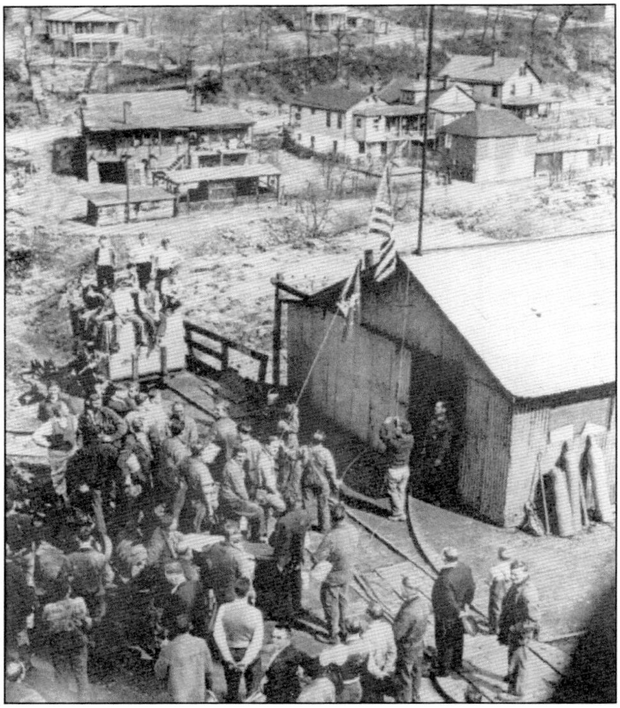

This photograph shows the Rural Ridge miners at a flag-raising ceremony held in celebration of most war bonds sold during World War II. The Rural Ridge mine was awarded the state flag, which is visible under the United States flag, and that was a very big deal to them. (Courtesy of Mary Yelich.)

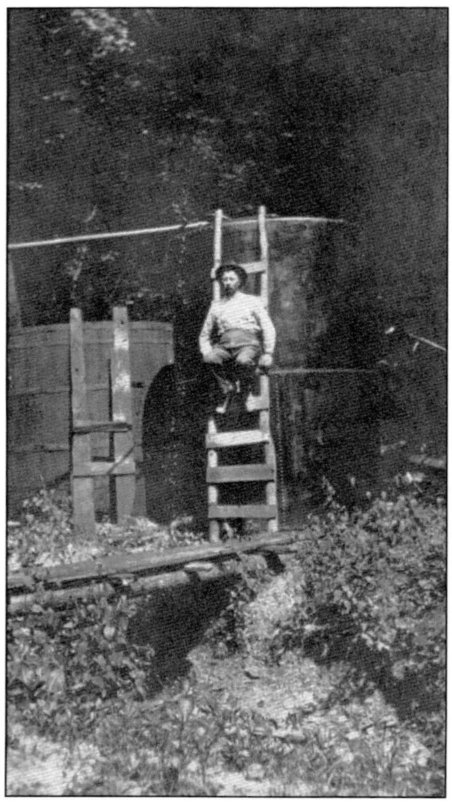

This oil well, located on the Prager property, was not the main source of income for the family. John P. Prager, son of George Prager, is pictured sitting on the family's oil well off of Mill Dam Road. As with most families in Indiana Township, farming provided the Pragers with the bulk of their income. John died on the homestead at the ripe old age of 99.

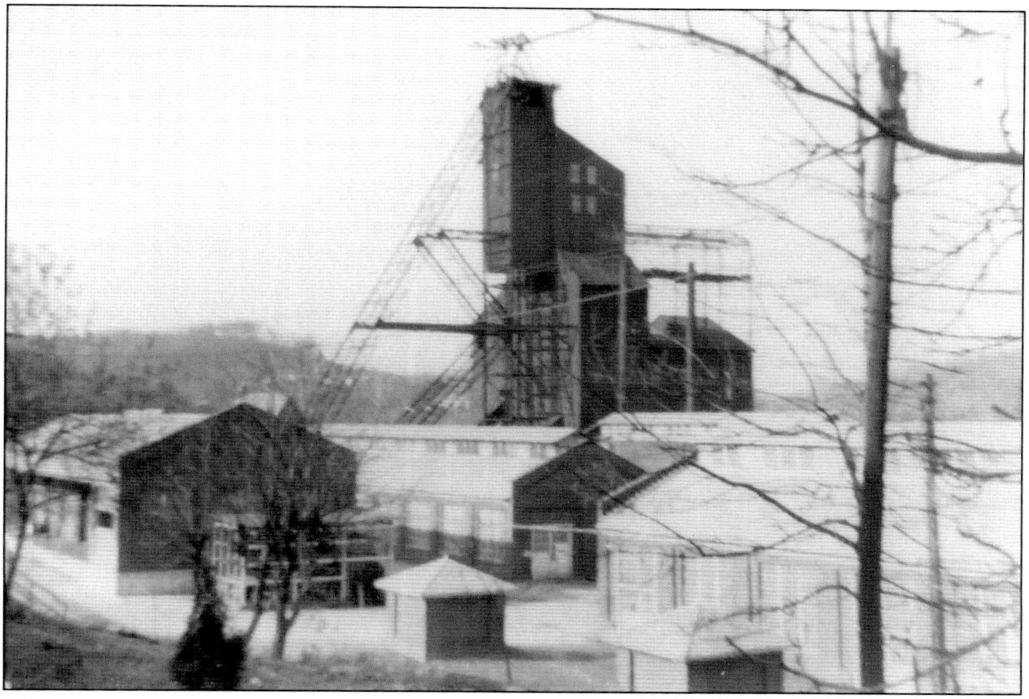

The Indianola mine tipple was erected in 1918. Here, mine cars were placed on a lift and carried up a conveyor belt. At the top, they were "tipped" and emptied of their coal, then the coal was sorted and distributed to its appropriate destinations.

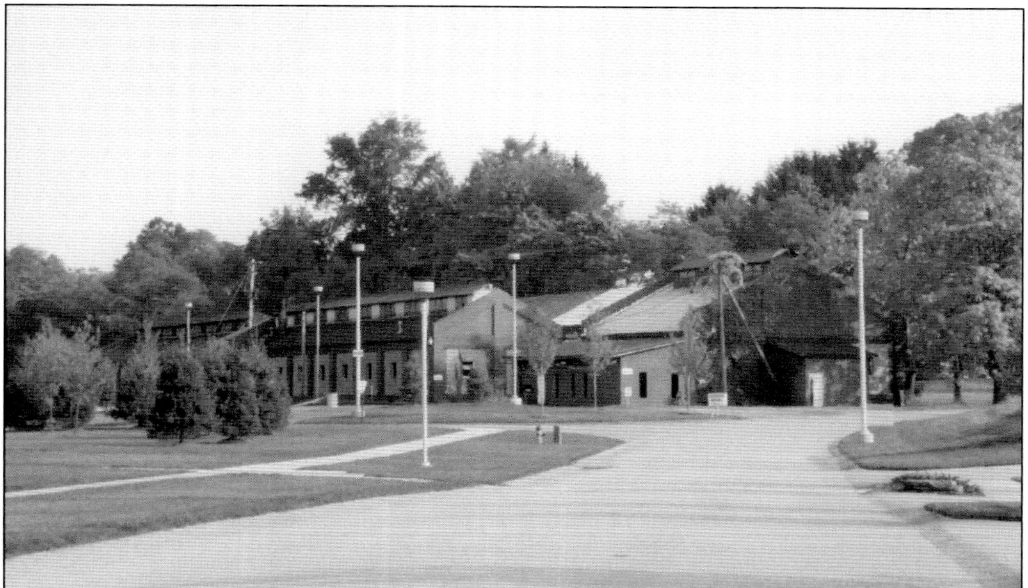

This 1990s photograph shows the old mine buildings on present-day Medrad Drive in Indianola. One of them contained the pump house, another the hospital, and another housed the mine office. Only the former mine hospital (the building closest to the right side of the image) is still standing. (Courtesy of Karen Sue Haley.)

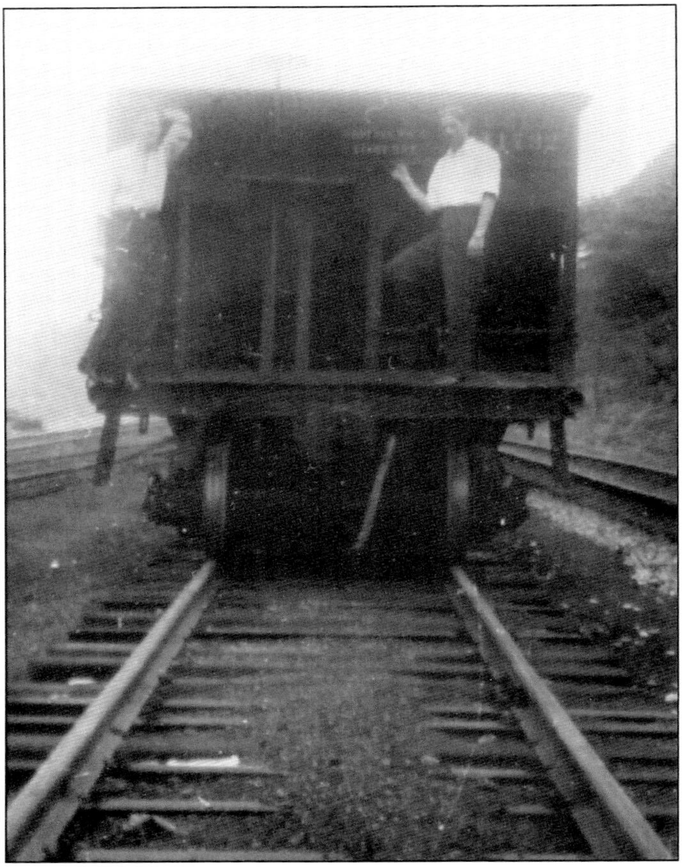

Joe Sabatini (left) and an unidentified person ride on the back of a coal car at Rural Ridge Mine. Upon close inspection, part of the writing on the coal car can be read: "B&L.E. [Bessemer & Lake Erie] 11732." A gentleman named Saxman and his two sons first developed the Rural Ridge mine in 1922. (Courtesy of Mary Yelich.)

This is a 1947 view of Rowe Street in the Rural Ridge development as seen from the hayfield. A note on the back of the photograph states, "village owned by Pittsburgh Consol. Then transferred into J.R. & Hilda & Russ Montgomery's name. Then transfers to individuals." (Courtesy of Mary Yelich; photograph by Russ Montgomery.)

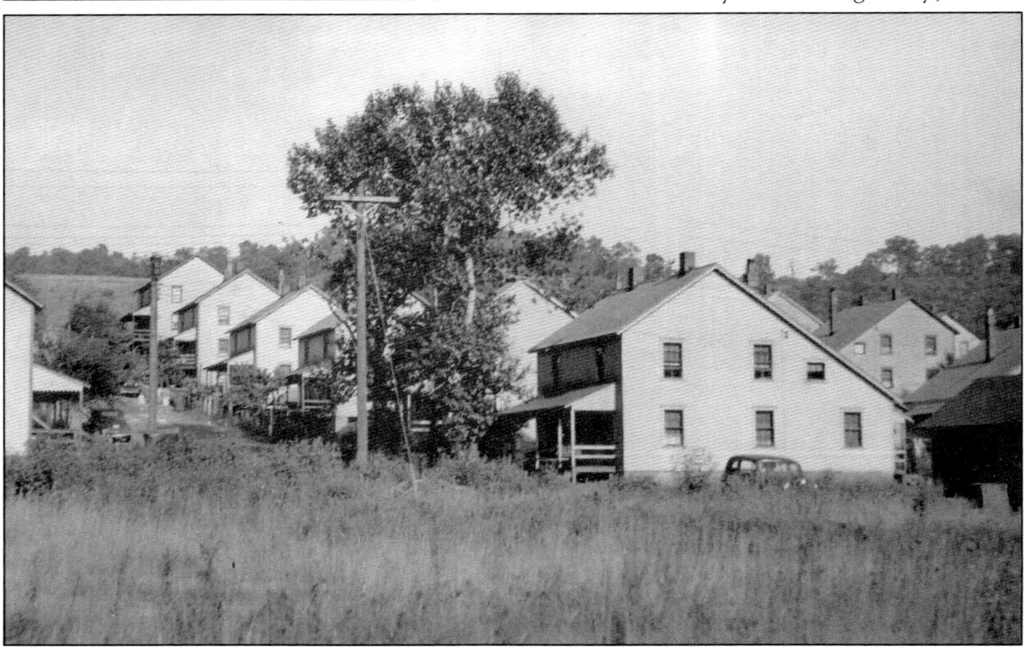

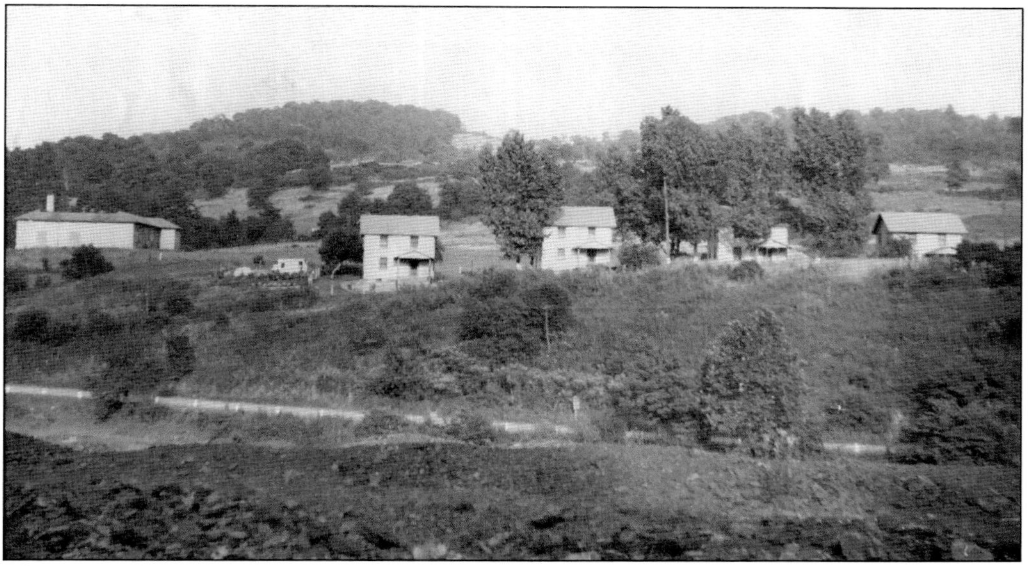

This is a good representation of Rural Ridge's landscape and topography in 1947. Little Deer Creek Road, one of Rural Ridge's main arteries, runs along the bottom of the photograph, and Hiles Farm is visible at upper left. The homes, which were located on Hays Street, are nearly identical in architecture. (Courtesy of Mary Yelich; photograph by Russ Montgomery.)

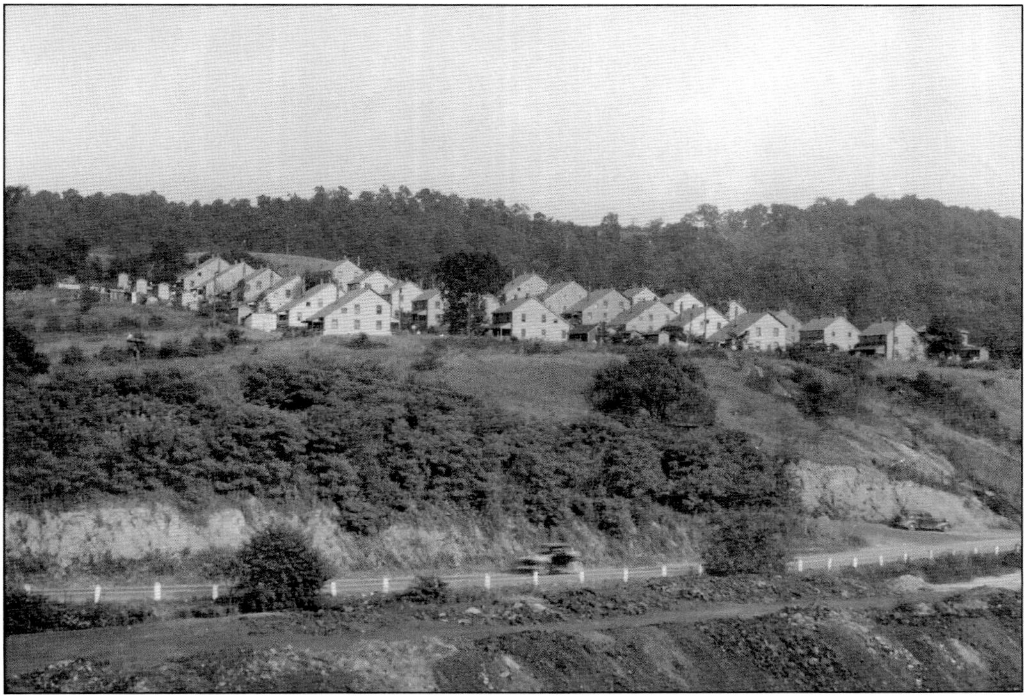

This photograph of Ring and Rowe Streets, in "the patch" of Rural Ridge, was taken from below Little Deer Creek Road in 1947. Barnhart Street leads up to these housing developments from Little Deer Creek Road. "The patch" was the name given to the area where the miners mostly lived and worked. (Courtesy of Mary Yelich; photograph by Russ Montgomery.)

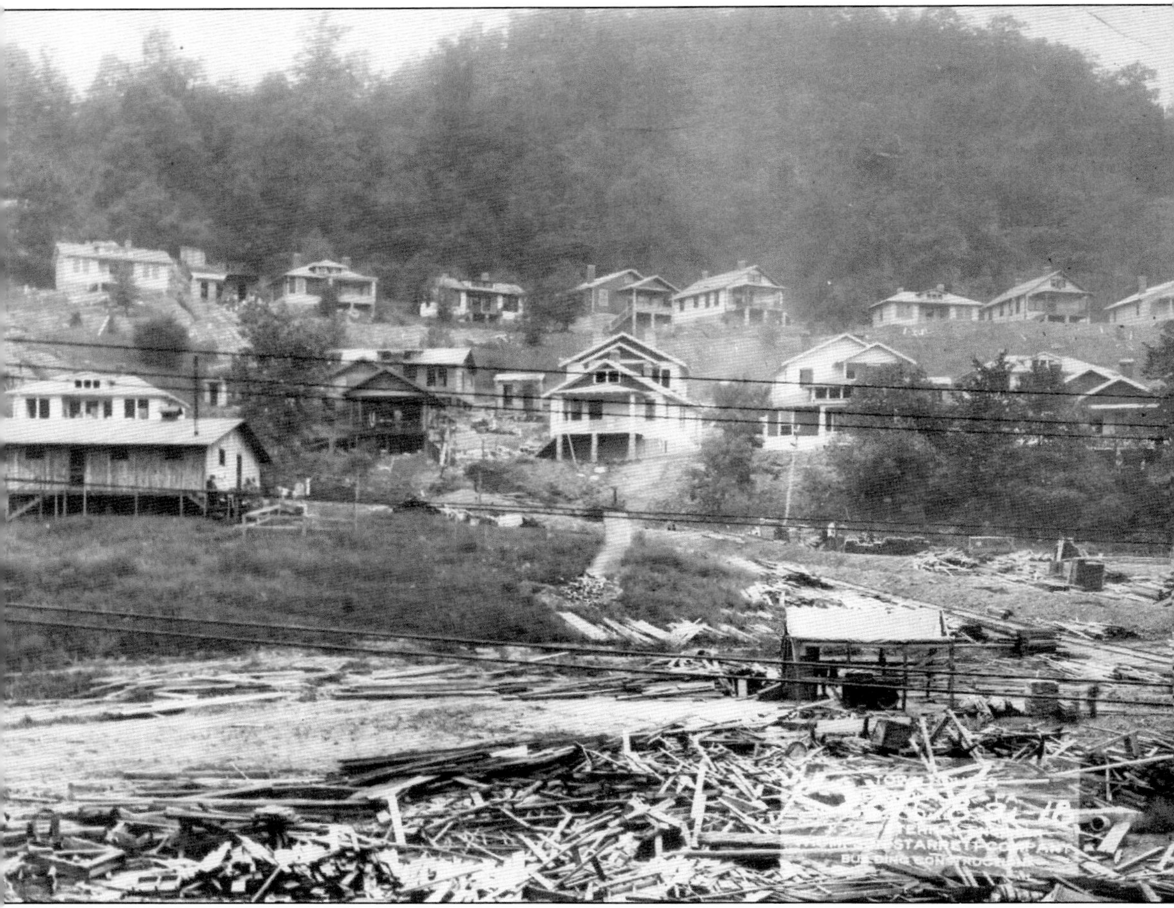

This is a close-up of the sawmill constructed in Indianola in order to finish building company homes. At the time, it was not unusual for mining companies to purchase a few catalogue homes and then build their own sawmill to try and recreate the same homes for less money, although it is not certain if Inland Collieries practiced this. The tracks running up the hillside were built to

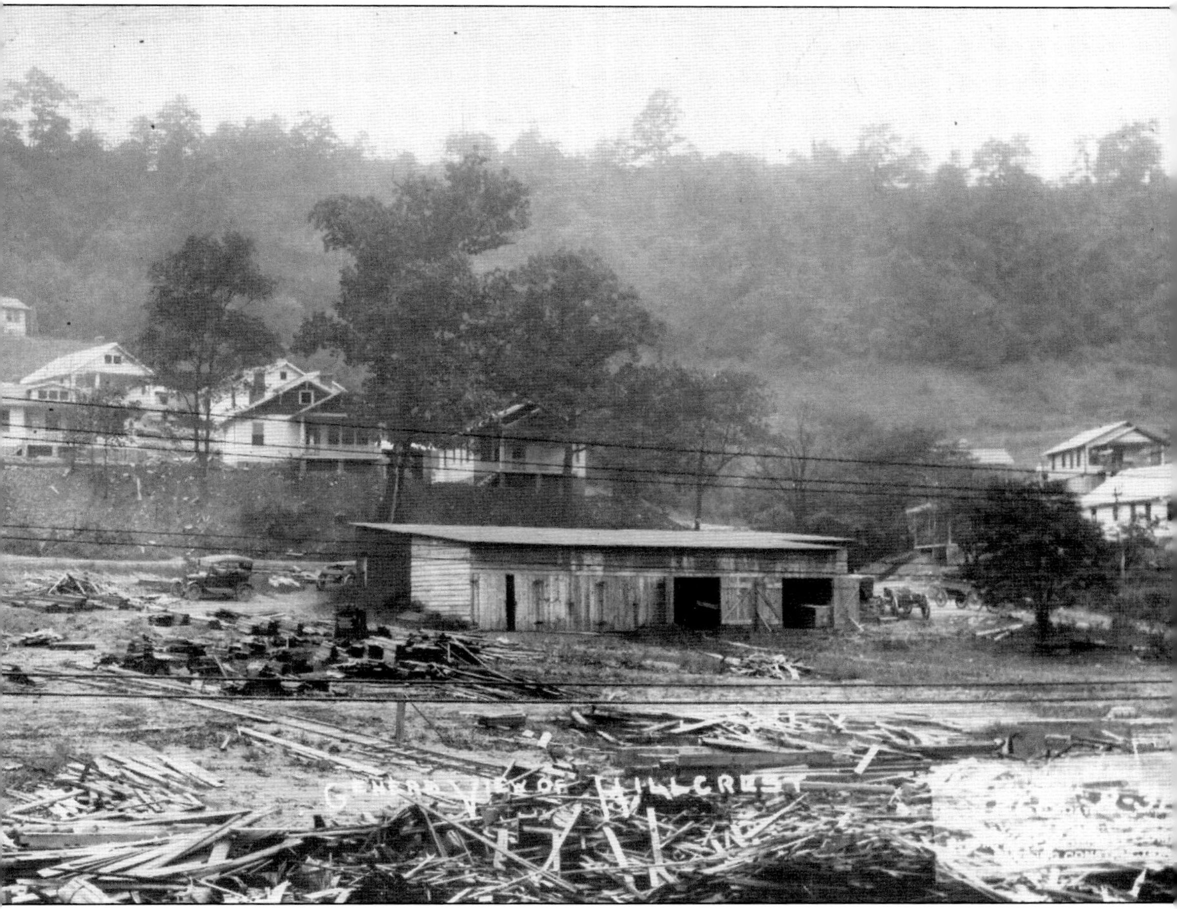

transport lumber to the top of the hill. Note the sheer amount of lumber on the ground around the sawmill ready to be put to use in building a home. Notice the car to the left of the building in the foreground. The houses in the background are along State Route 910 above the mine complex. (Courtesy of Karen Sue Haley.)

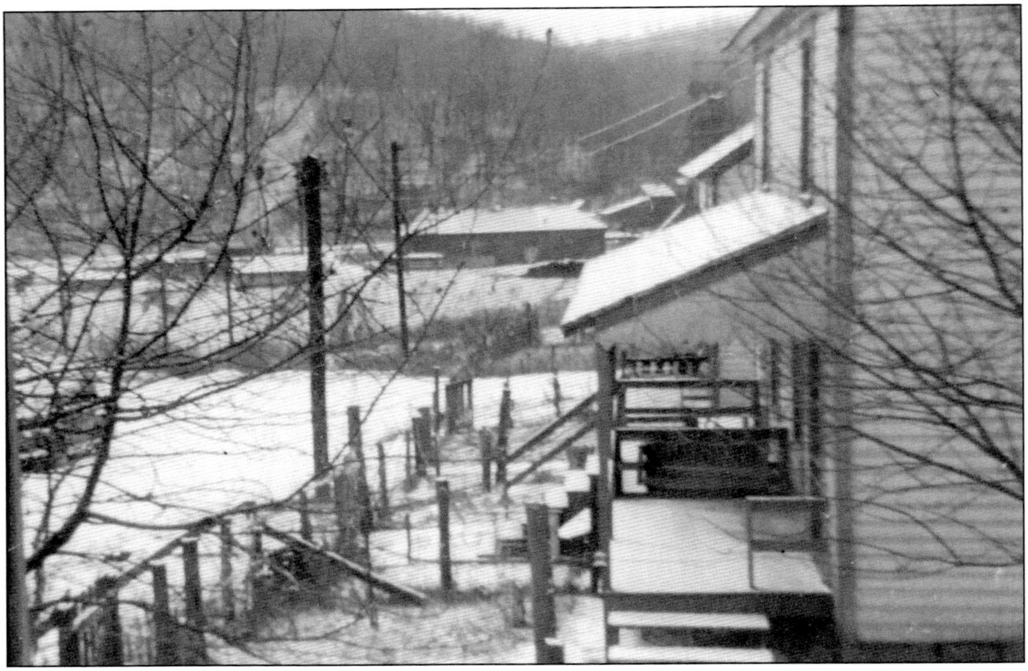

It is obvious how close the backyards were at the housing developments constructed in Rural Ridge. These houses appear to be on Little Deer Creek Road, below where "the patch" used to be, with the railroad and tipple in the background. (Courtesy of Mary Yelich.)

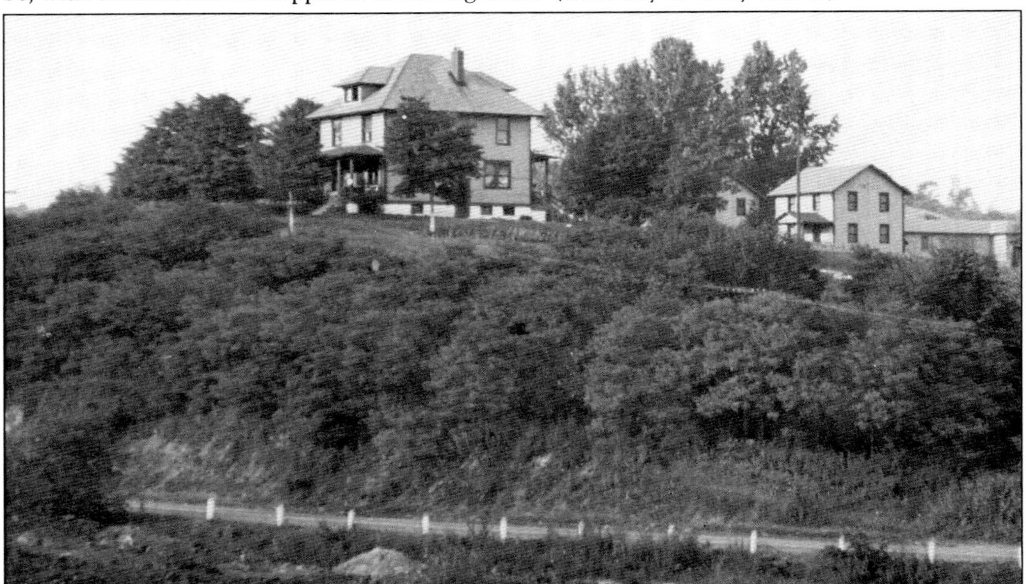

This 1947 view of Little Deer Creek Road shows an unknown street running up the hill to the large house. According to Mary Yelich, this home belonged to a Dr. Torin. A note on the back of the photograph reads: "Village owned by Pittsburgh Consol. Then transferred into J.R. & Hilda & Russ Montgomery's name. Then transfers to individuals." (Courtesy of Mary Yelich; photograph by Russ Montgomery.)

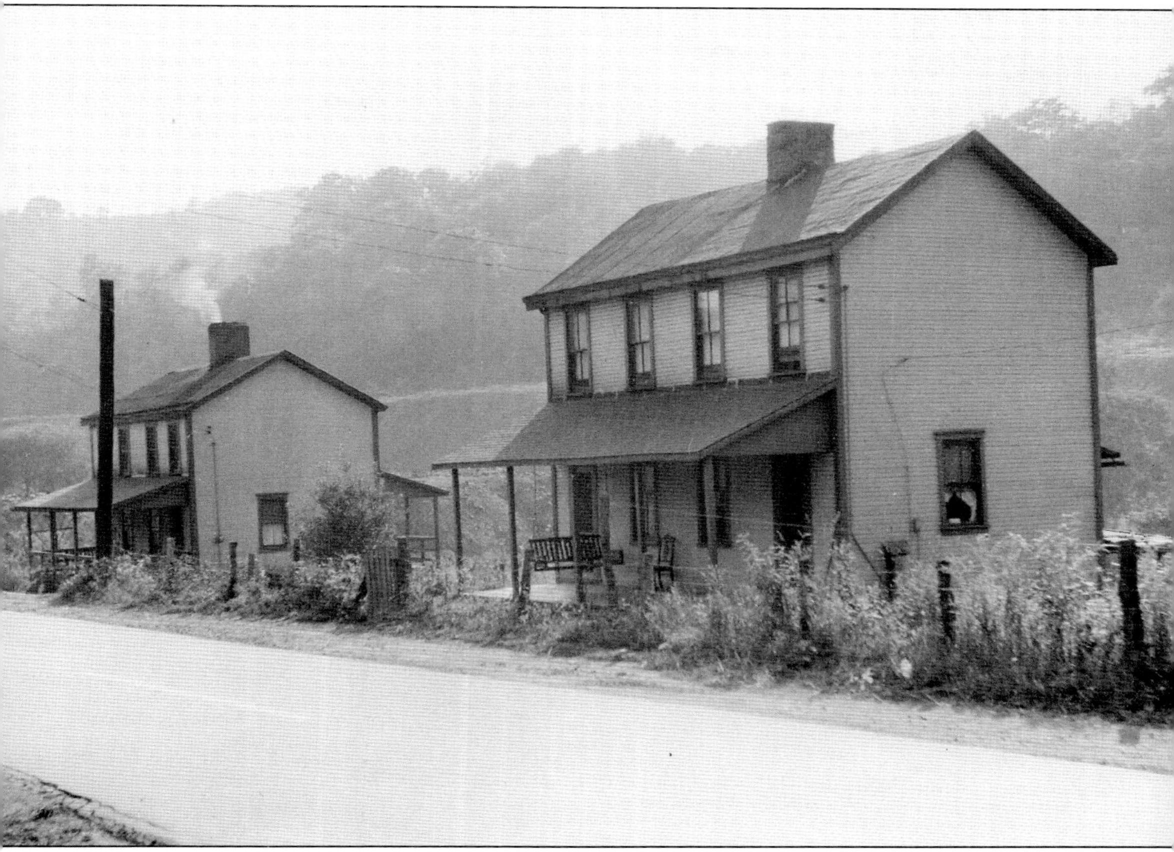

These two near-identical houses are on Little Deer Creek Road in Rural Ridge. This 1947 image shows the Yaworsky (left) and Bokach homes. (Courtesy of Mary Yelich; photograph by Russ Montgomery.)

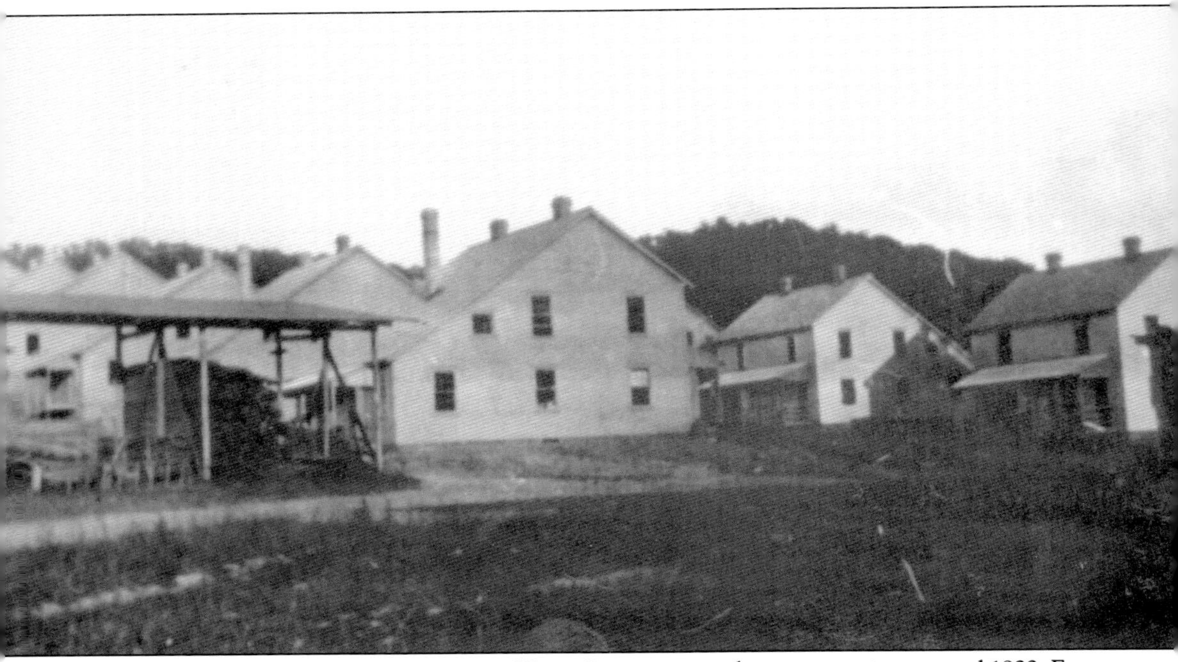

In this image, patch houses on Rowe and Ring Streets are under construction around 1922. Every mining town had its "patch," and a sawmill was usually constructed in order to build the patch housing. Rural Ridge's patch contained four rows of frame, double-family houses. Four-frame, single-family houses were built on Hays Street for the mine bosses. (Courtesy of Mary Yelich.)

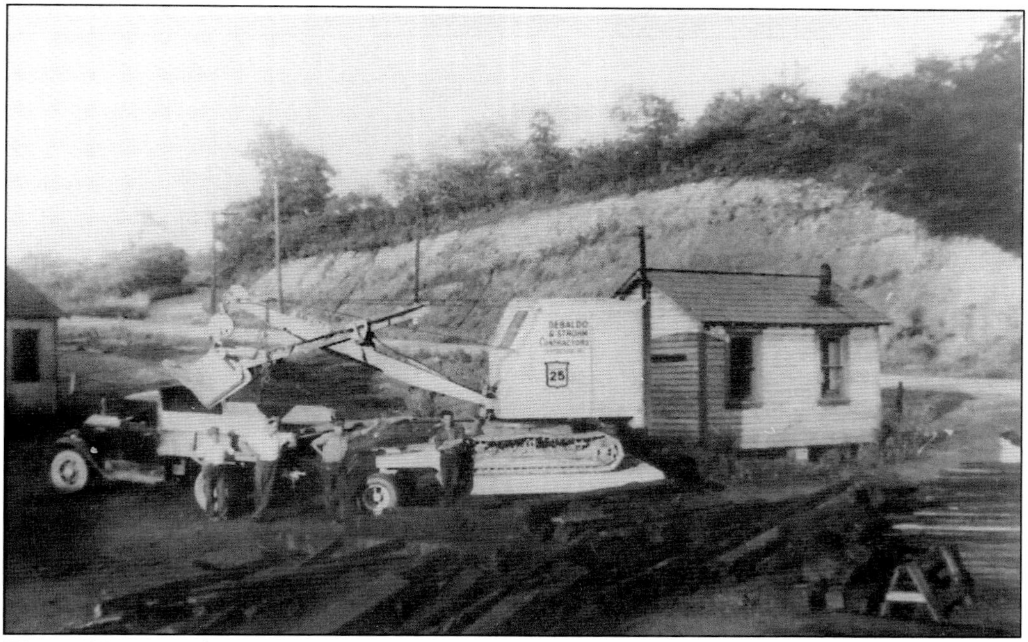

This 1939 image shows Pete, Windy, Carl, Amie, and Alice Strohm (in no particular order) closing and filling at the Harrison and Quinette coal mine on Saxonburg Boulevard. The mine was actually called the Thomas Mine, but was owned by the Harrison and Quinette Coal Company. Not much is known about this mine other than that it opened in 1938; according to the photograph, it was disassembled in 1939. (Courtesy of Eden Harris.)

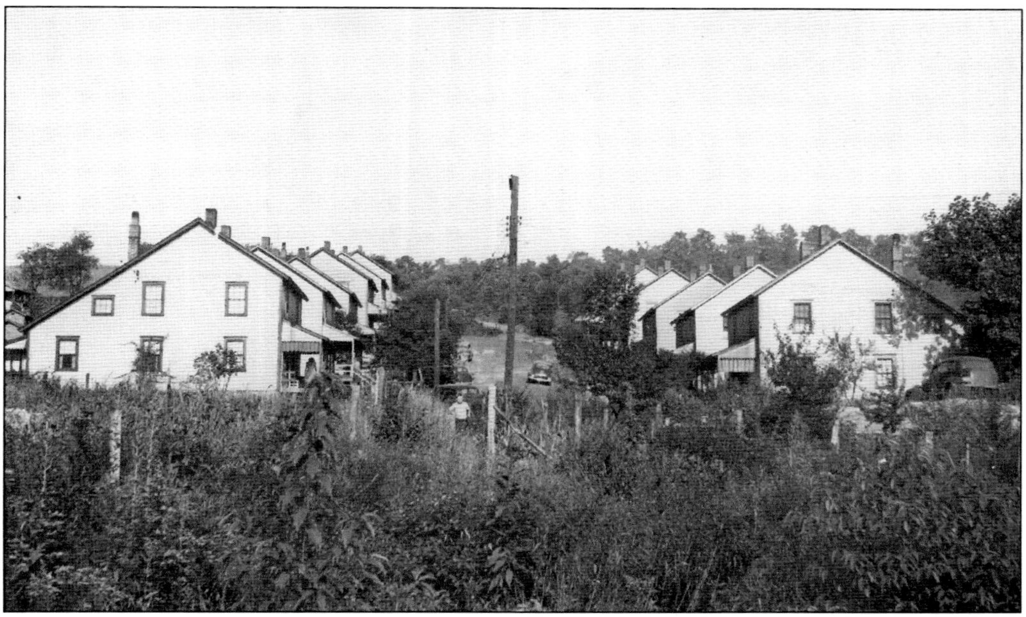

This 1947 photograph offers a good view of Ring Street in the Rural Ridge "patch." Miners paid $11 per month for one half of a double house in the patch. The streets were dirt and would turn to mud in wet weather, making it difficult to walk anywhere. (Courtesy of Mary Yelich; photograph by Russ Montgomery.)

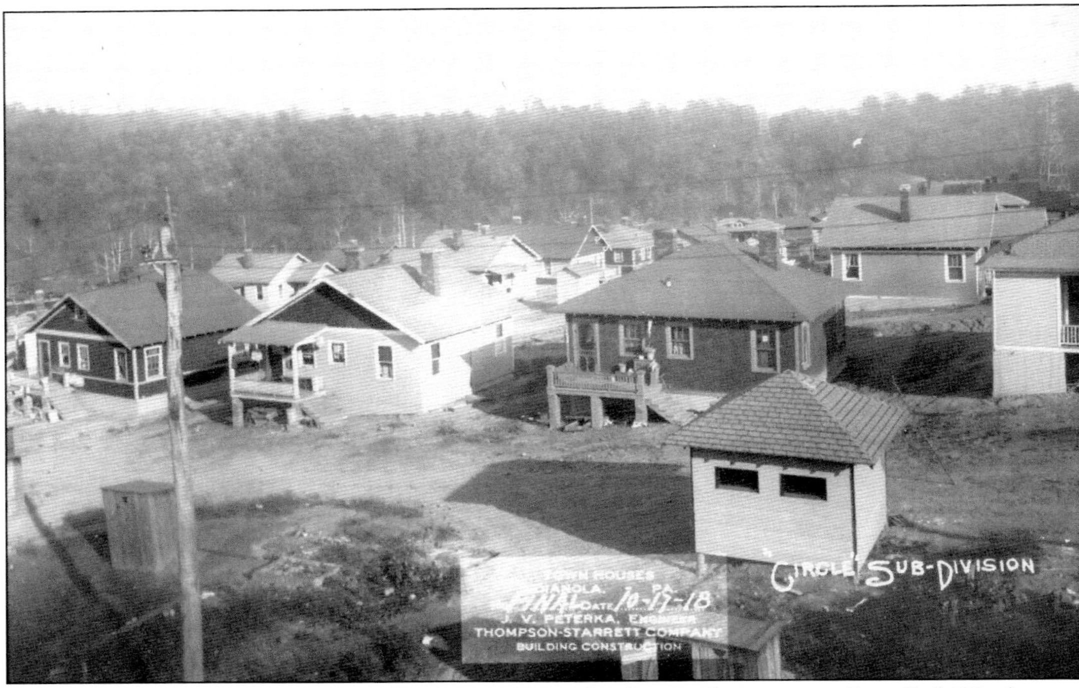

This area of Indianola is closest to the Harmar Township line and was originally called "Circle Subdivision." This October 17, 1918, image shows State Route 910 running through the

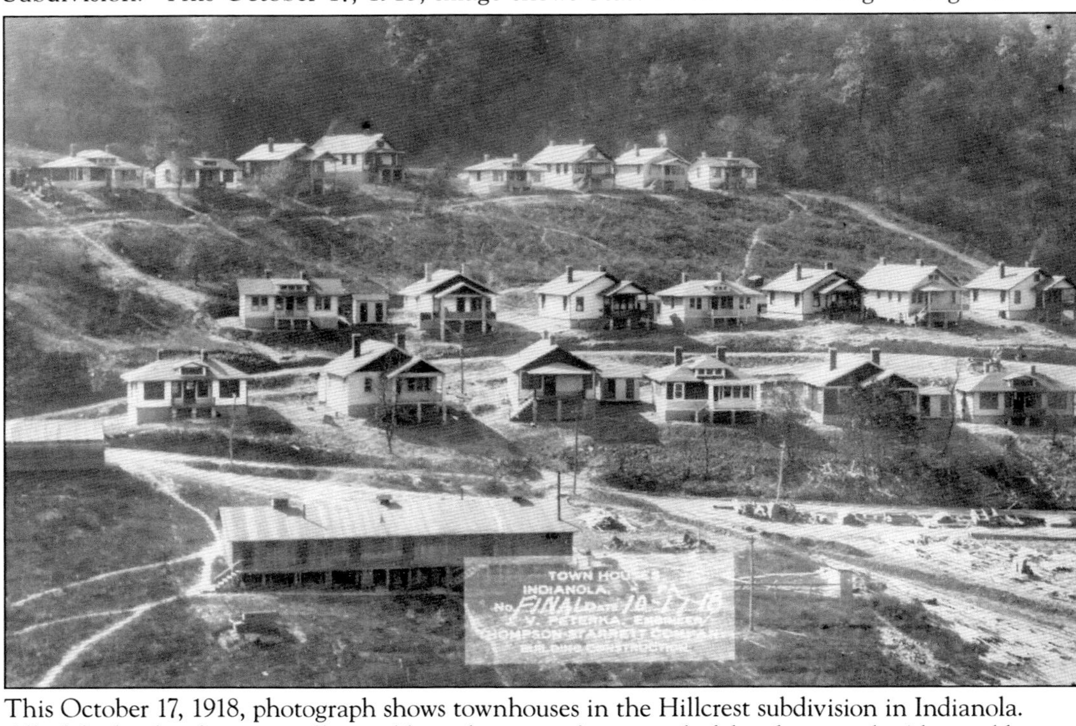

This October 17, 1918, photograph shows townhouses in the Hillcrest subdivision in Indianola. All of the lumber for a sawmill is visible in the center foreground of the photograph. Also visible are the tracks built to haul or, more accurately, roll the lumber up the hill for home construction.

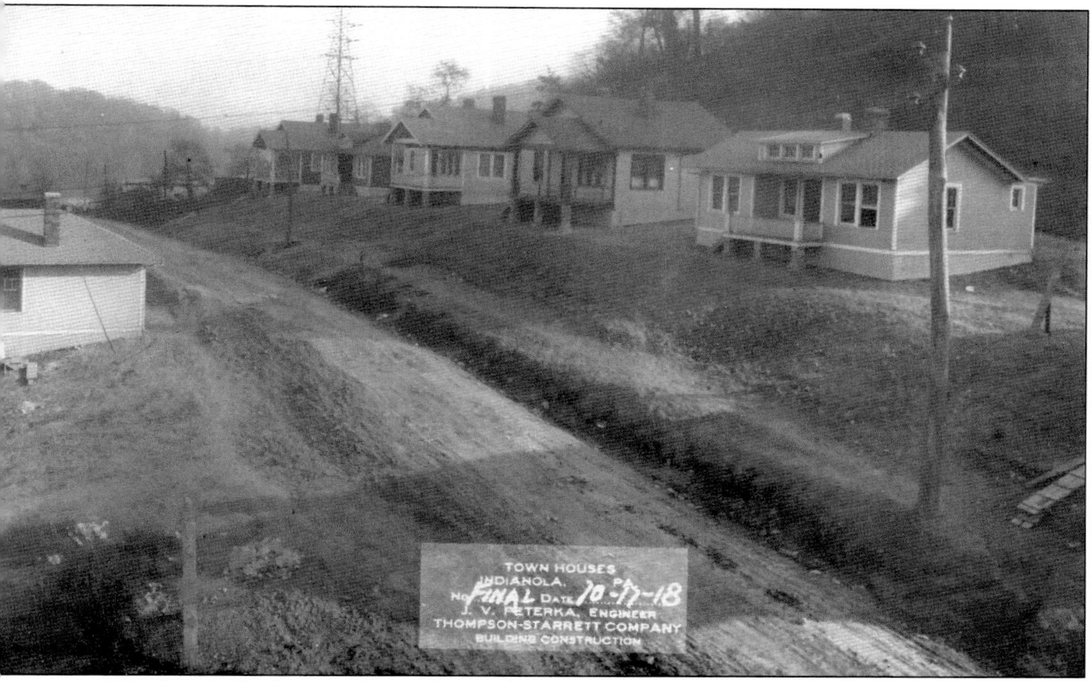

neighborhood; the houses above the road (at right) were torn down when State Route 910 was widened. (Courtesy of Karen Sue Haley.)

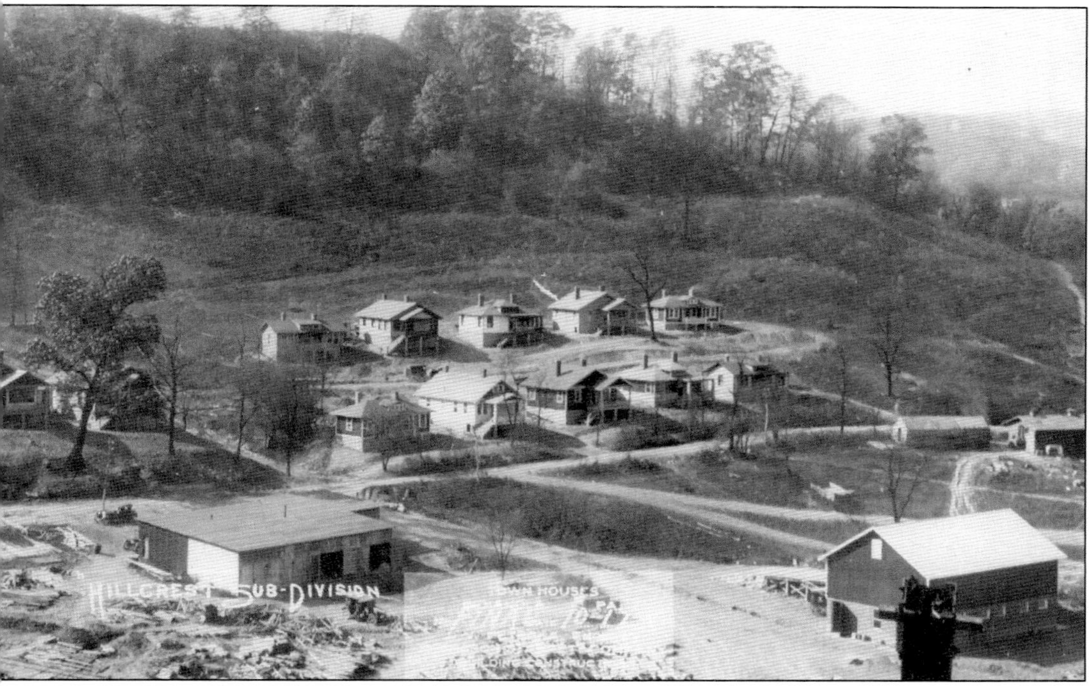

A mine barrack is in the foreground; this is where some of the miners—mainly bachelors—stayed. The barracks were more of a bunkhouse, with many beds to accommodate the miners. The mule barn is shown in the lower right corner. (Courtesy of Karen Sue Haley.)

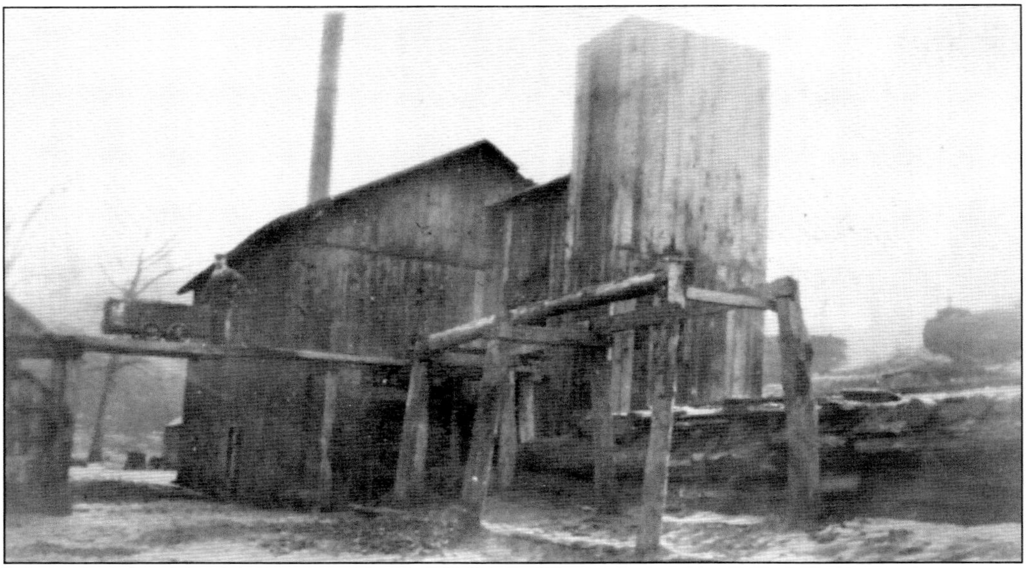

Peter and Henry Mink opened their coal mine in 1905 on State Route 910, near the intersection of 910 and Cedar Run Road, where it crosses over the present-day Pennsylvania Turnpike. One of the Mink brothers is pictured with a coal car on their coal mine and shaft. The Mink brothers had to shut down operations in 1930, possibly because of the Depression.

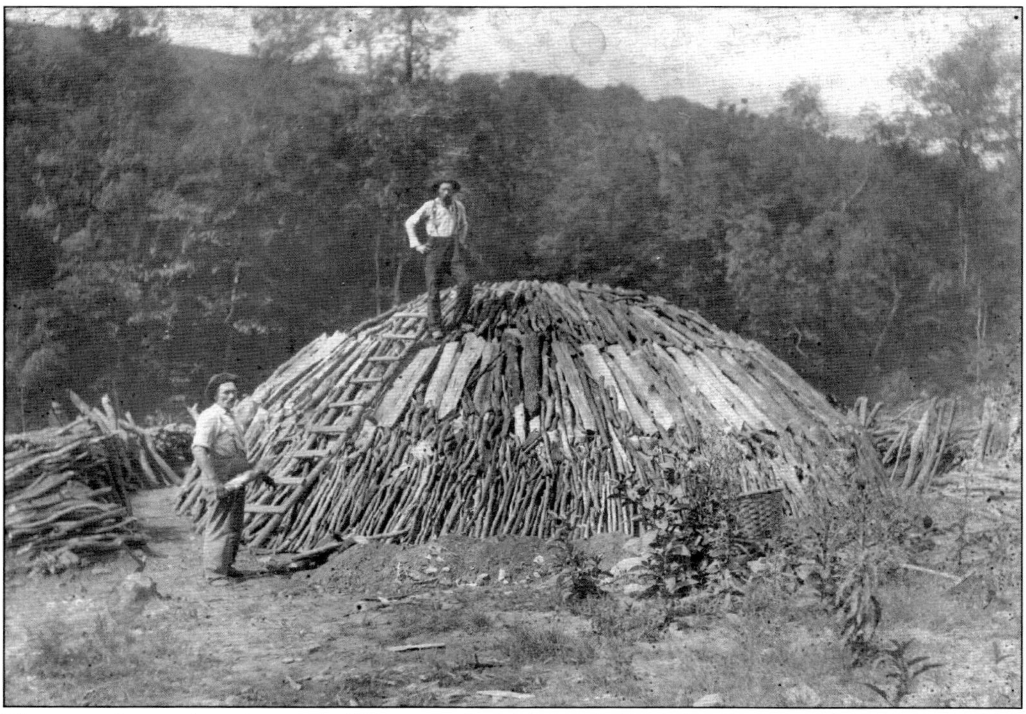

This is a charcoal pit located off Fairview Road behind the Arbuckles' woods. The Arbuckles resided on Fairview Road, across the street from the Fosters. Charcoal was processed in a pit like this and then sold to various companies in Pittsburgh. (Courtesy of Dorothy Preston Bauer via John F. Bauer III.)

Three

DISASTERS

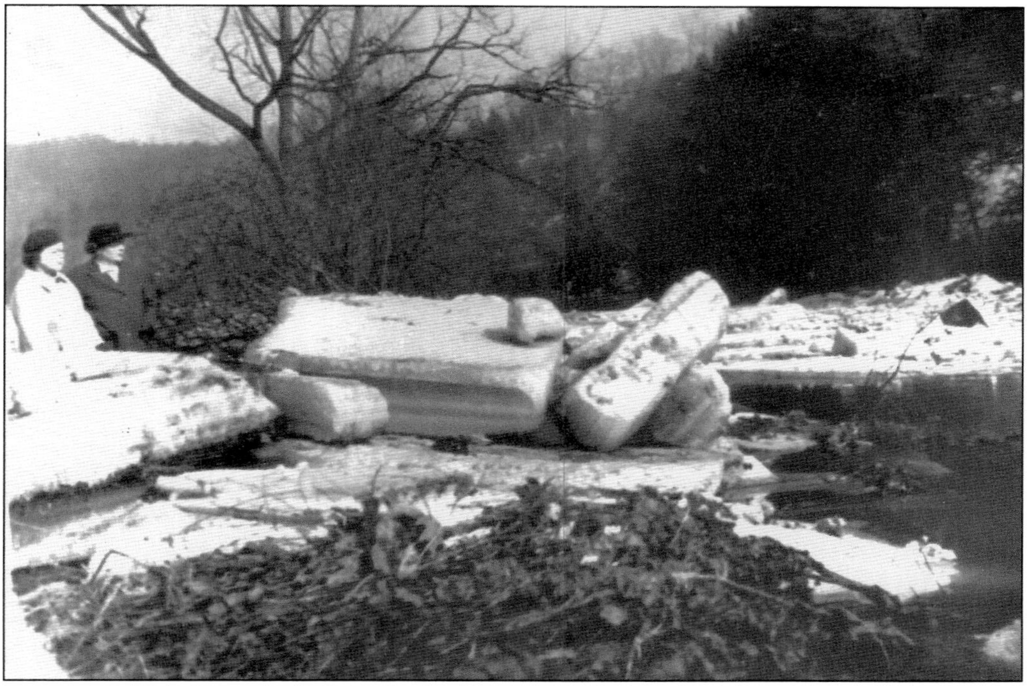

This photograph shows Little Deer Creek at the Emmerling House in Emmerling Park off of State Route 910. Gretchen Emmerling Roth (left) and Jane Beeson Emmerling Witt are looking at ice blocks on Little Deer Creek. Gretchen is the sister of Dr. John F. Emmerling, for whom the park and home were named.

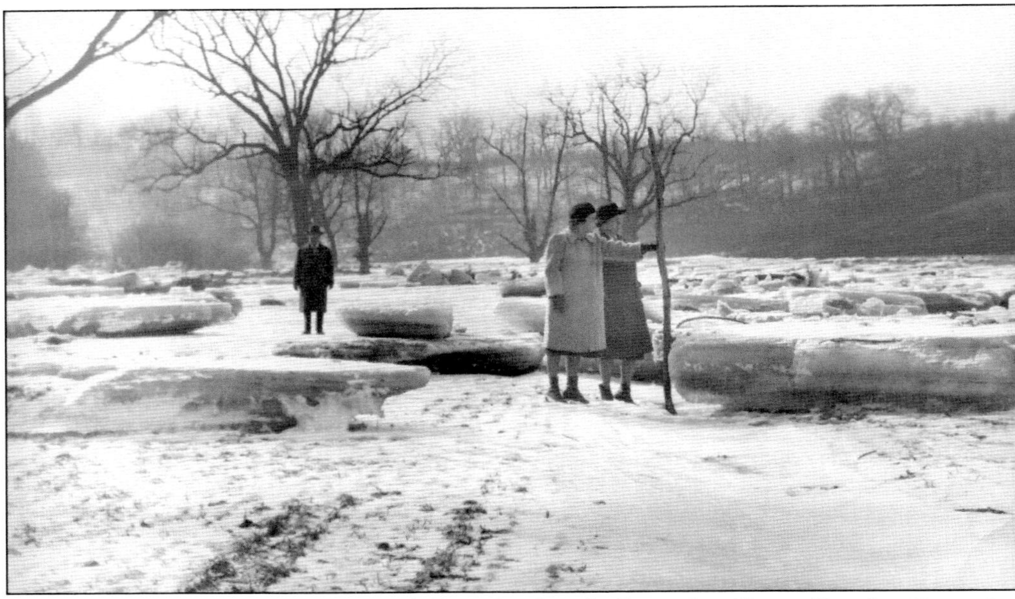

Charles V. Witt (left) looks at ice on Little Deer Creek at the Emmerling House. Gretchen Emmerling Roth (center) and Jane Beeson Emmerling Witt also look upon the weather anomaly. Charles was Jane's second husband. An ice floe like this has yet to happen again on Little Deer Creek.

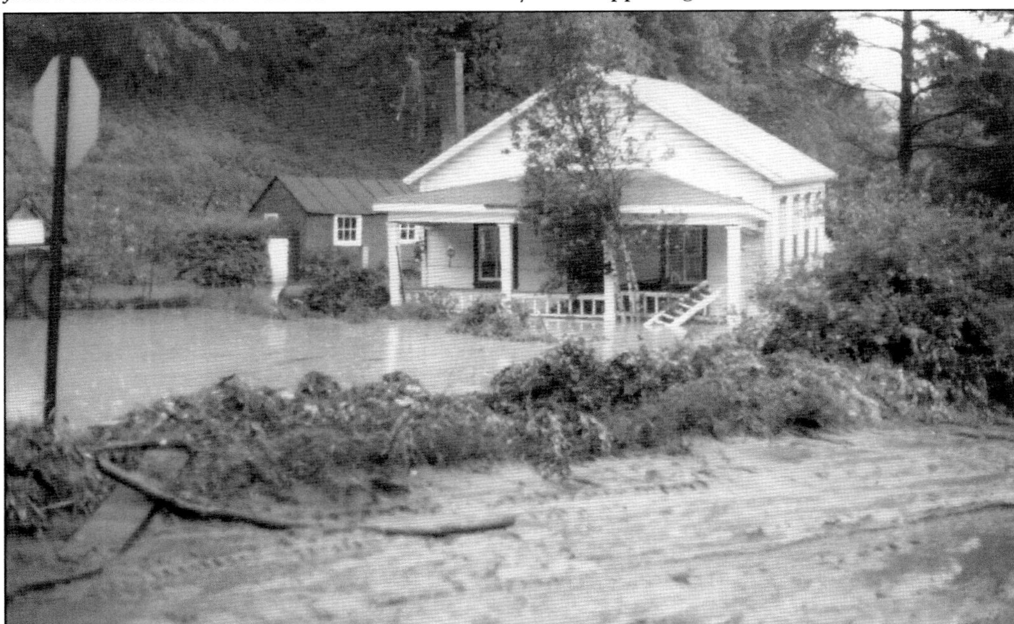

The old Valley View schoolhouse at the intersection of Cedar Run Road and State Route 910 was swept off its foundation during the flood of 1986 and ended up being a total loss. This was the home of Mary Ellen Boyle. She grew up there with her parents, brother, and sister. In 1986, Boyle was a 54-year-old nurse at the Harmarville Rehabilitation Center. Joseph Stephenson, chairman of the Indiana Township Historic Commission and lifetime resident of Dorseyville, said this was a two-room schoolhouse, which was unusual for the time period.

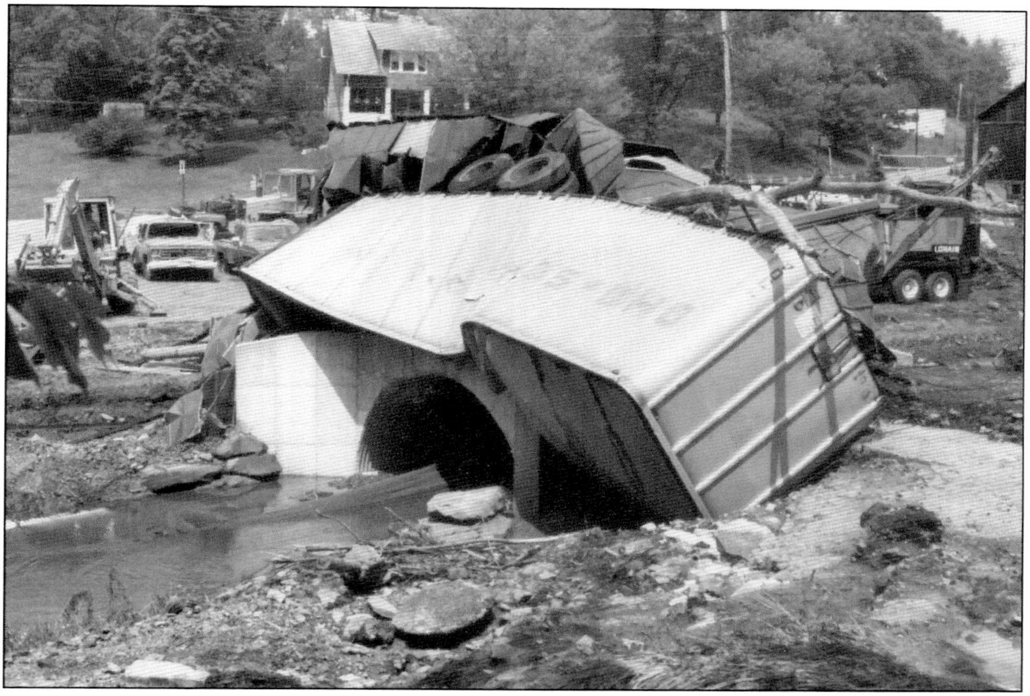

This is the intersection of Harts Run Road and Saxonburg Boulevard after the flood of 1986. The damage at DeBaldo's gas station on the corner clearly shows the forceful nature of the flood and the destruction it caused. Many vehicles that were housed inside the garage on the property ended up wrapped around other structures or marooned in peculiar places.

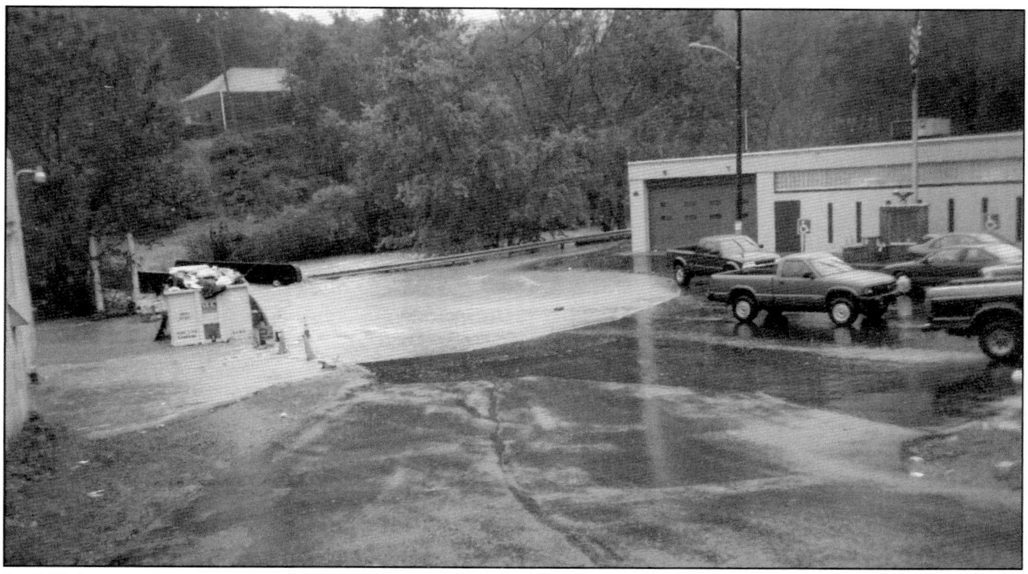

In 2004, rising waters after Hurricane Ivan resulted in flooding that almost reached Rural Ridge's Volunteer Fire Department (VFD). The VFD was founded in 1953, and the fire hall pictured above was constructed in 1963. Before this structure was erected, the VFD used the former Kosta Radich house. (Courtesy of Mary Yelich.)

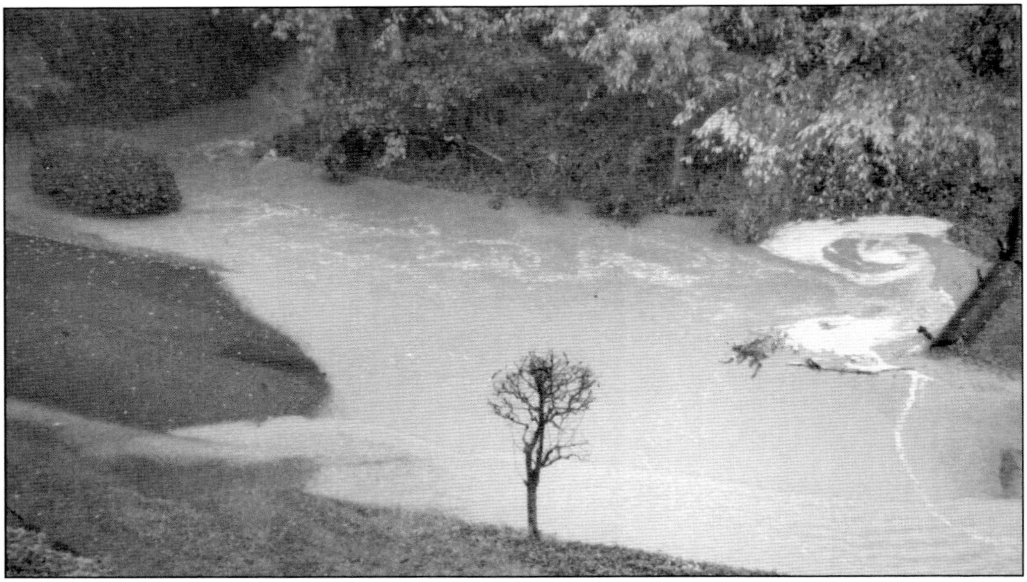

This is Voskamp Road in Rural Ridge after Hurricane Ivan came through in 2004. Deer Creek's waters rose and flooded many areas throughout the community. With all of the valleys and rivers running throughout Indiana Township, flooding is likely when there is heavy rain. (Courtesy of Mary Yelich.)

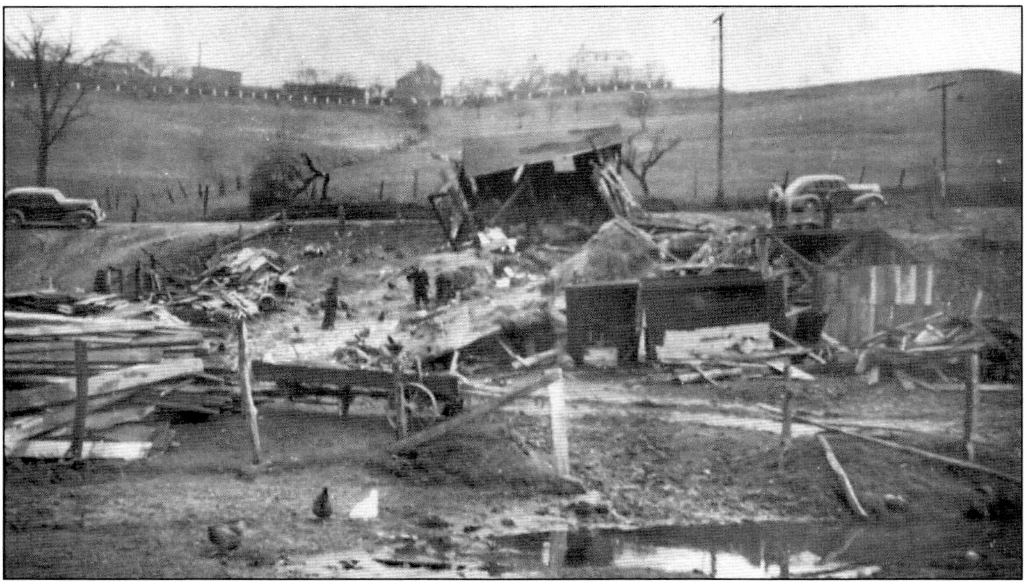

This photograph shows the tornado damage done to the Smith (Schmith) barns along Saxonburg Boulevard in 1938. Note Halter Farm at the top of Dorseyville Road in the background. In an interview with Pearl Margaret Smith, one of the children recalled the time during the tornado: "The temperature rose to about 80 degrees. About 2 a.m. we were awakened by the roar of wind and debris hitting the house . . . my brother pulled open the door and mother screamed fearing the electric wires might be down . . . the big barn had blown down on top of the cows and horses."

Four

EARLY HOMES

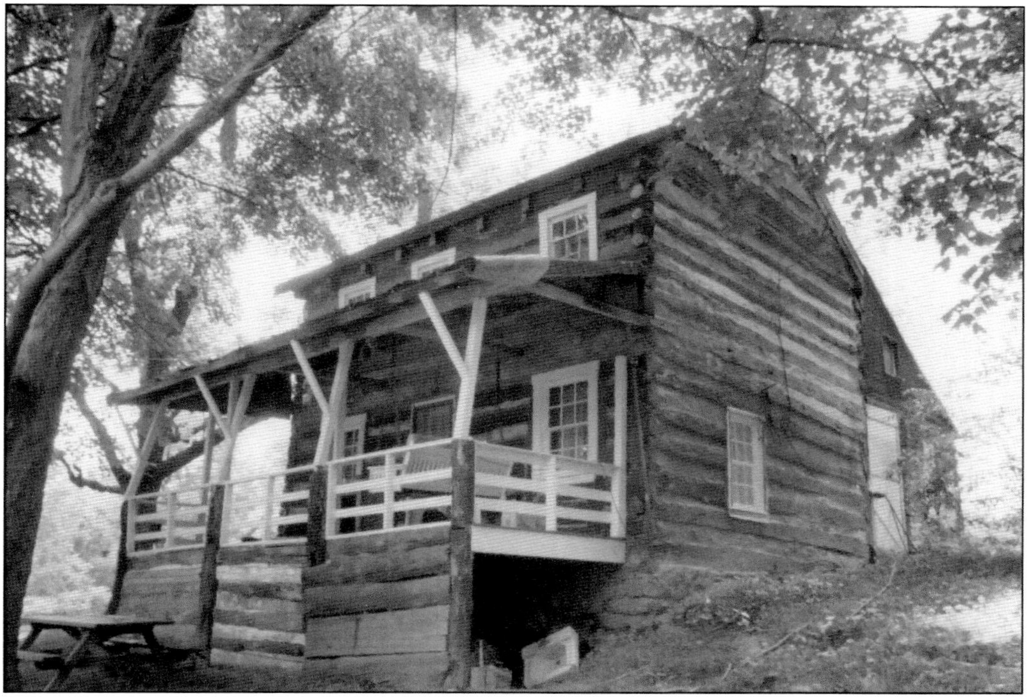

Martin Giesy's log home, a nostalgic site, is the epitome of a "pioneer house." The structure is rumored to be over 250 years old, making it the oldest log home in Allegheny County. According to an interview with Giesy, one of the home's earliest tenants used to chase Indians up near Deer Creek and would occasionally run into some of Guyasuta's scouts; Guyasuta was a Seneca chief and a guide and hunter for George Washington.

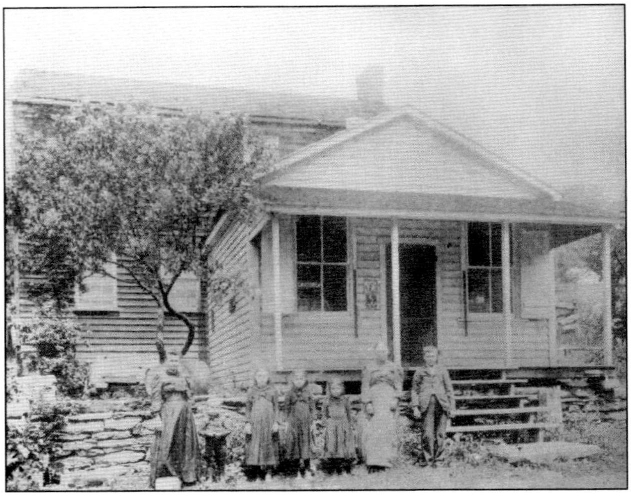

The John Frederick Farmhouse was built around 1850, and the address is listed as 129 Saxonburg Boulevard (before 9-1-1 re-addressing). The general store was attached sometime between 1890 and 1920. Pictured here are, from left to right, Louisa C. (Dietrich) Frederick, John B. Frederick, Bernice (Frederick) Kindelberger, Bessie (Frederick) Kelly, Elnora Frederick, Elizabeth Dietrich, and Willy Dietrich. (Courtesy of John Frederick.)

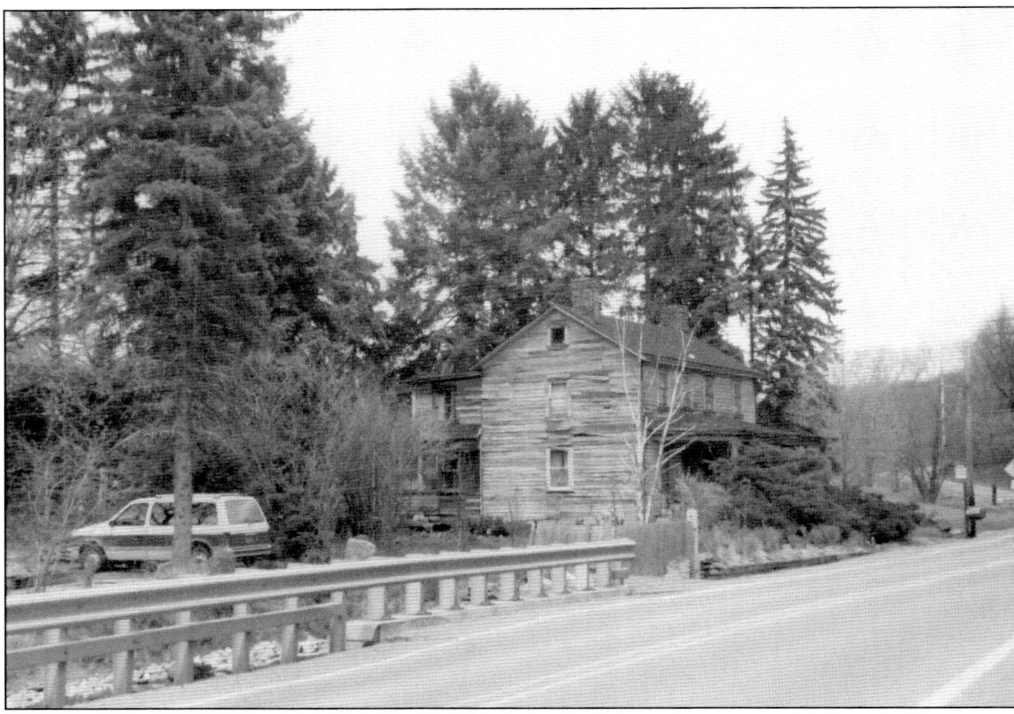

The Frederick House, located at 129 Saxonburg Boulevard (before 9-1-1 re-addressing), originally belonged to John Dietrich. He acquired several parcels of land in Indiana Township and sold parts of it to family. His parcels totaled 164 acres and dominated the intersection of Harts Run Road and Saxonburg Boulevard, which became known as "Dietrich's Crossroads." According to an interview with Pearl Sallade (who turned 90 in 1994), the family still has the sheepskin that states the land was first deeded to a soldier for payment for his services in the Revolutionary War. This photograph was taken during a 1989 bus tour orchestrated by the Indiana Township Historic Commission.

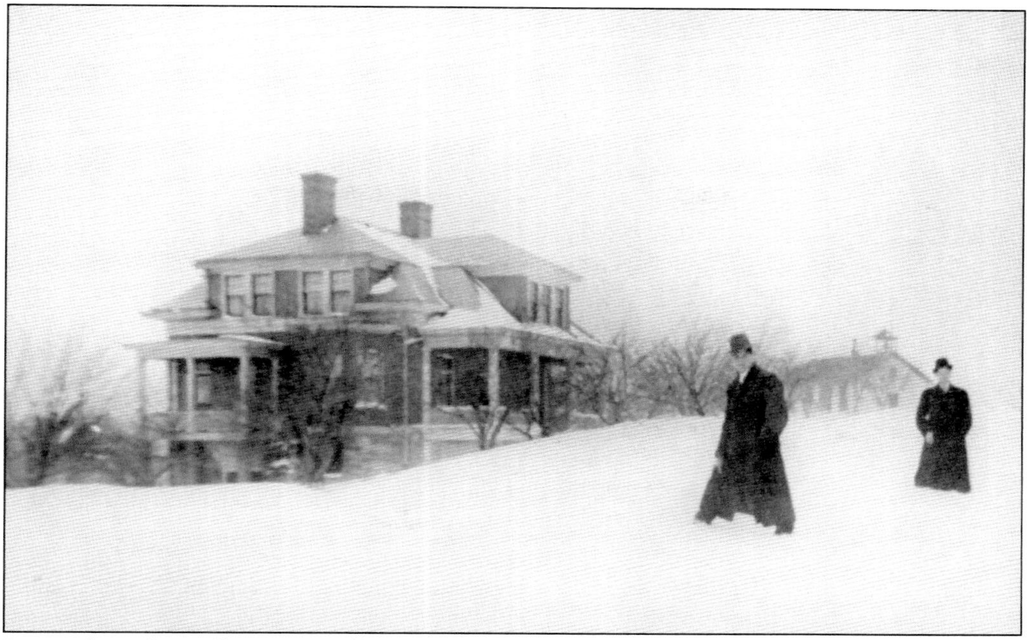

Pictured are the Gallenz House (foreground) and the Bailiff School (background). The Gallenz House was built in the late 1800s and is located at 2105 Middle Road. The Bailiff School, also known as Pleasant View School, was across the street from the Middle Road Fire Hall. The two men in the photograph are said to be Regis Soeder's uncles.

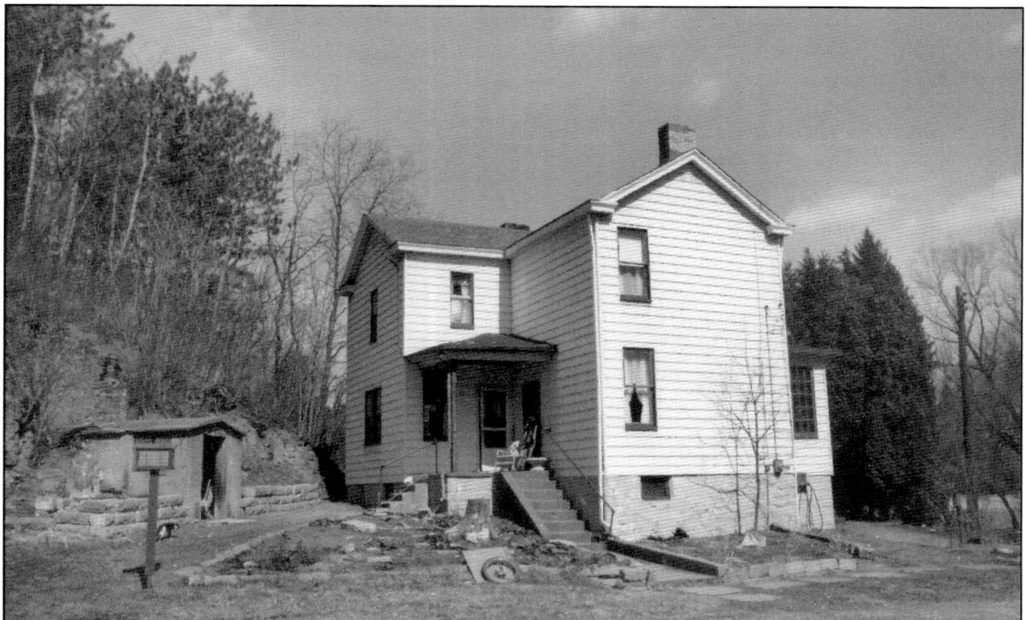

This structure is a remodeled, 100-year-old farmhouse owned by Anthony DeBaldo and located on Bigler Drive. The bake oven at left was built in 1930. DeBaldo's ancestors Peter and Lucia and their four sons bought the house from the Emerick family in 1920.

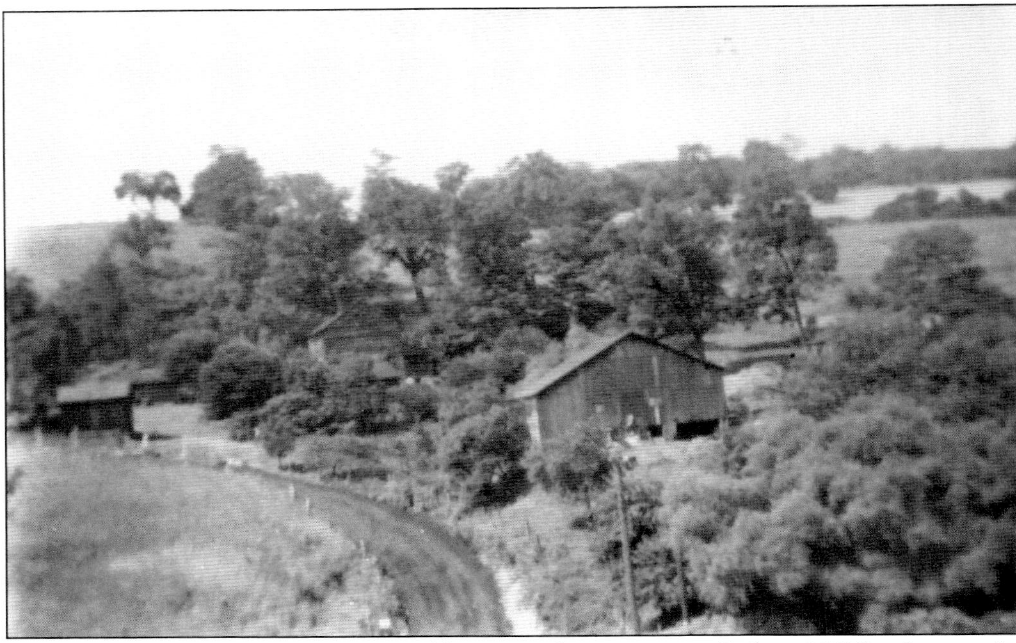

Lloyd and Helen Wachter built a second house on the property on Lefever Hill Road across the road from the original log house (the center structure in the above image), which was built in the early 1800s. Their daughter Elma Wachter Baker was born in the new house (not pictured). Lefever Hill was known for its many oil wells, which Lloyd helped to run and maintain.

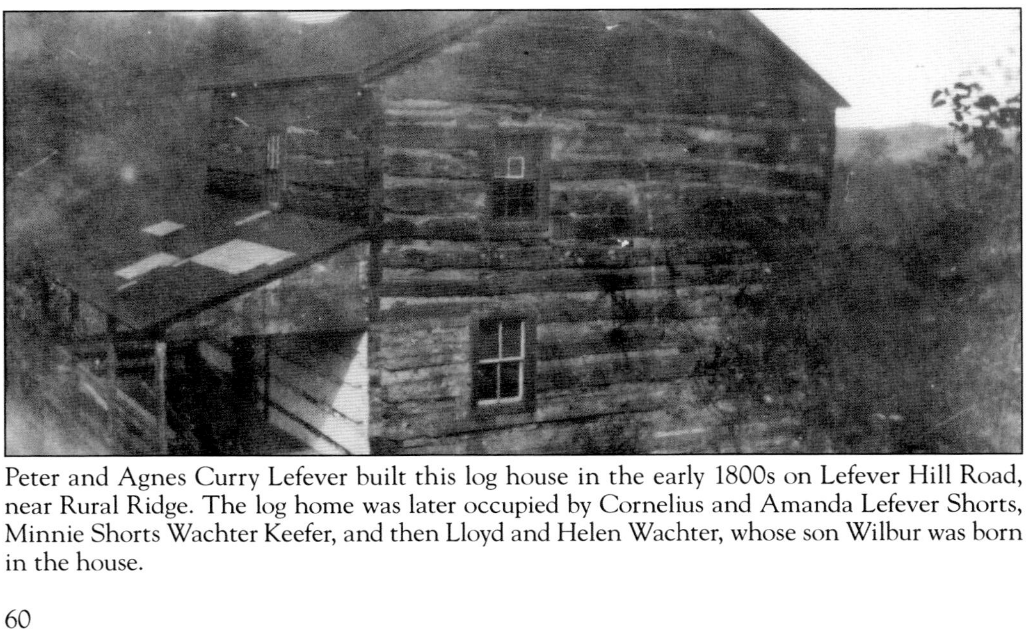

Peter and Agnes Curry Lefever built this log house in the early 1800s on Lefever Hill Road, near Rural Ridge. The log home was later occupied by Cornelius and Amanda Lefever Shorts, Minnie Shorts Wachter Keefer, and then Lloyd and Helen Wachter, whose son Wilbur was born in the house.

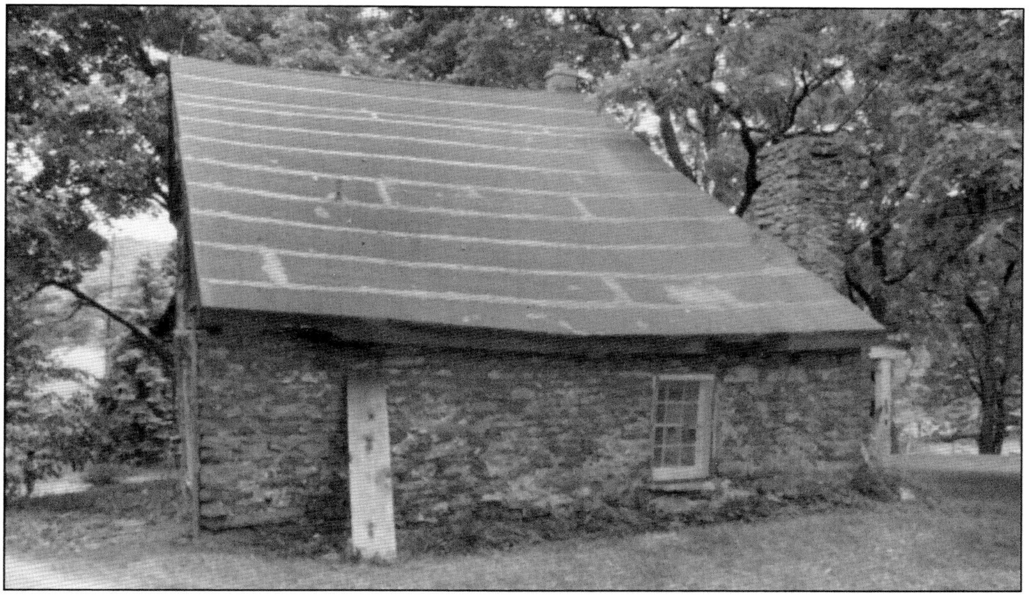

The Martin Giesy log house is possibly the oldest in Allegheny County. Giesy recalled that as a boy, an old man named Peter Neff talked about how his (Neff's) grandfather built the log house. Judging from that recollection, the log house would be over 250 years old. This photograph shows the 1847 stone kitchen addition at the back of the log home.

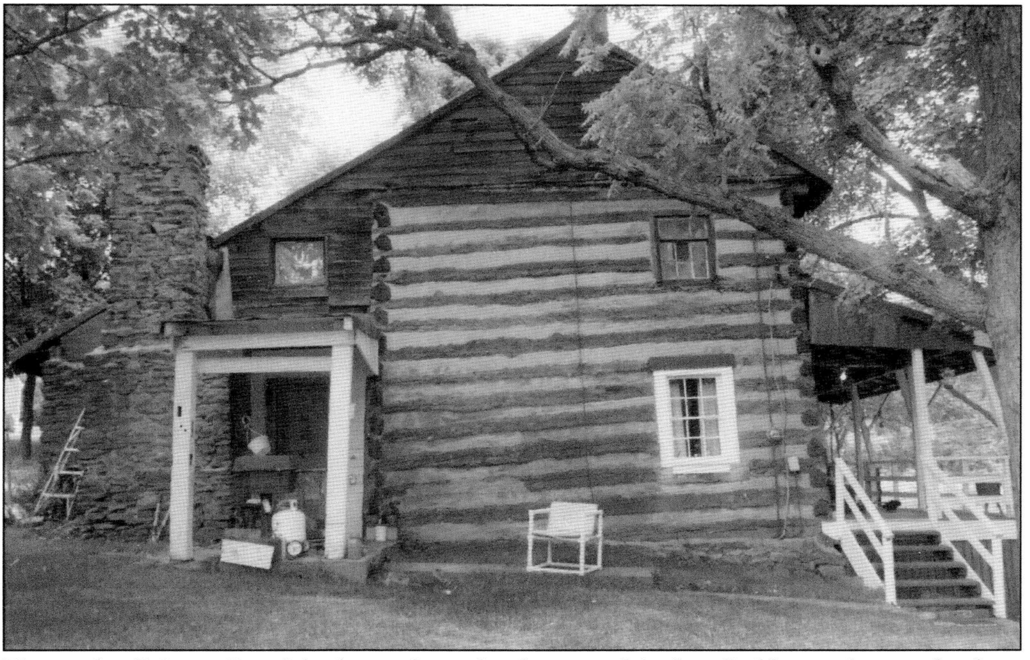

This angle of Martin Giesy's log home shows the chimney of the "new" addition of a stone kitchen. The log home is now the site of Camp Deer Creek, Pittsburgh's oldest children's day camp, which accepts children between the ages of 4 and 15. Sarah May Giesy Newcamp, granddaughter of Martin Giesy, grew up here and remembers sleeping upstairs and that the stairway from the kitchen to the upper level was not a "regular stairway."

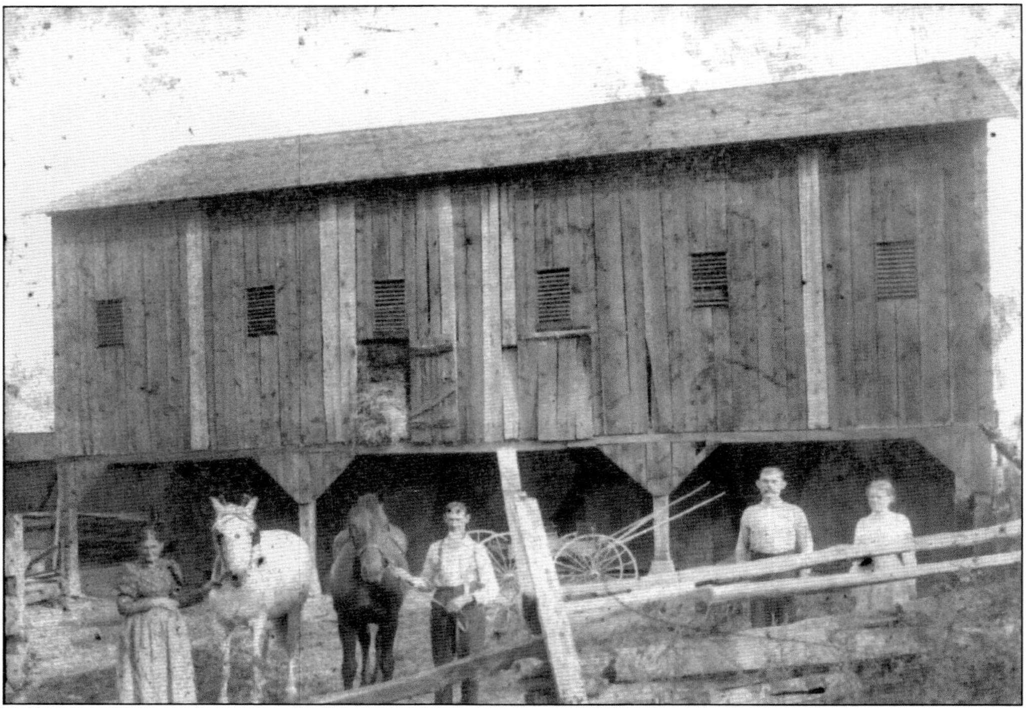

This is known as the William Marshall Barn, which was constructed from 1862 until 1864. William Marshall's father is Samuel Marshall (1786–1864), and census records indicate that he was a native of Pennsylvania and resided in Indiana Township. According to land records, Samuel purchased a total of 447 acres of land in the northeast corner of Indiana Township.

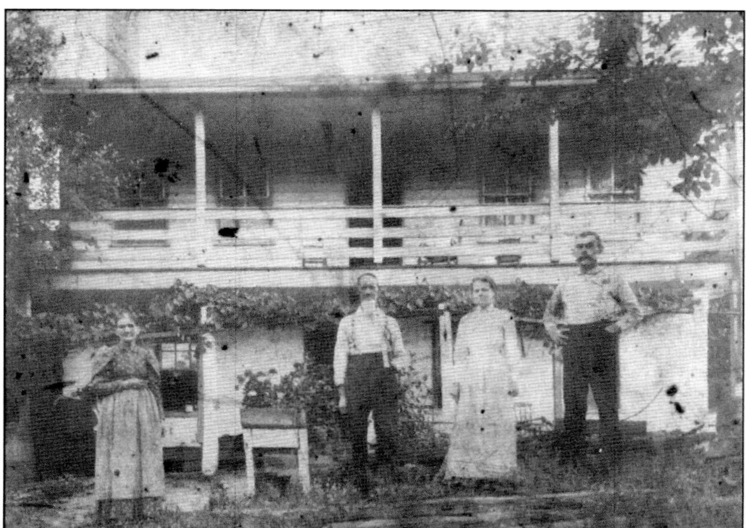

William Marshall also built a home while constructing the barn. Samuel Marshall divided his 447 acres between his seven children. William Marshall is the father of Sarah Elizabeth Marshall Greenwald, who married Philip Jacob Greenwald. In 1920, Philip purchased Sarah's original homestead from the Marshall heirs. The barn and farm are located on Rich Hill Road.

This is the original log house that John Dietrich moved into upon his return from Oil City around 1877. Dietrich and his wife and children lived here with the Emericks. This property, later known as the Emerick property, was located off Harts Run Road. The entire Dietrich clan lived on the properties located at the intersection of Saxonburg Boulevard (then called Little Creek Road) and Harts Run Road. (Courtesy of Pearl Sallade.)

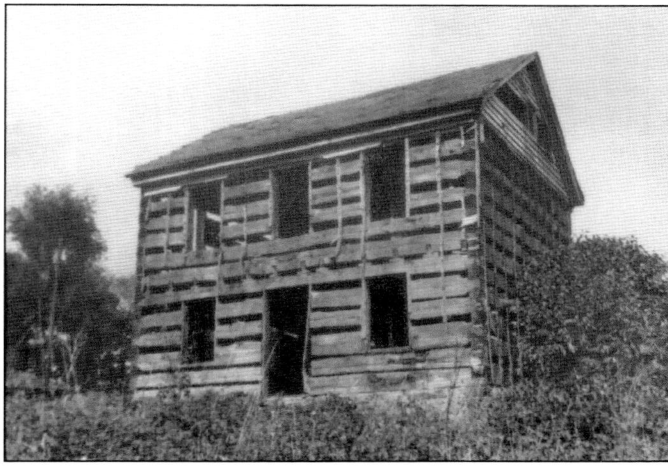

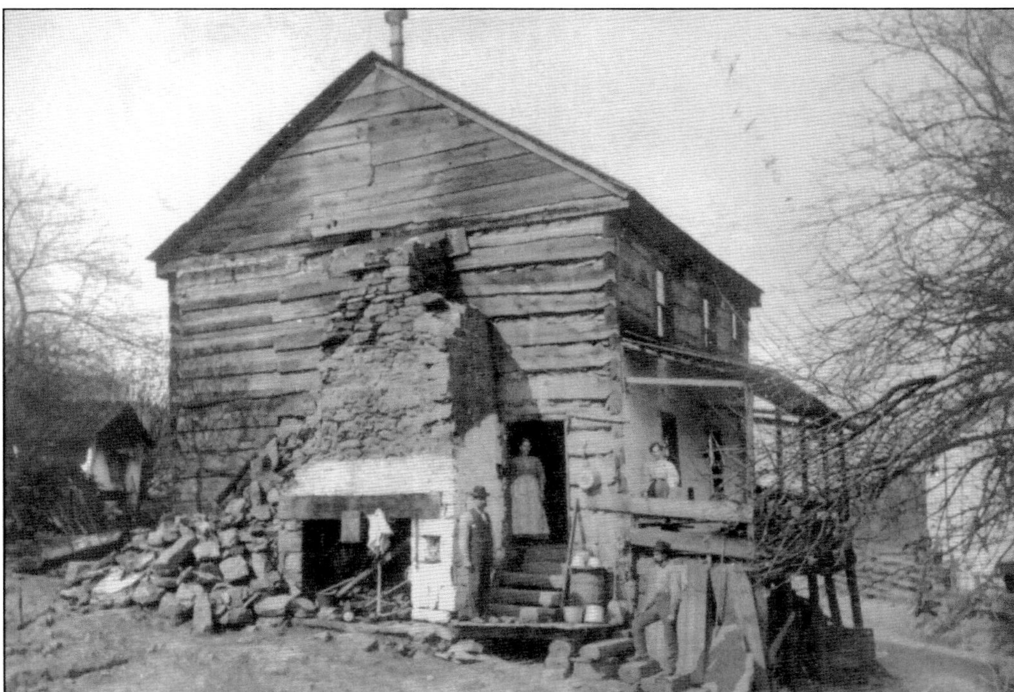

John Dietrich lived in this log house before leaving for Oil City in 1863. Dietrich left for Oil City intent on becoming a major player in the oil fields, and he also wanted to open a hotel in town. This did not happen, and he and his family returned to Indiana Township around 1877. The house was later occupied by John's son William C. Dietrich. (Courtesy of Pearl Sallade.)

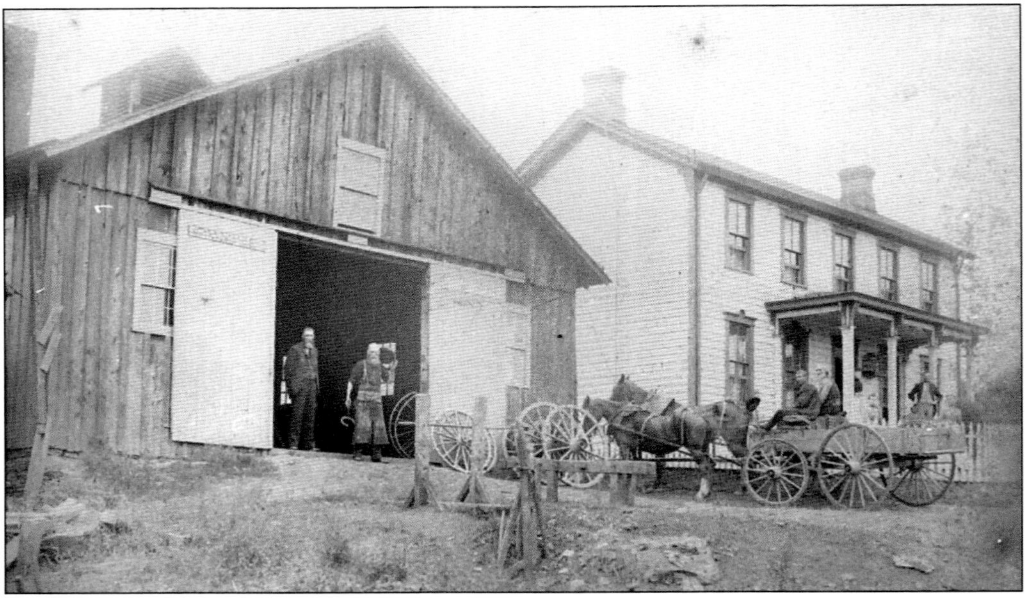

William McIntyre purchased property in Dorseyville in 1876 and built a log house on a stone foundation. He also built a large, two-forge blacksmith shop located right next to the house. In 1884, William dismantled the log structure and erected the present-day two-story frame house on the same stone foundation. In this 1905 photograph, William's daughter Edith McIntyre Hodel is on the porch holding infant Marguerite Hodel, with Wilverda Hodel standing on her left. Anthony Hodel stands at the foot of the porch steps.

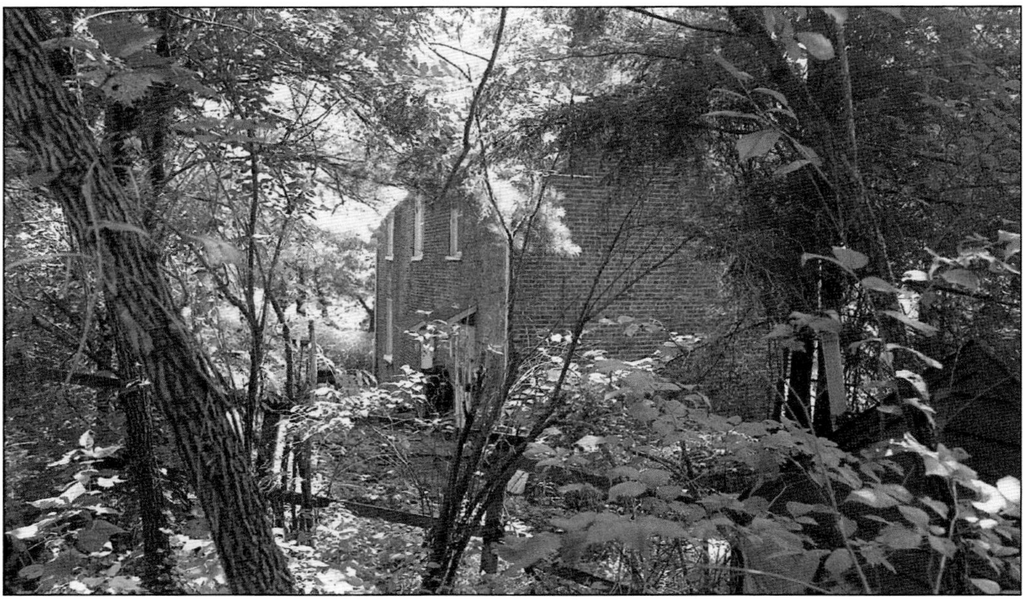

The Emmerling House is visible through the foliage at Emmerling Park in this 1990 photograph. In the 1864 deed for this property (54.75 acres), it mentions a two-story brick dwelling (probably the Emmerling House as seen today) and a steam-powered flour mill. The Emmerlings purchased 10.11 acres from Luther and Florence Foust of Aspinwall in 1941 and donated the land to Indiana Township in 1972. No one currently resides in this historic home.

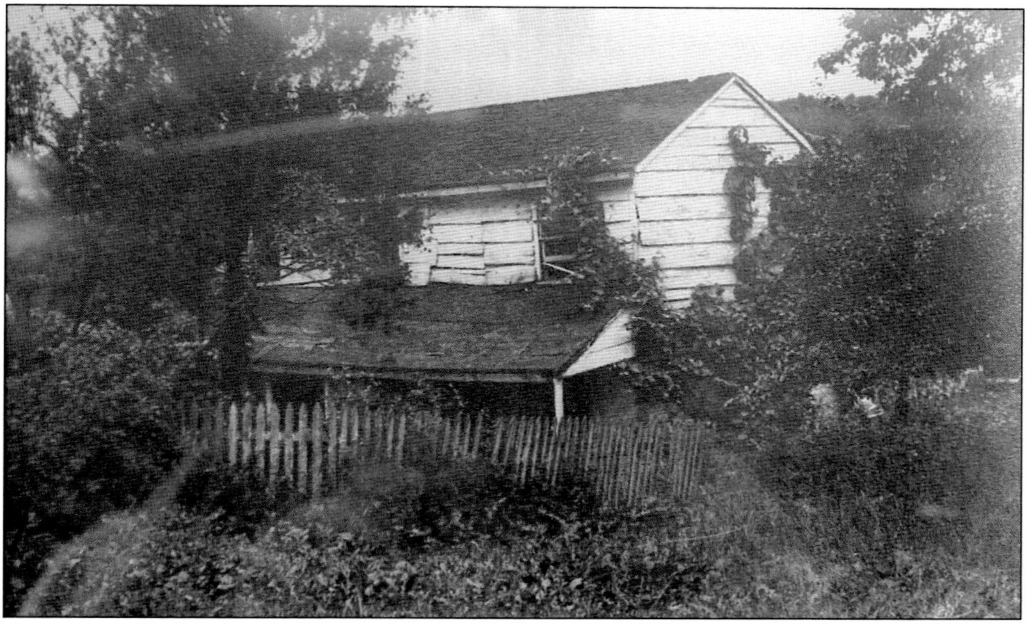

Edward J. McCague III is the current owner of this property at 825 Dorseyville Road. McCague obtained the property from the Neesons, who obtained the property from a caretaker by the name of Charles Feiertag. Feiertag had the property deeded over to him from the Flaccuses, who had purchased the property from the original landowners, the Peter Claus family. Siding covers the original logs in this undated photograph. (Courtesy of Edward McCague.)

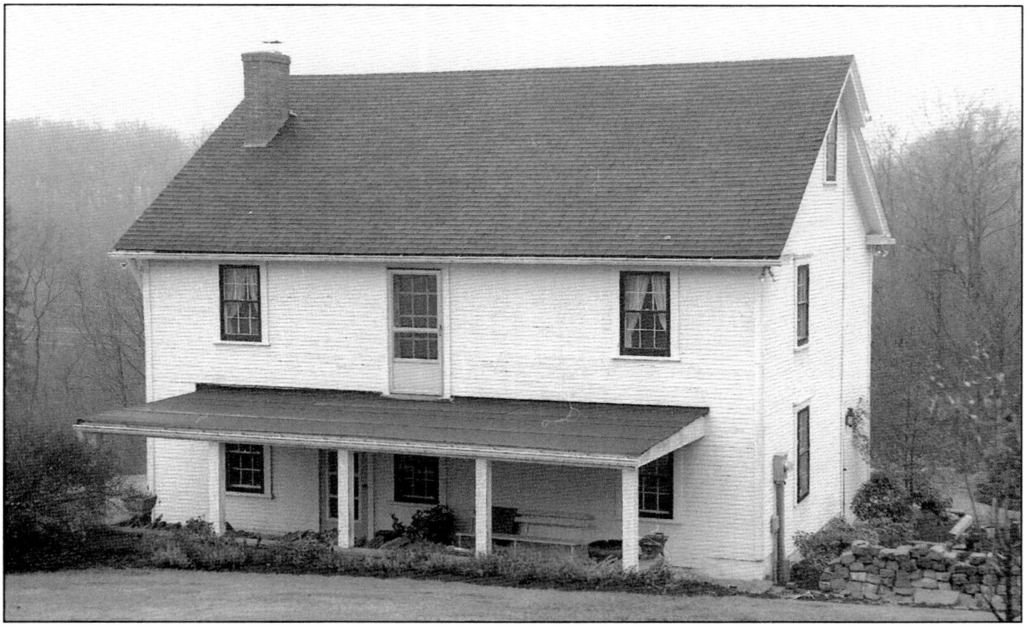

The architect and date of construction are unknown for the 825 Dorseyville Road log home (pictured here in 1991). The second floor was added on top of the original log home, but the date of the addition is unknown. The entire house is now encased in clapboard siding. A modern kitchen now stands in place of the lean-to at the back of the house.

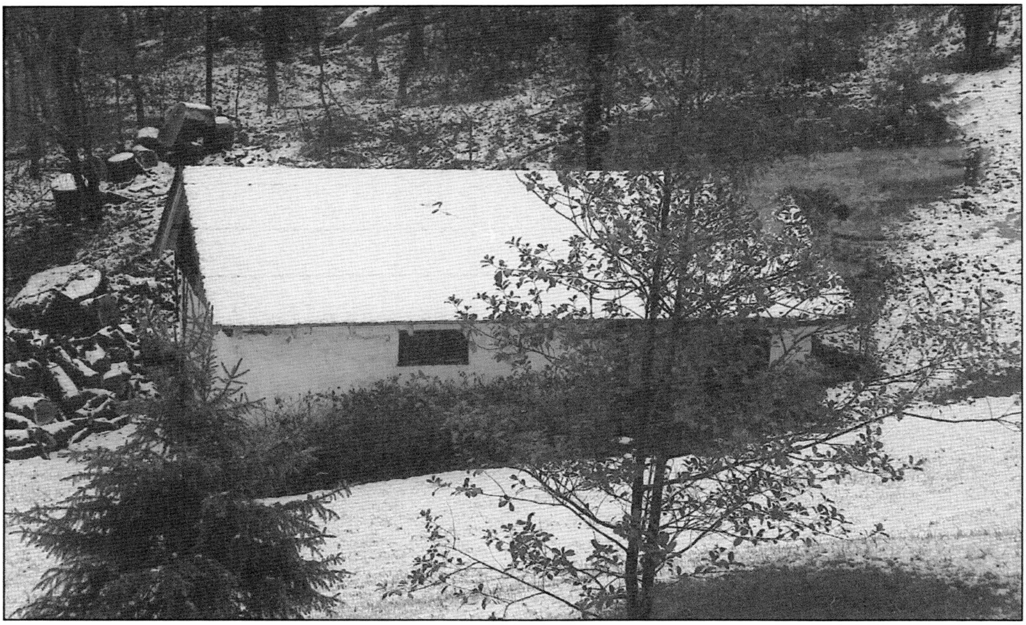

As of 1991, the springhouse associated with the 825 Dorseyville Road log house still maintained a good water supply. The springhouse is located on the original six acres of land deeded over to the McCagues from the Neesons in 1984. Springhouses were used to keep items cool in the summertime before widespread use of the refrigerator, or "icebox."

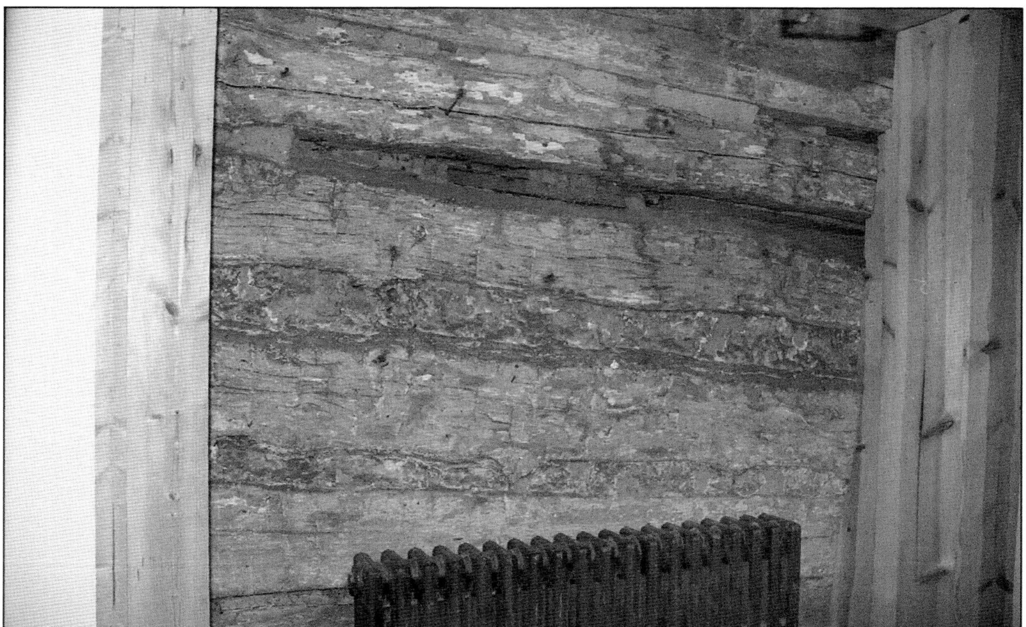

These are the red logs used to build the house at 825 Dorseyville Road. The only other original feature still associated with this modern structure is the stone foundation used to lay the groundwork for construction. The home's owner, Edward McCague, has taken care to maintain these historic aspects.

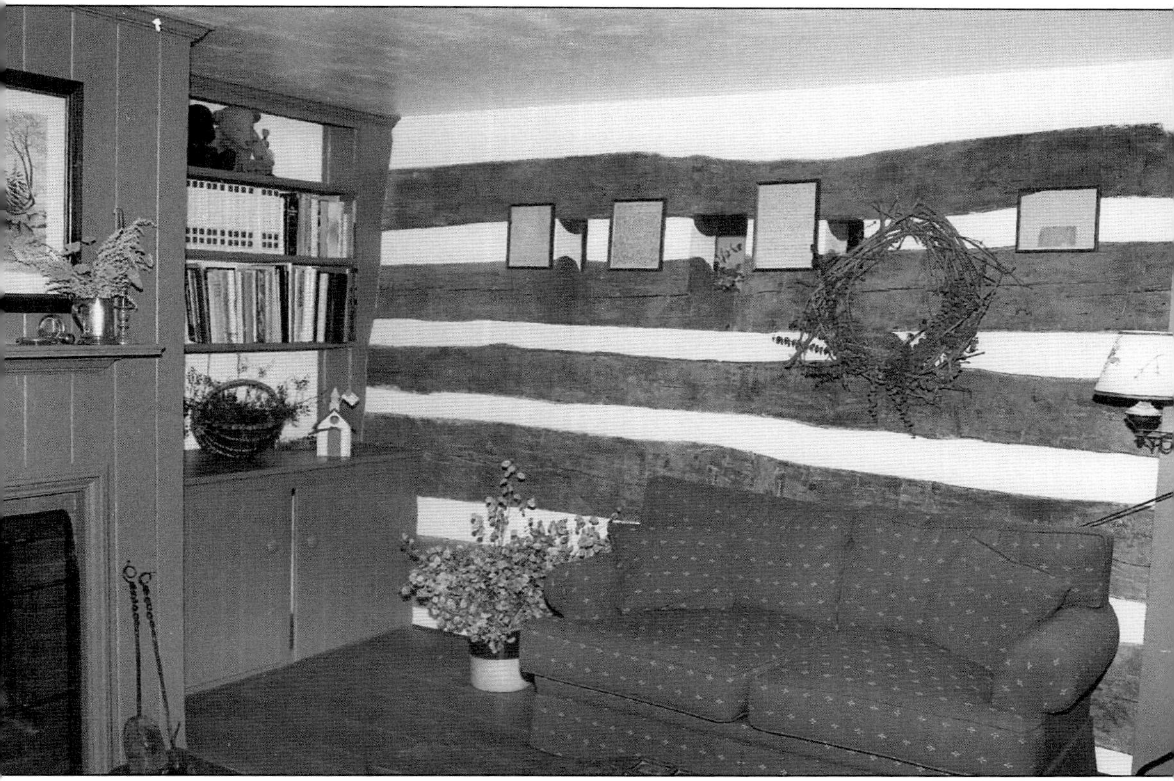

This 1991 photograph shows the interior of the 825 Dorseyville Road log home after restoration. In *Landmark Architecture of Allegheny County, Pennsylvania*, James D. Van Trump and Arthur P. Ziegler Jr. stated in the article "Neeson Log House" that "the chief mystery of the house is a set of three openings in the back wall of the original structure. These square holes are symmetrically placed, the middle one being rather larger than those at either side of it. They have been tentatively identified as gun ports; perhaps with an excess of romantic historical zeal, and in tenuous support of this theory the openings seem at the right height for a man to sight a musket against stealthily advancing Indians. Nowadays one has merely a good view of the kitchen from these mysterious embrasures."

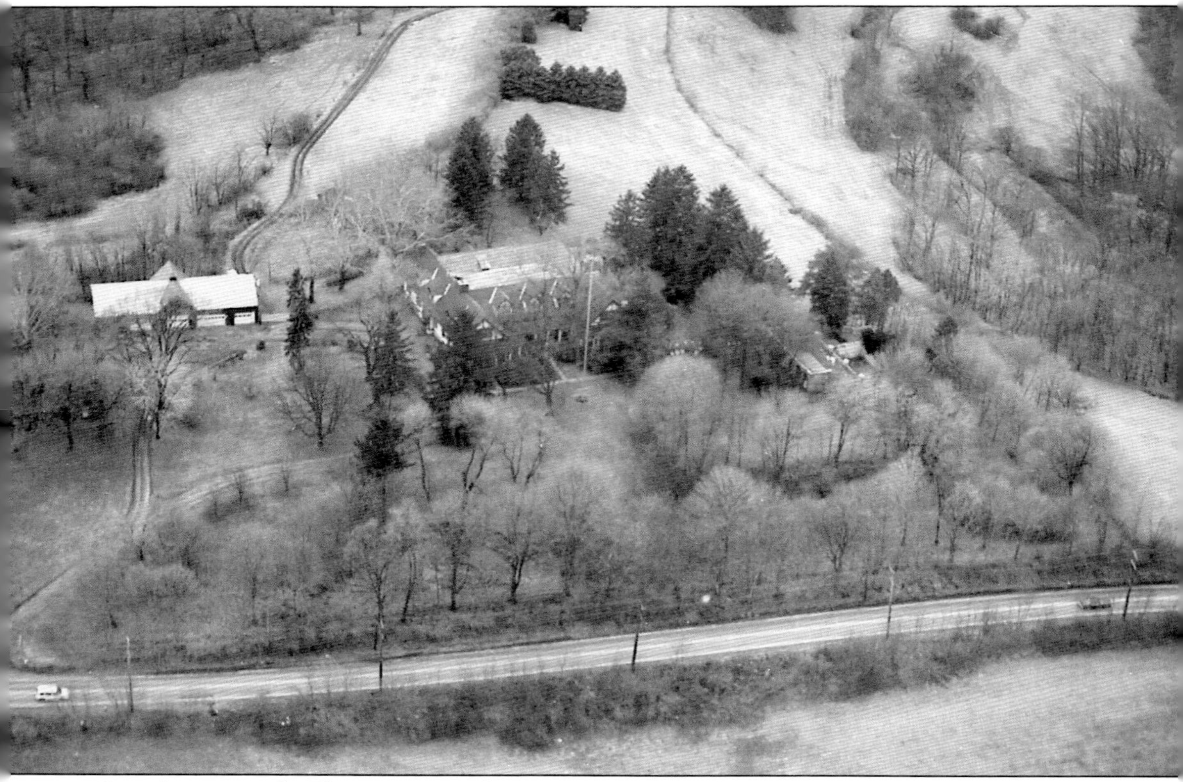

Once known as the Flaccus Estate, this structure goes by the name of Red Gables Farm because of its type of roofing. Located at the crossroads of Fox Chapel and Dorseyville Roads, this 18,000-square-foot house, which sits on a 105-acre estate, was built in 1905 as a summer retreat for the Charles L. Flaccus family and is quite an architectural marvel. The estate went up for sale when Charles's granddaughter Jane Louise Flaccus passed away in 1997; she resided in the home for 73 years and never married. This 1991 aerial photograph shows the immense size of the estate and its outbuildings. Among the amazing amenities of the estate were a trapdoor in the living room, which once provided an area for guests to enjoy a drink during Prohibition; a dining room that could comfortably seat 30; and a glass roof in the solarium that provided ventilation for the whole house before the advent of air-conditioning. The house also had nine bedrooms and bathrooms and a large nursery on the second floor. The family relied heavily on servants and cooks to keep the place running. The property and buildings, which are boarded up, are still around today but are in disrepair.

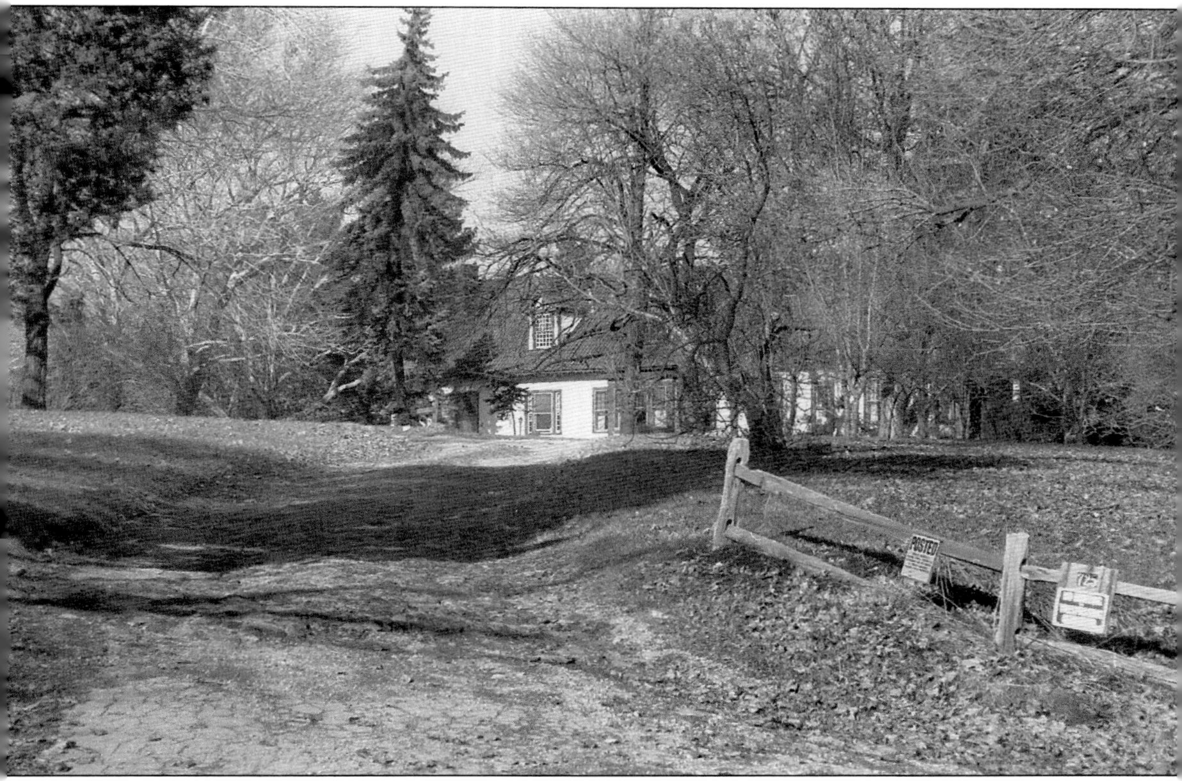

This is another 1991 view of the Flaccus Estate, aka Red Gables Farm. A 20-horse stable occupied part of the 105-acre estate, along with a field once used as a skeet and trap range. This is where Jane Louise Flaccus, granddaughter of Charles L. Flaccus I, honed her riding and marksmanship skills. Charles Flaccus III, who inherited the estate when his aunt (Jane Louise Flaccus) died, remembers the estate as being a wonderful place to visit—he recalls that when he woke up in the mornings, his bed would be made for him and breakfast was served before he went out riding. Charles Flaccus I was born in 1850 and built the estate for his family. He held the rights for glass bottling by machinery in the United States and was considered a pioneer of the industry. His company, C.L. Flaccus Glass Co., was one of the nation's largest glass companies in the late 19th and early 20th centuries.

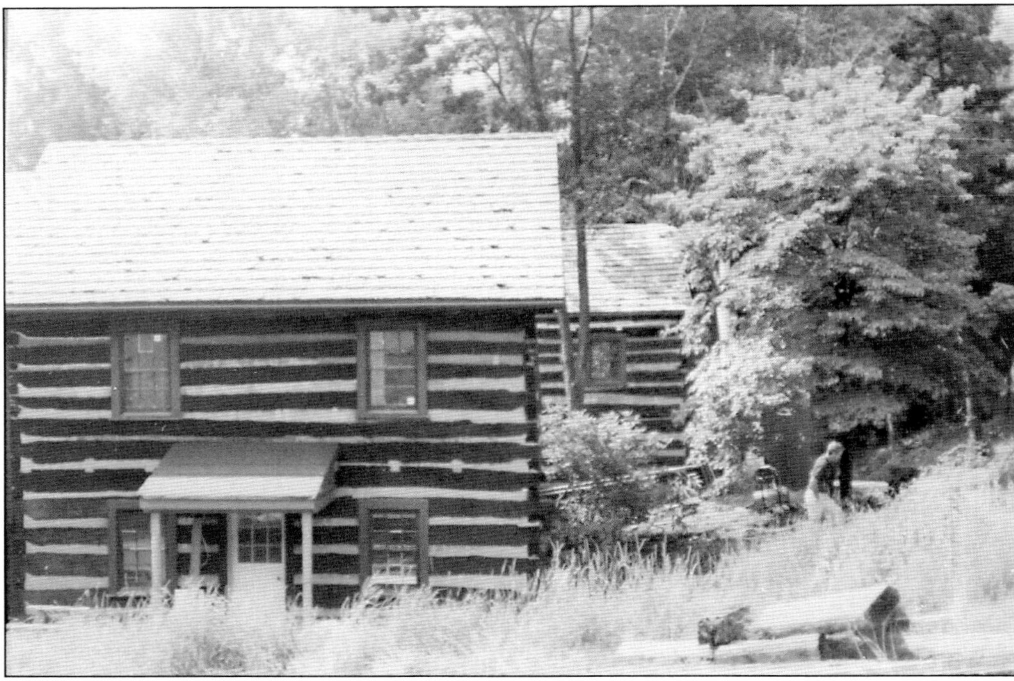

Located in present-day Fox Chapel on Kakakitty Lane, between Squaw Run Road East and Old Mill Road, this old log house is one of five log houses in the area built by George Hodil in the early 1800s. Even though Kakakitty Lane is in Fox Chapel, when the homes were built, the land was considered Indiana Township. Dr. Peter and Sandra Kyne were the last known owners (in 1989).

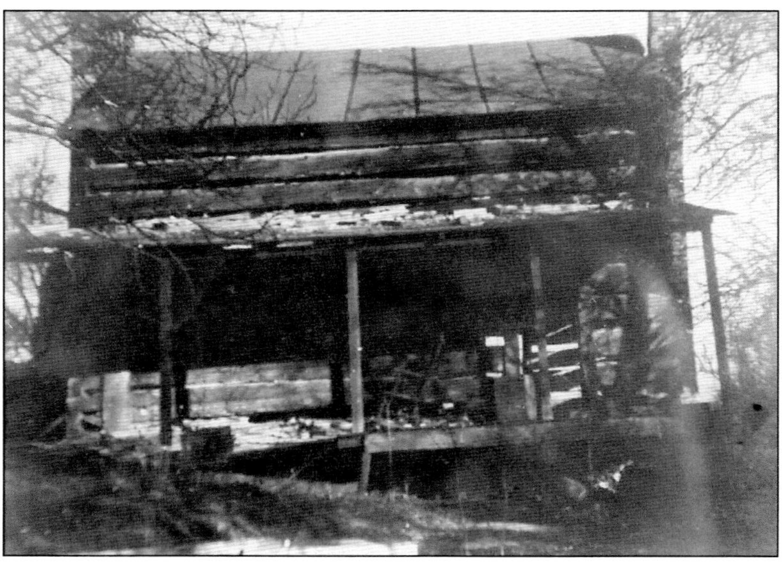

This cabin, called Limestone Hill, is located on Rawlins Run and Old Mill Roads and is pictured before it was restored in the 1940s. Early 1851 maps indicate that this is one of the earliest log homes built by the Hodil family. The dilapidated condition of this old log home is clearly visible. (Courtesy of Bonnie Anderson.)

Limestone Hill is pictured here during a 1940s or 1950s restoration. Bonnie Anderson and her husband, John, purchased Limestone Hill from a family named Riley in 1982. The Andersons have in their possession an original deed dated June 29, 1805, that names their tract of land Limestone Hill, so the Andersons adopted the name for their home. (Courtesy of Bonnie Anderson.)

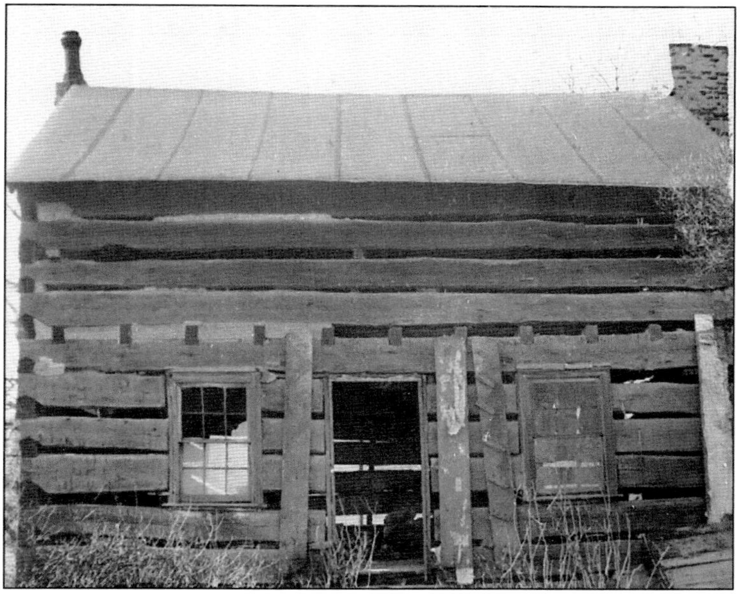

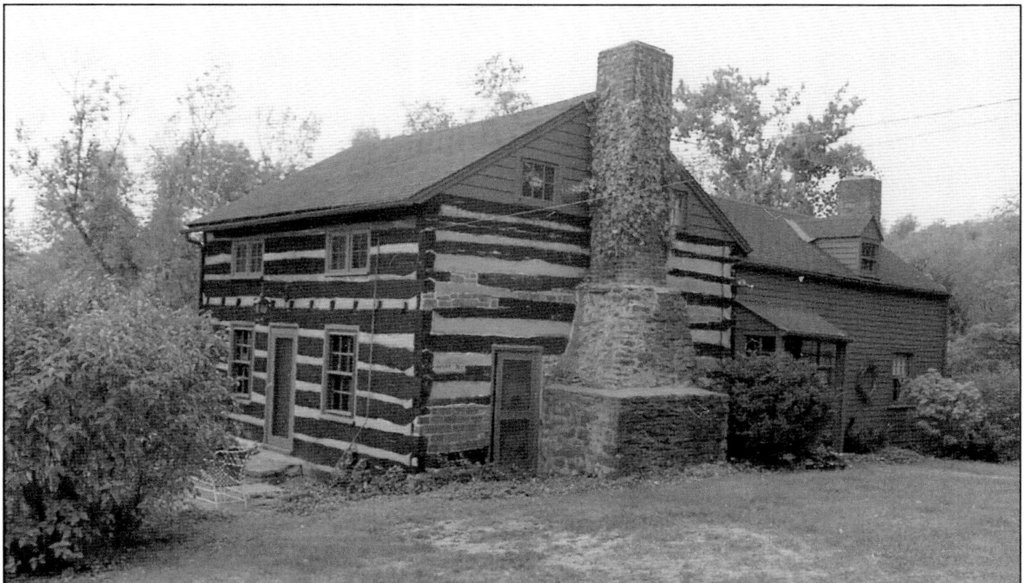

Limestone Hill is pictured here in 1991. The Rileys purchased this log cabin "as is" sometime in the 1940s and restored the original log cabin into a home, adding the frame seen in the photograph. Bonnie Anderson, who owned the home as of 1991, is an antiques dealer and has furnished the home in a manner consistent with its history and architecture. (Courtesy of Bonnie Anderson.)

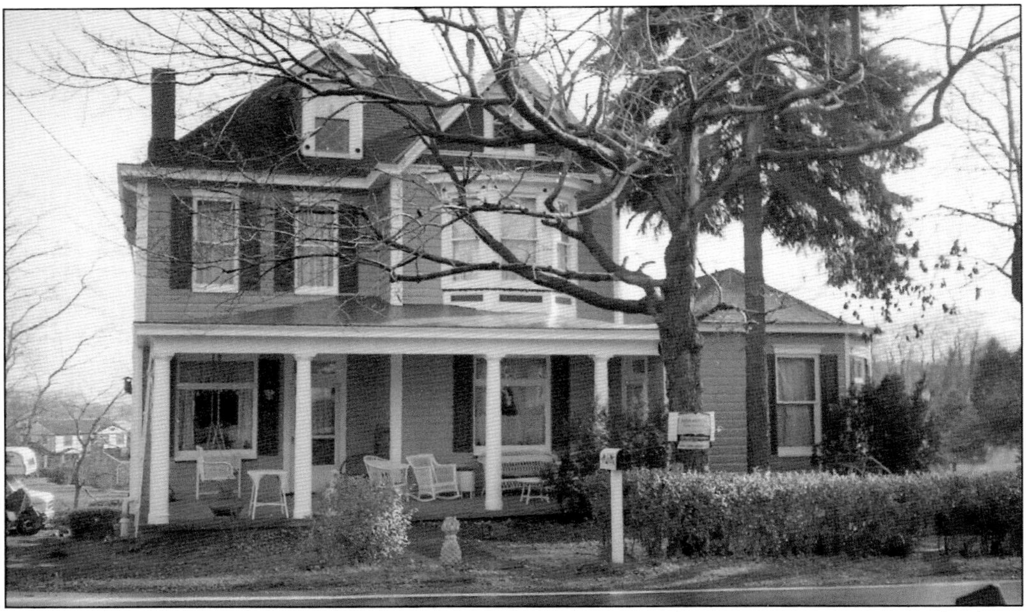

This building at 630 Saxonburg Boulevard, once the home of Dr. W.J. McGeary, was built in 1902, according to the Allegheny County Assessors' Office. The addresses changed when the township implemented the new 9-1-1 system, and this home is currently listed as 3772 Saxonburg Boulevard. Doctor McGeary was the local doctor in Dorseyville in the early 1900s.

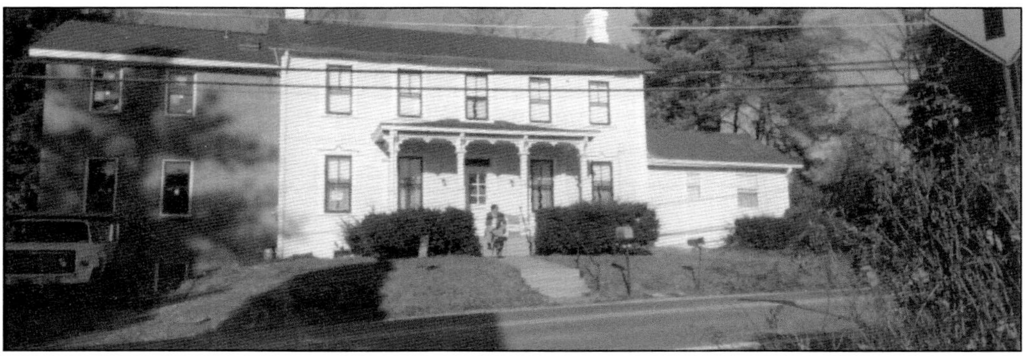

The McIntyre House is pictured in the 1990s. The addition at right was added by the third generation of McIntyres, and the wing on the left was added by the fourth generation, which is currently still living there. Joseph Stephenson, chairman of the Indiana Township Historic Commission and fourth-generation resident of this historic home, sits on the front steps. (Courtesy of Joseph Stephenson.)

Five

Education and Religious Life

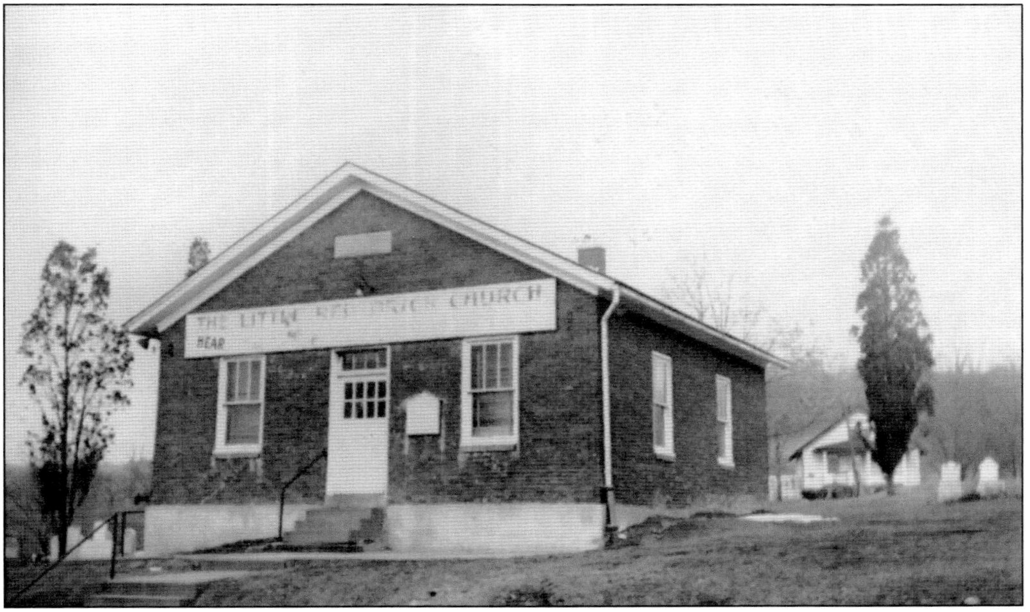

In 1869, the United Brethren Church in Dorseyville leased this land, located on Saxonburg Boulevard, from Jacob Weber to build the Blue Run Cemetery and the accompanying building, which is labeled "Little Red Brick Church." This church, a small, one-room meetinghouse that had a cemetery next to it, was a landmark of sorts in its heyday. The Little Red Brick Church was razed in 1960, and Dorseyville Alliance Church now stands next to the original plot.

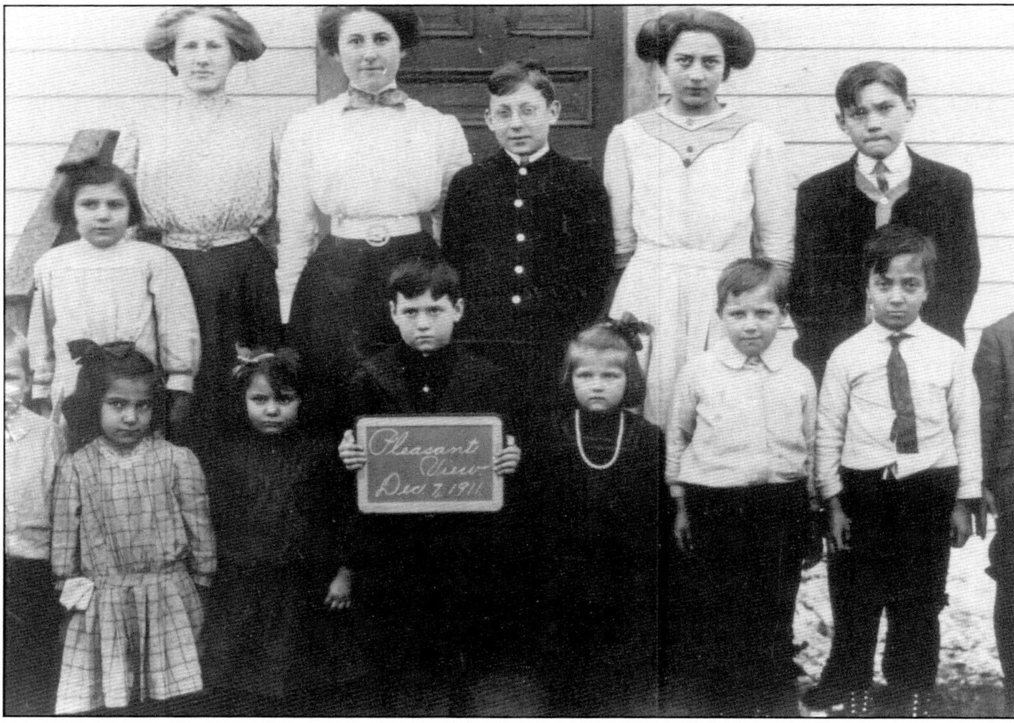

This is a December 1911 photograph of a class from Pleasant View School, which was located on Middle Road across the street from Middle Road Fire Hall. This school was also called Bailiff School because it stood on the corner of the Bailiff property. (Courtesy of Mary Jeffrey Giudici.)

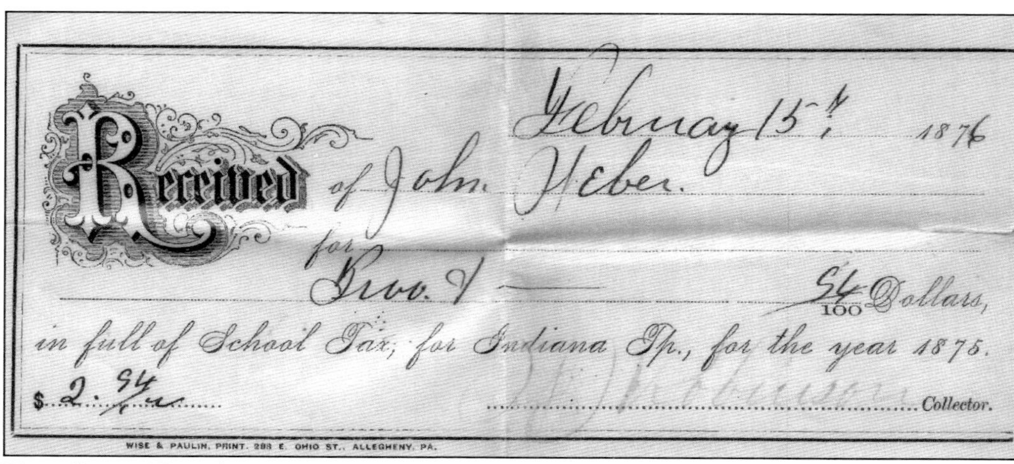

February 15th 1876

Received of John Weber

for [illegible] 54/100 Dollars,

in full of School Tax, for Indiana Tp., for the year 1875.

$2.94 .... Collector.

WISE & PAULIN, PRINT. 288 E. OHIO ST., ALLEGHENY, PA.

Tax collector J.D. Robinson wrote this receipt to John Weber for payment of the Indiana Township school tax in the year 1875. Then, school tax was only $2.94. Note the evolution of penmanship over the last 100 years. (Courtesy of Ray Yute.)

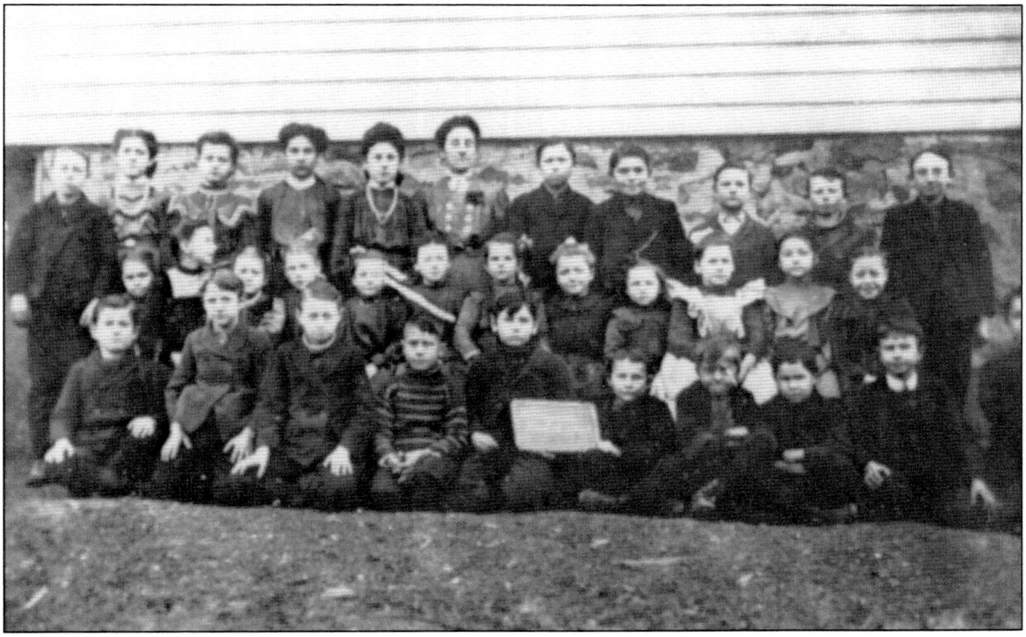

This is a December 1909 photograph of a class from Sunnyside School. Sunnyside School, aka Schoolhouse No. 1 in Indiana Township, was a one-room schoolhouse with a water pump outside that provided drinking water for the students and teacher. There was no indoor plumbing, so everyone used outhouses—one for girls and one for boys. (Courtesy of Pearl Sallade.)

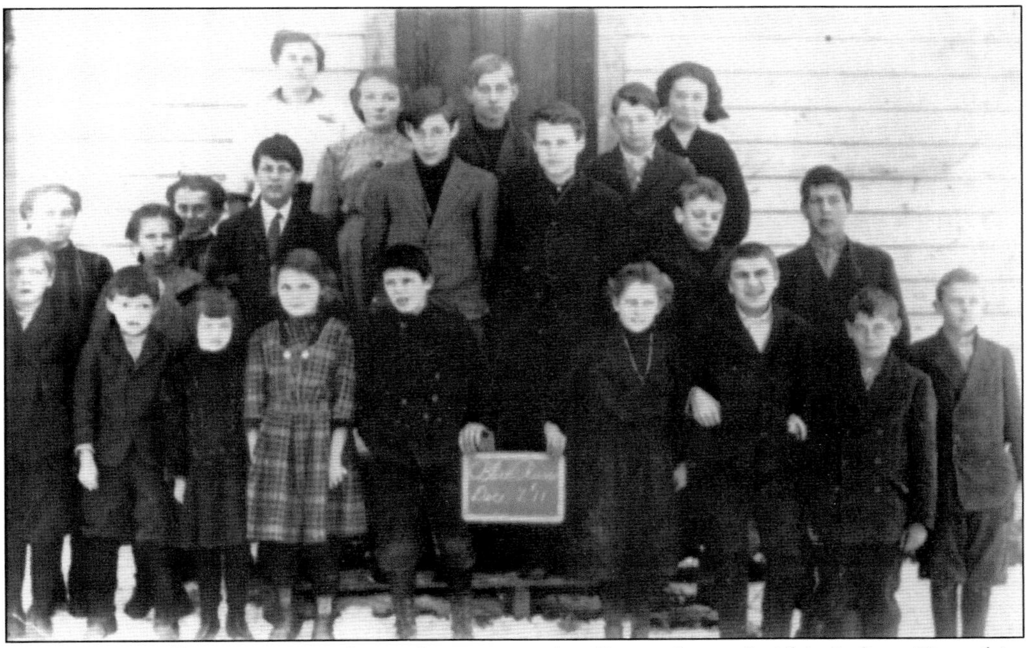

Blue Run Schoolhouse was one of several one-room schoolhouses located within Indiana Township. It had a potbelly stove in the center, and during the winter, students from all eight grades fought for a seat near the stove. This photograph was taken on December 7, 1911, as indicated by the sign held by the children in front.

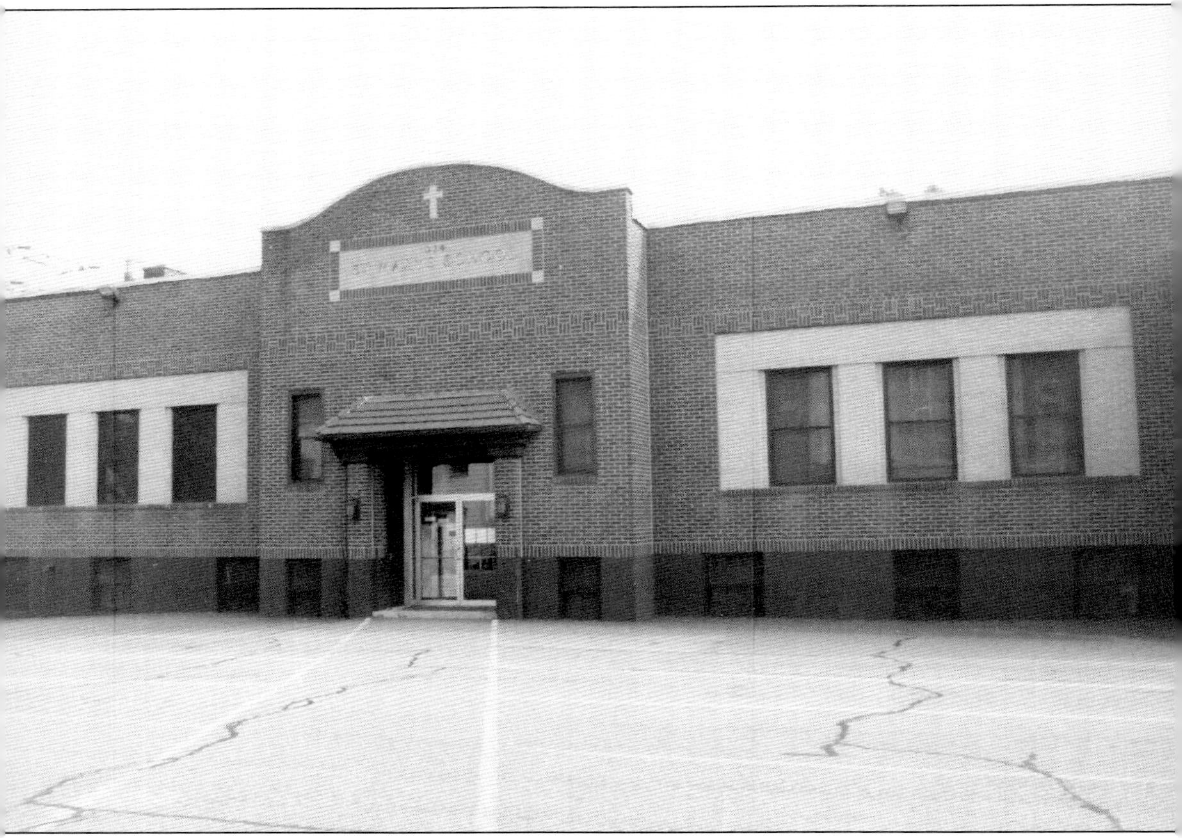

Since 1843, St. Mary School on Middle Road has provided education for children from kindergarten through eighth grade. Each year, students at St. Mary School test well above average for diocesan norms. The parish associated with the school, St. Mary of the Assumption, is on the same property but is located in neighboring Hampton Township. Children attend the school from several nearby communities, including Shaler, Hampton, O'Hara, Fox Chapel, Richland, and West Deer. The first St. Mary church for was made of logs and built in 1835. Shortly after, the people of the parish found that they needed a school, and St. Mary School was established. It originally stood two stories high, was 36 feet long by 24 feet wide, consisted of stone taken from the premises, and used logs for crossbeams. The first floor served as the classroom, while the second floor housed priests attending the parish.

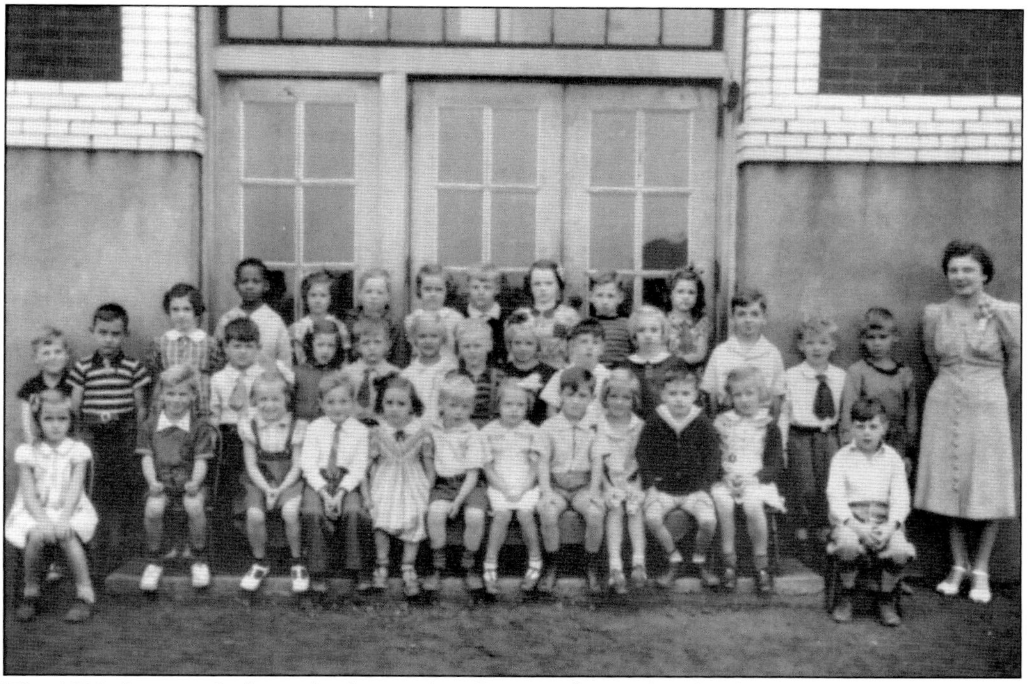

This 1938 photograph shows the first grade at Dorseyville Grade School. Dorseyville Grade School (or Dorseyville Elementary School) was founded and built in 1925 and replaced all of the small one-room schoolhouses throughout the township. (Courtesy of Pearl Sallade.)

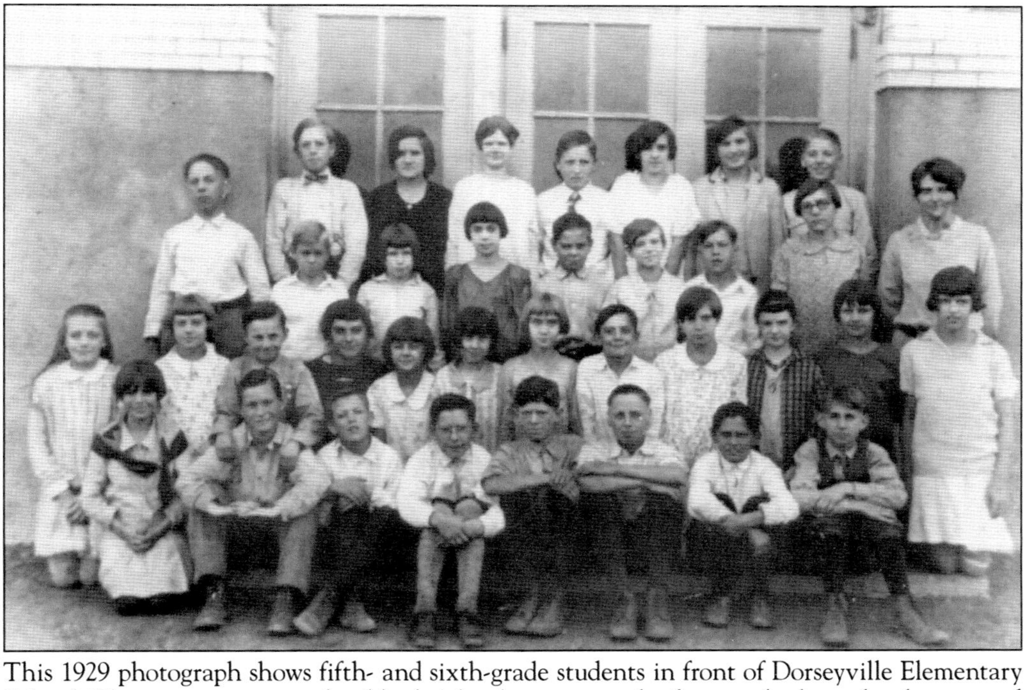

This 1929 photograph shows fifth- and sixth-grade students in front of Dorseyville Elementary School. The new, two-story school had eight classrooms—the four on the lower level were used for grades one through four, while the rooms on the second floor were for grades five to eight.

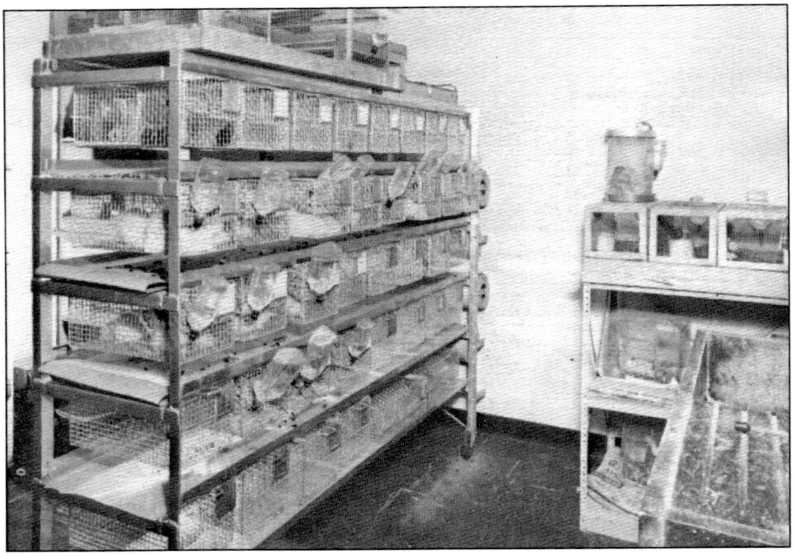

Fox Chapel High School opened in 1961 with state-of-the-art classrooms, which were pictured in the "Fox Chapel Dedication and Open House" booklet from 1962. This room, with a sink and exhaust fan, was adjacent to the biology room. Animals used in a cancer research project were housed in these cages.

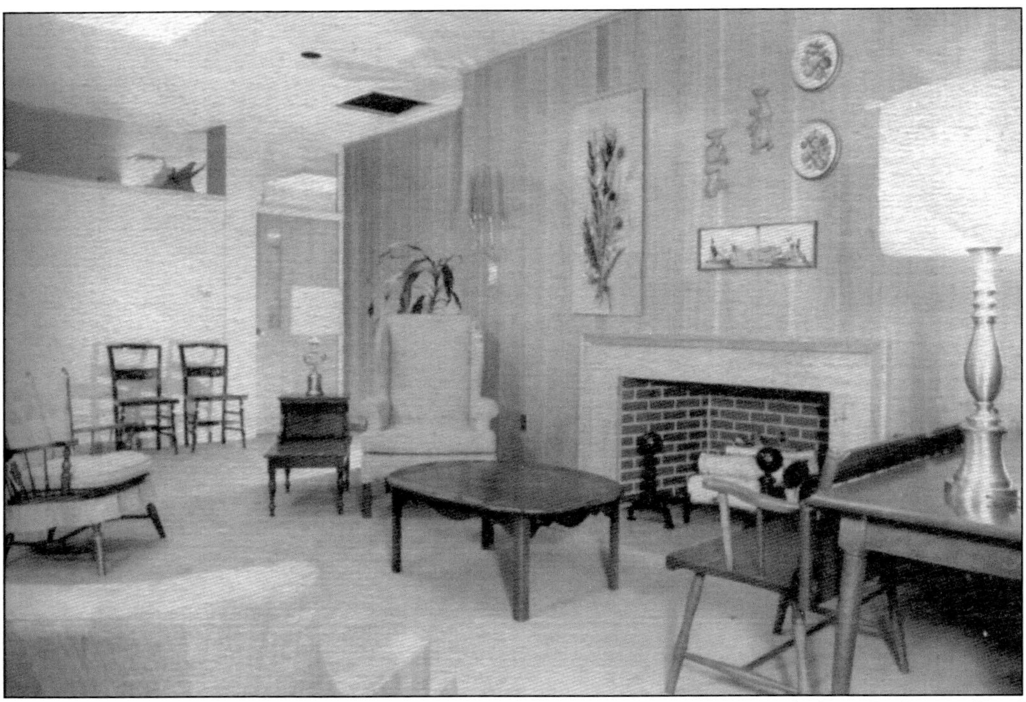

Fox Chapel High School educated young adults from many communities, including the boroughs of Aspinwall, Blawnox, and Fox Chapel, and the townships of Indiana and O'Hara. This photograph, which is also from the 1962 "Fox Chapel Dedication and Open House" booklet, shows the family-living instruction center.

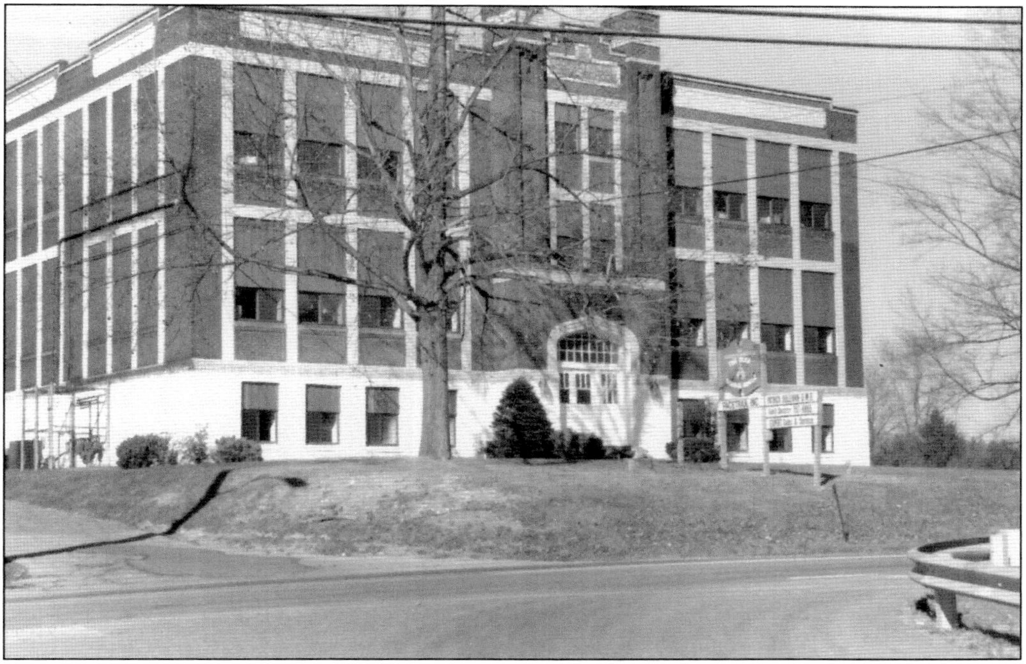

The eight-room Dorseyville Elementary School, built in 1925, replaced schoolhouses located throughout the area. Many residents were slow to accept one large school, and parents were hesitant to let their children ride public transportation when, before, they had safely walked to school.

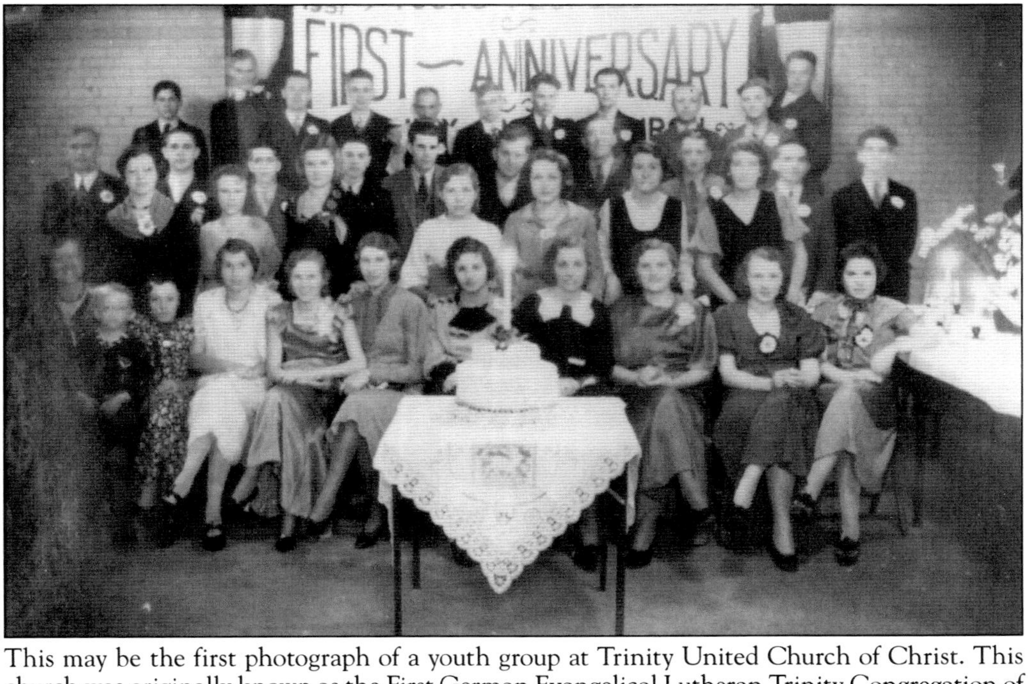

This may be the first photograph of a youth group at Trinity United Church of Christ. This church was originally known as the First German Evangelical Lutheran Trinity Congregation of Indiana Township. Rumor has it that the church started in 1831, but no records have been found that date it earlier than 1851.

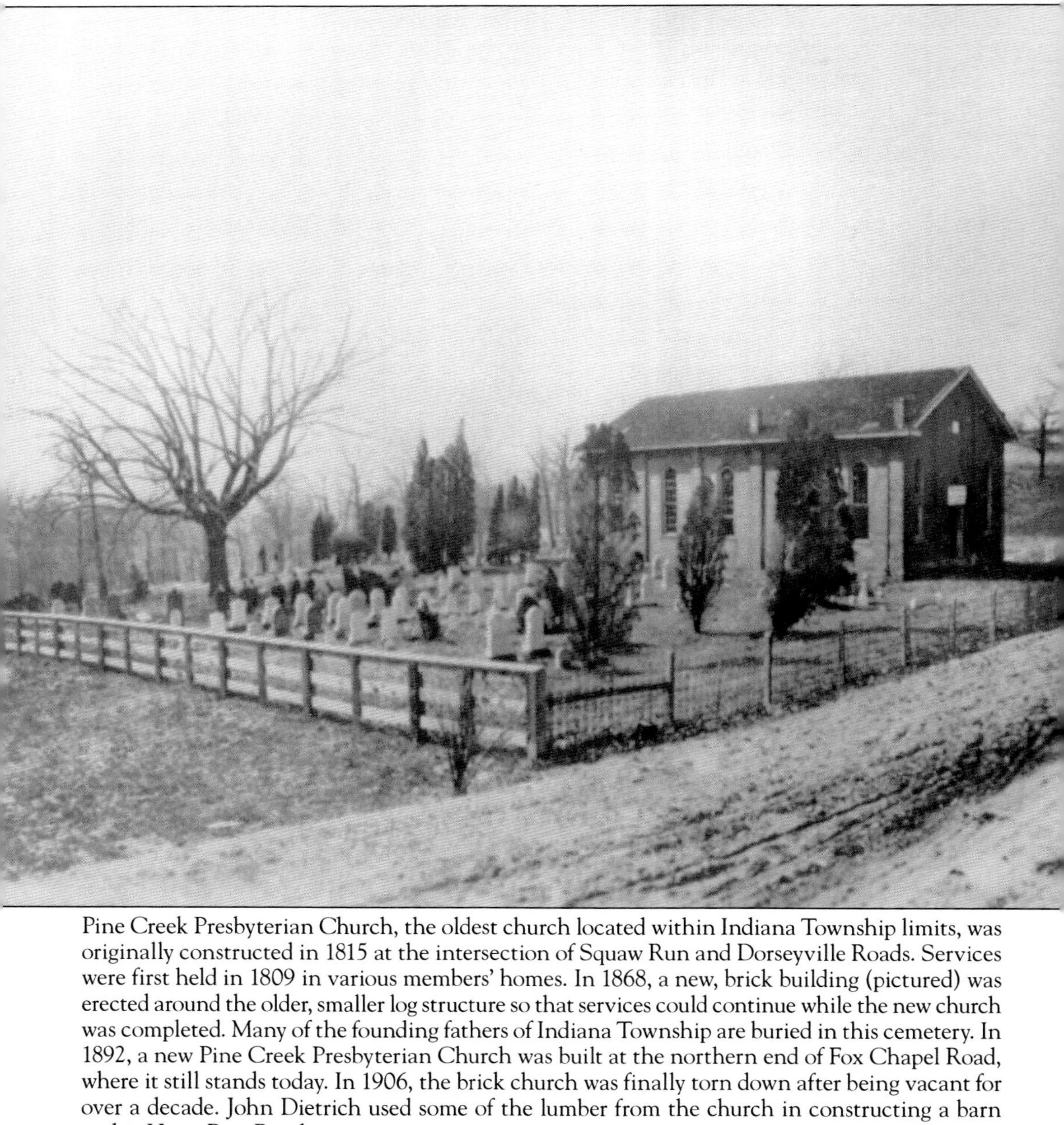

Pine Creek Presbyterian Church, the oldest church located within Indiana Township limits, was originally constructed in 1815 at the intersection of Squaw Run and Dorseyville Roads. Services were first held in 1809 in various members' homes. In 1868, a new, brick building (pictured) was erected around the older, smaller log structure so that services could continue while the new church was completed. Many of the founding fathers of Indiana Township are buried in this cemetery. In 1892, a new Pine Creek Presbyterian Church was built at the northern end of Fox Chapel Road, where it still stands today. In 1906, the brick church was finally torn down after being vacant for over a decade. John Dietrich used some of the lumber from the church in constructing a barn on his Harts Run Road property.

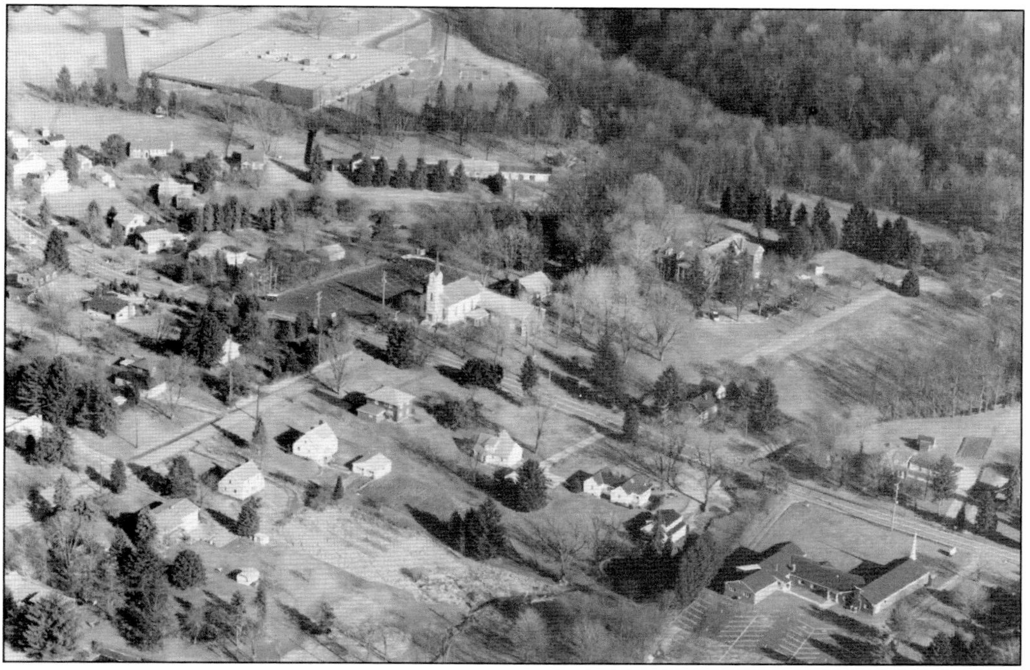

This is a 1990 aerial view of the center of Indiana Township—Dorseyville, Pennsylvania. Trinity United Church of Christ is located in the center. The old Blue Run schoolhouse is to the right of Trinity United Church of Christ. The intersection of Church Lane and Saxonburg Boulevard is directly in front of Trinity United Church of Christ. Dorseyville Alliance Church is visible in the lower right-hand corner.

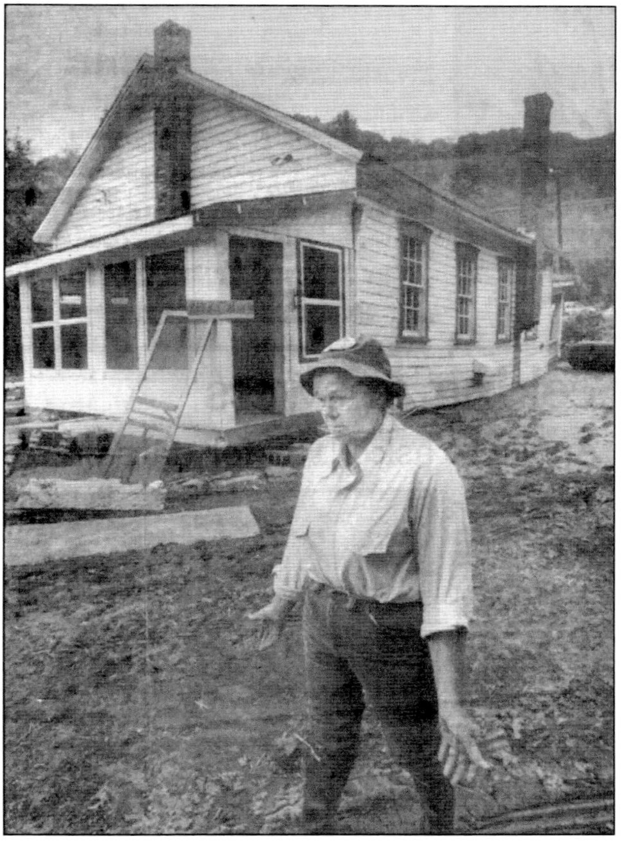

In 1938, Mary Ellen Boyle's parents, Dale S. Boyle Sr. and Mary E. Creese Boyle, purchased the old Valley View schoolhouse for use as a dwelling. In 1986, floodwaters twisted the Indiana Township home of Mary Ellen Boyle (pictured) off of its foundation; this photograph shows the back of the old Valley View schoolhouse. (Courtesy of the *Pittsburgh Press*.)

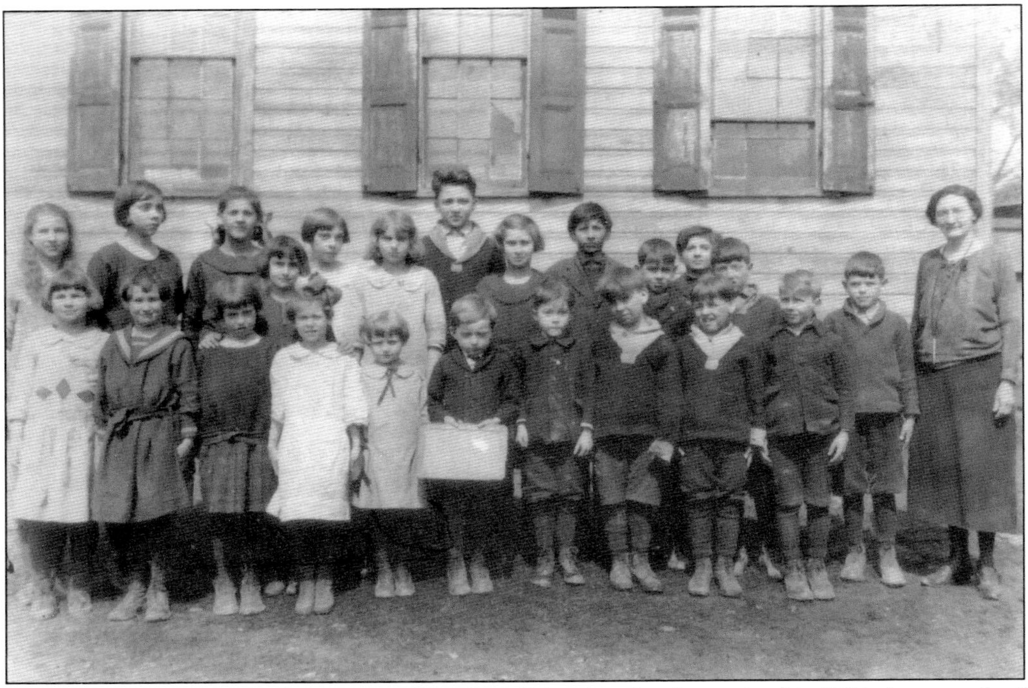

Amelia Weber taught for four years at Blue Run School and is shown in this 1924 photograph of a Blue Run School class. According to a 1987 interview with Margie Baumgartel, there was an outside toilet for the school, and the boys always had to carry a log in for the stove. (Courtesy of John Myers and Lester Strohm.)

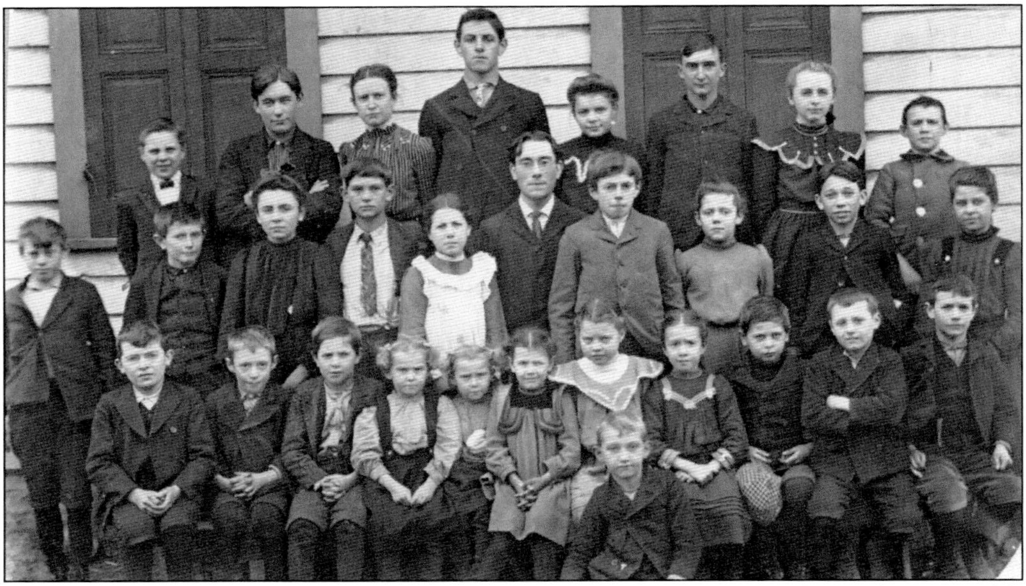

The date of this Blue Run School class photograph is unknown. However, the teacher is possibly a Mr. Kinkeade. Blue Run School was a typical one-room schoolhouse, except it was painted grey, according to Pearl Doerzbacher, instead of the usual red.

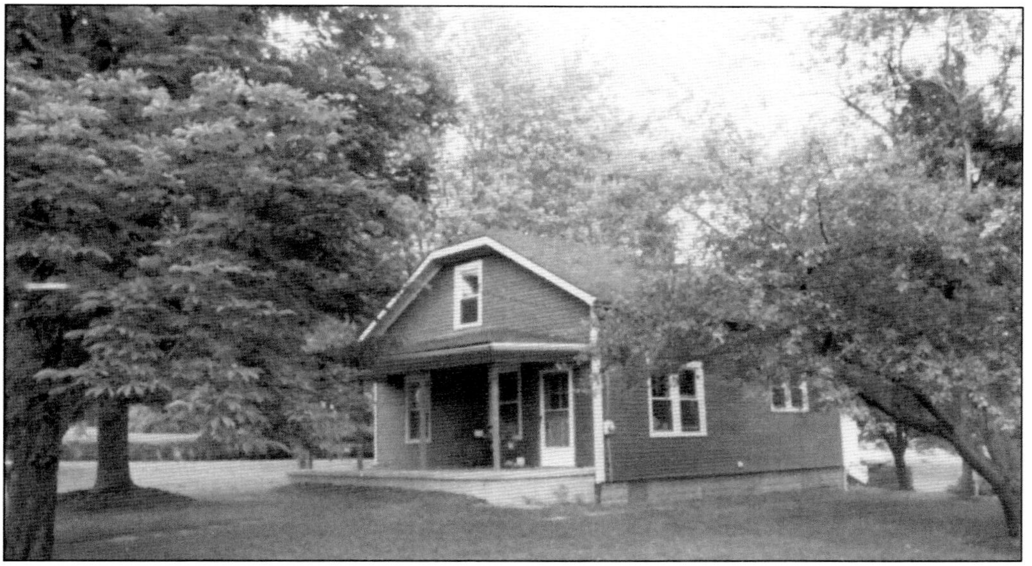

This is a modern photograph of the Blue Run School. Blue Run also used to be known as "School No. 2." Most of the one-room schoolhouses in Indiana Township were numbered. This building still stands and is located beside Trinity United Church of Christ on Saxonburg Boulevard.

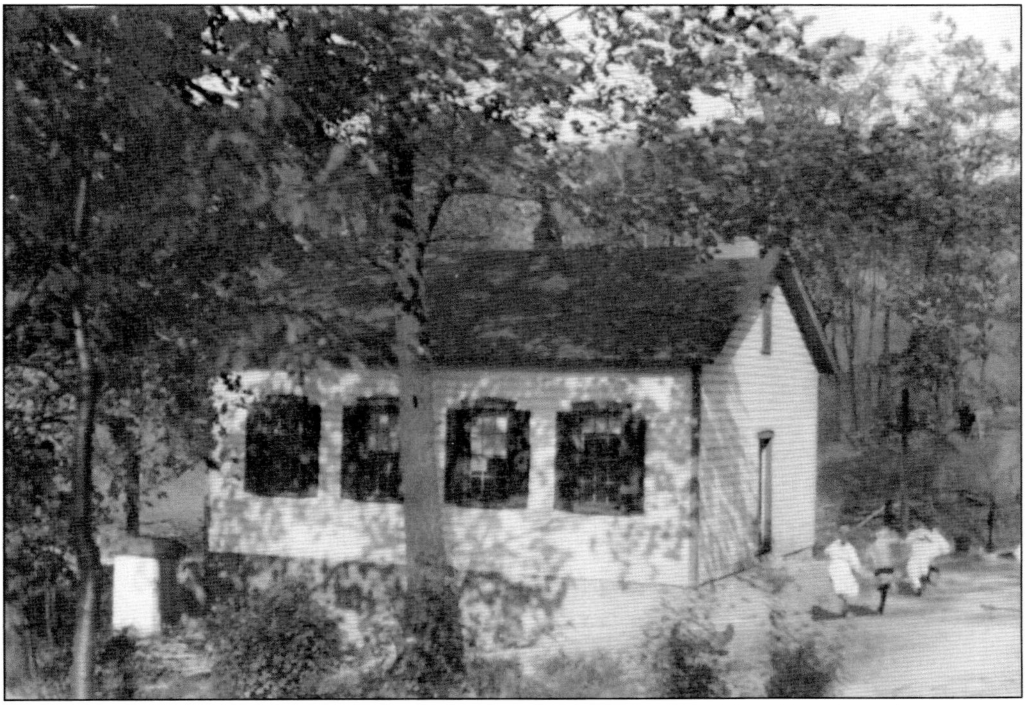

The Cross Roads ("School No. 5") also went by the name "Grubb's School" and was located near the corner of Fox Chapel and Old Mill Roads. It is not known when it was founded, but there is evidence that the structure existed as early as 1896. A pail of water filled from the water pump provided children with drinking water, and each child had his or her own drinking cup.

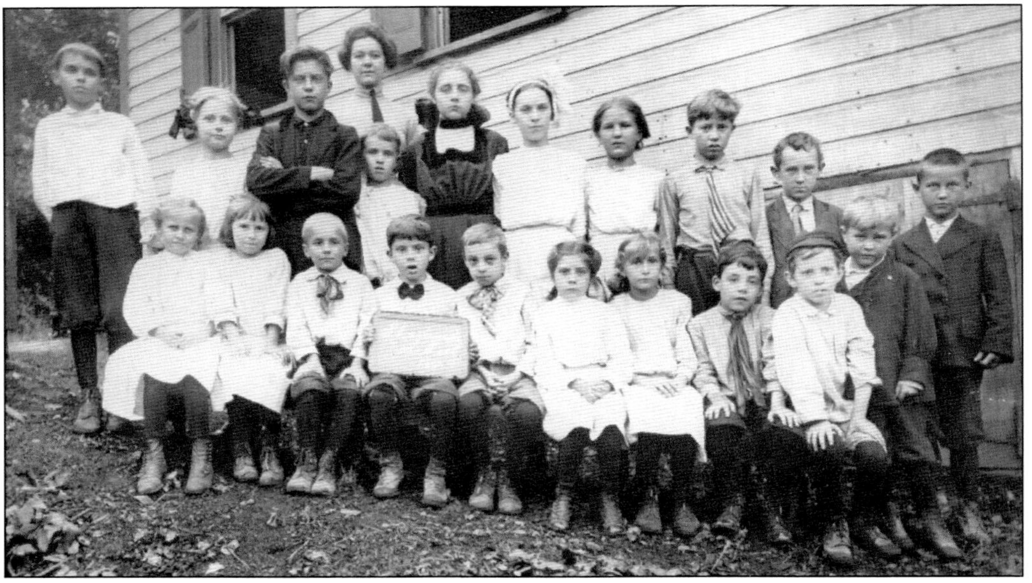

The plaque held by the boy in the center reads, "Shadyside School No. 4." Pictured here are, from left to right, (first row) unidentified, unidentified, unidentified, Mackey Marshall, Lloyd Shaner, unidentified, unidentified, unidentified, unidentified unidentified; (second row) unidentified, ? Collier, unidentified, unidentified, Margaret Cunningham, Elva Morath, unidentified, Hessie Walter, unidentified, and two Leslie boys (first names unknown). Shadyside School (also known as Pigeon Hollow School) was the hub of social life, since it was centrally located and the only school in the area. The Walter Chapel United Methodist Church began here, where the congregation held services and meetings before the church was built. The teacher was Ethel Mellon.

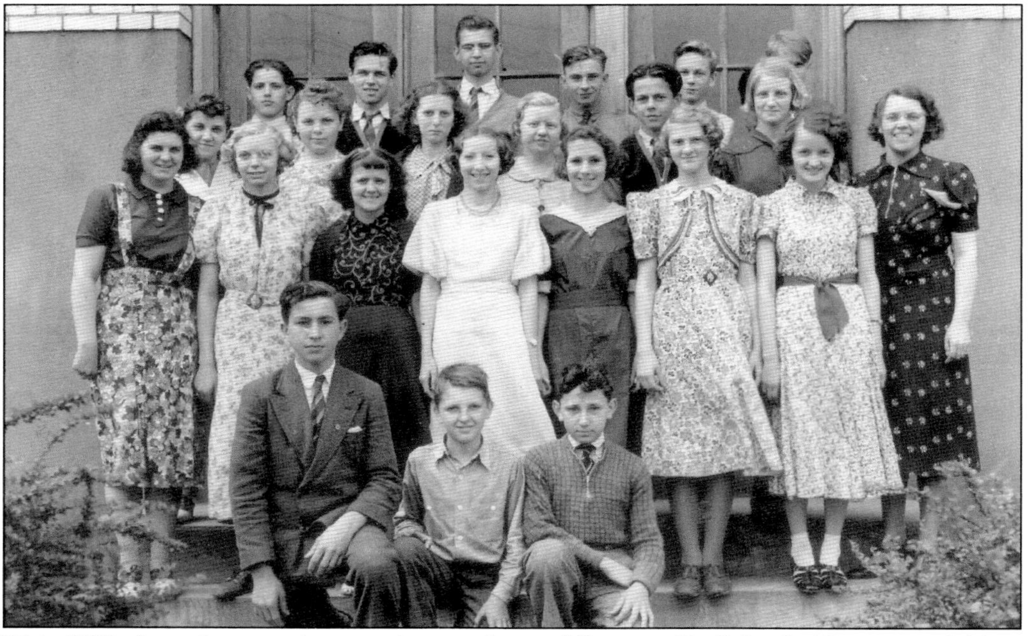

This 1938 class photograph was taken in front of Dorseyville School. (Courtesy of Alice B. Foster.)

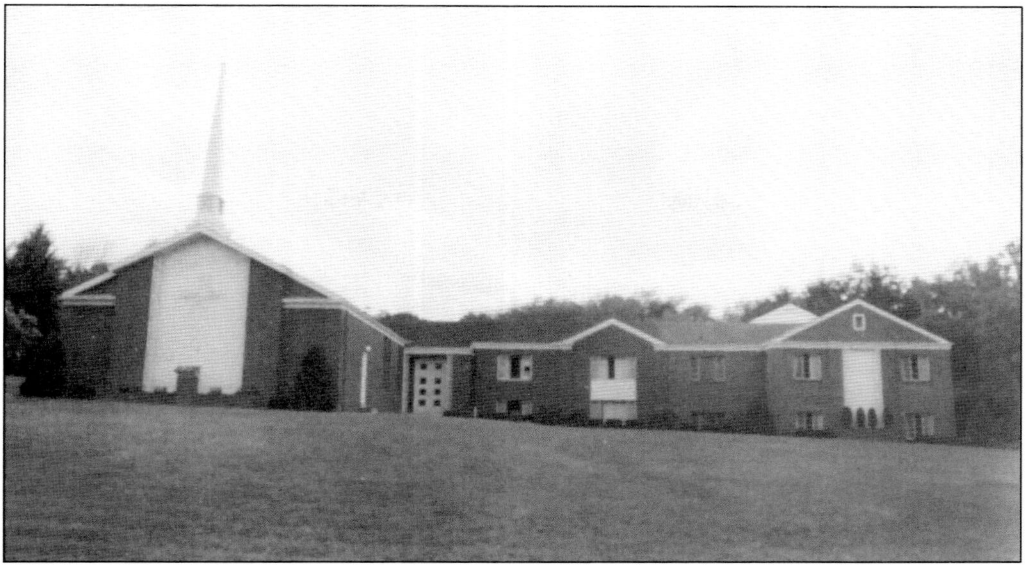

Over many years, a number of different congregations merged, split, and/or dissolved, making way for today's Dorseyville Alliance Church. In 1960, this building replaced the Little Red Brick Church, which was adjacent to Blue Run Cemetery. The congregation of the Little Red Brick Church donated whatever they could every Sunday to raise enough money to begin construction of the Dorseyville Alliance Church. Children even gave their candy money for the cause.

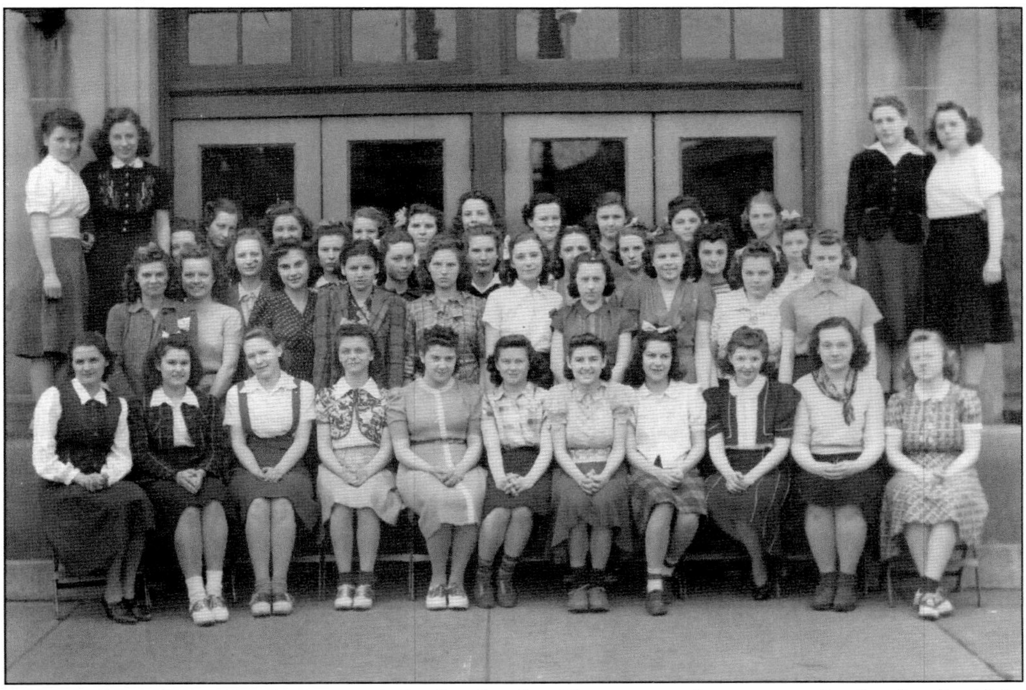

Many Indiana Township kids went to high school in Etna, since there was no high school within the boundaries of the township. The other area high school was located in Aspinwall. In the early years, many children could not go to high school because the bus system that was in place cost money, and families could not afford to pay the bus fare. (Courtesy of Alice B. Foster.)

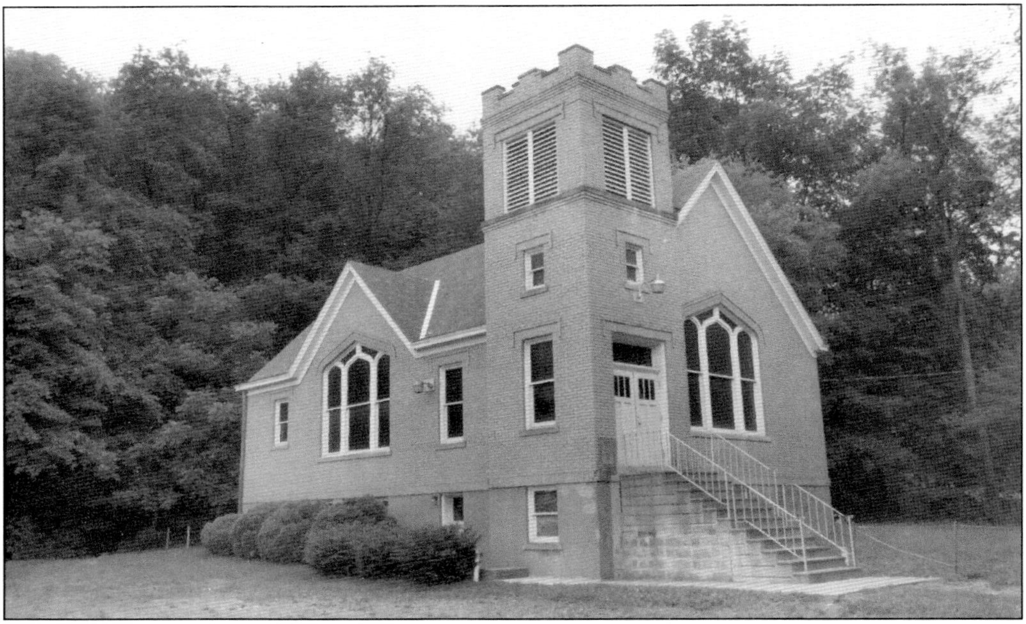

Indianola United Presbyterian Church was built in 1923, mainly by volunteers from the mine. The volunteers did everything by hand with the only assistance coming from a team of horses. T.G. Fear, a superintendent of the mine owned by Inland Collieries Co., designed the plans for the church. Kathleen Walker, a parishioner, said in a 1988 interview that their congregation is small, but they have a slogan: "A place where a carpenter still mends broken lives."

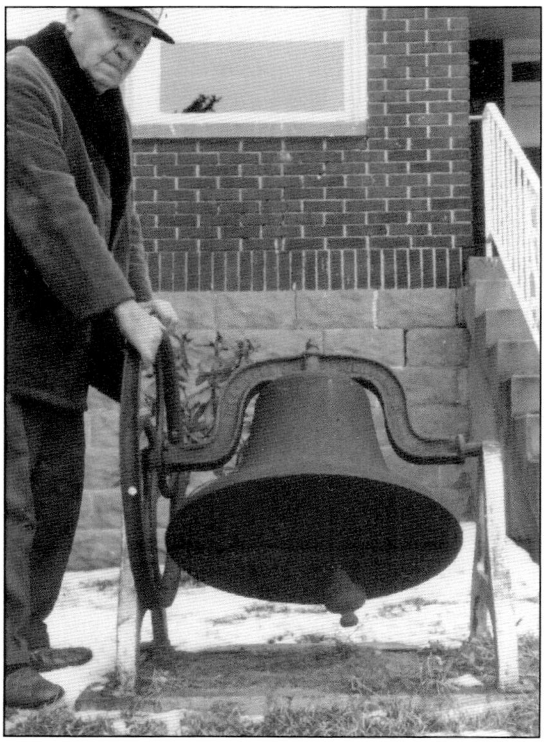

This is an old school bell that Michael Hertz (pictured) purchased from John Prager's scrap pile on Mill Dam Road. According to interviews conducted by former members of the historic commission—June Einnes, Emily Allison, and Navie Burgi—Hertz stated that the bell was from the first school built in Dorseyville and that Prager was the school director at that time. The bell, which is 26 inches wide and sat on top of the schoolhouse, is inscribed with "The C.S. Bell Co., Hillsboro, Ohio."

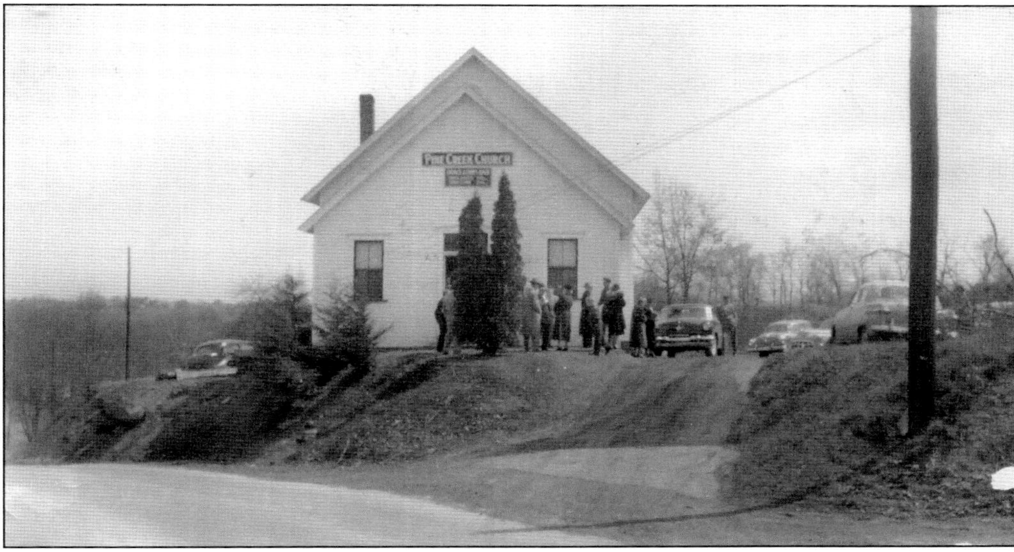

The Pine Creek Presbyterian Church is pictured in 1957, shortly before it was moved 50 yards away from Fox Chapel Road (shown in the foreground). This image illustrates how close the church was to Fox Chapel Road; due to increased traffic, the church needed to move back from the main drag. This move also enabled the church to increase the size of the parking lot in order to accommodate the increasing size of the congregation. (Courtesy of Dorothy Preston Bauer via John F. Bauer III.)

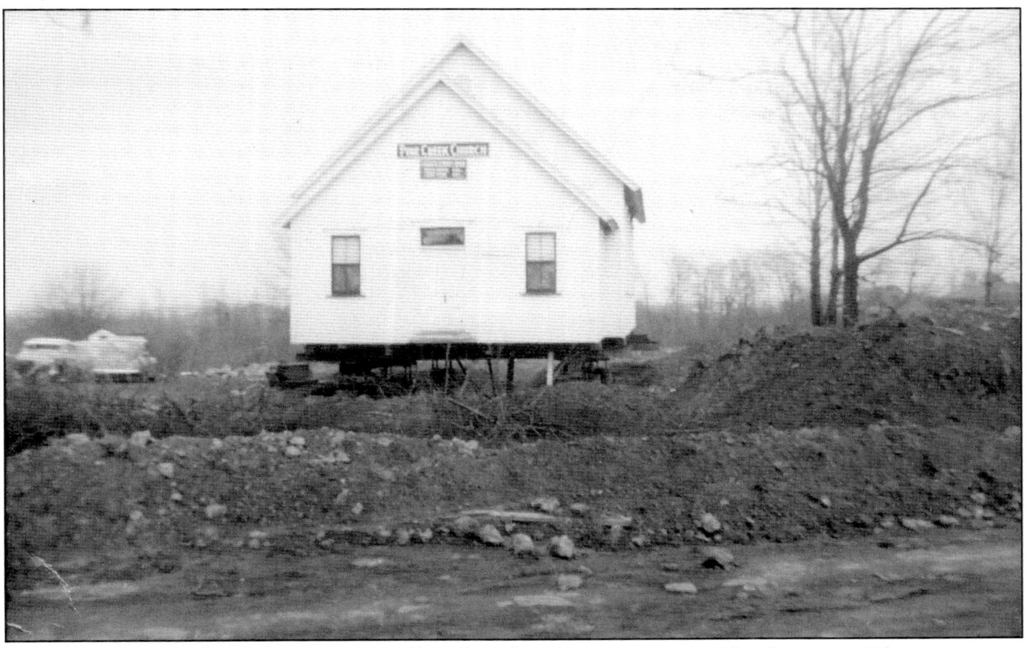

The elevated Pine Creek Presbyterian Church is shown in preparation for the move. The contractor jacked up the church, set it on logs, and rolled it about 50 yards to its present location. In addition to the new basement the church acquired during the course of this move, it also got a furnace room, bathrooms, and a stage. The road in the foreground is Oak Knoll Drive. (Courtesy of Dorothy Preston Bauer via John F. Bauer III.)

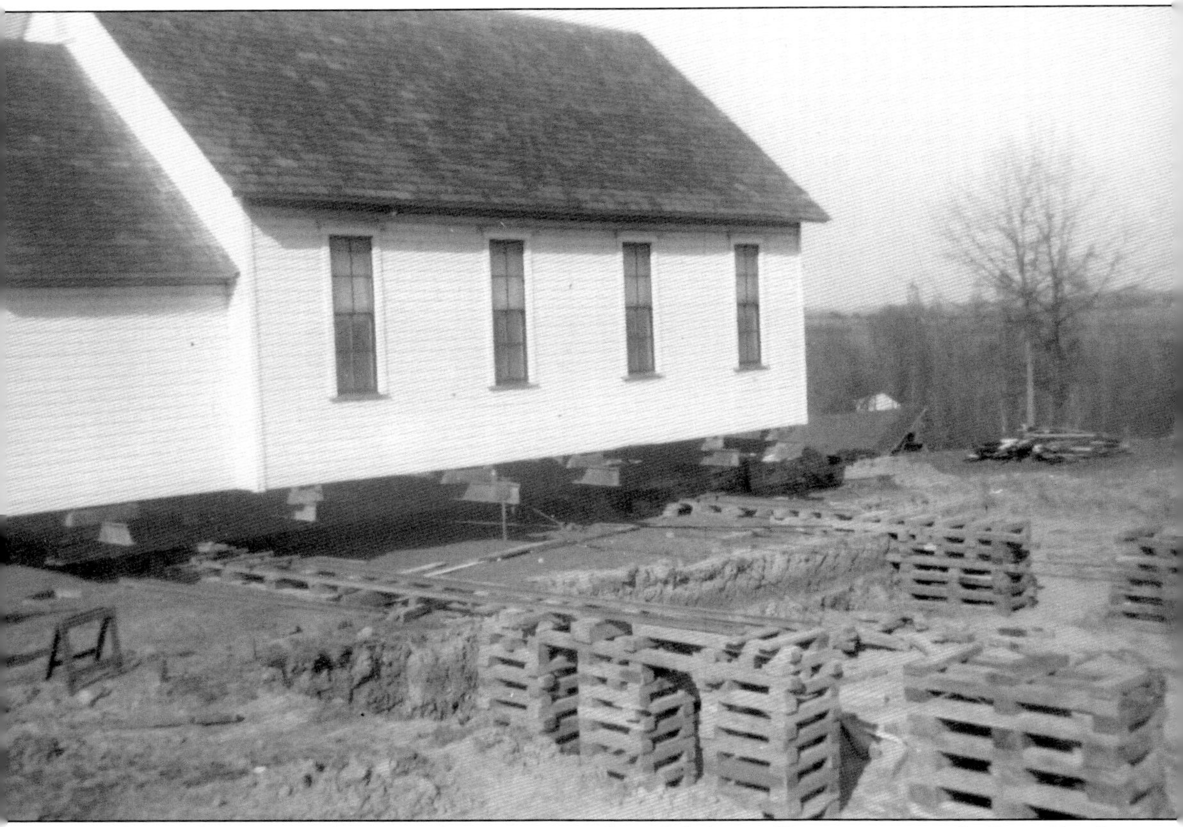

When Indiana Township's population increased, so did the traffic on major roads. Pine Creek Presbyterian Church had to be moved back to make way for the construction of the new Fox Chapel Road. This is a detailed look at how the foundation was shifted. When the congregation relocated the building, they decided it was a good time to give the church a basement, so a basement was dug in preparation for the move. The building was initially erected in this location in 1892. Due to changes in the neighborhood and the nearness of Sharpsburg and other churches, the original site of the church—on the corner of Squaw Run and Dorseyville Roads—became too far removed from the majority of the congregation. (Courtesy of Dorothy Preston Bauer via John F. Bauer III.)

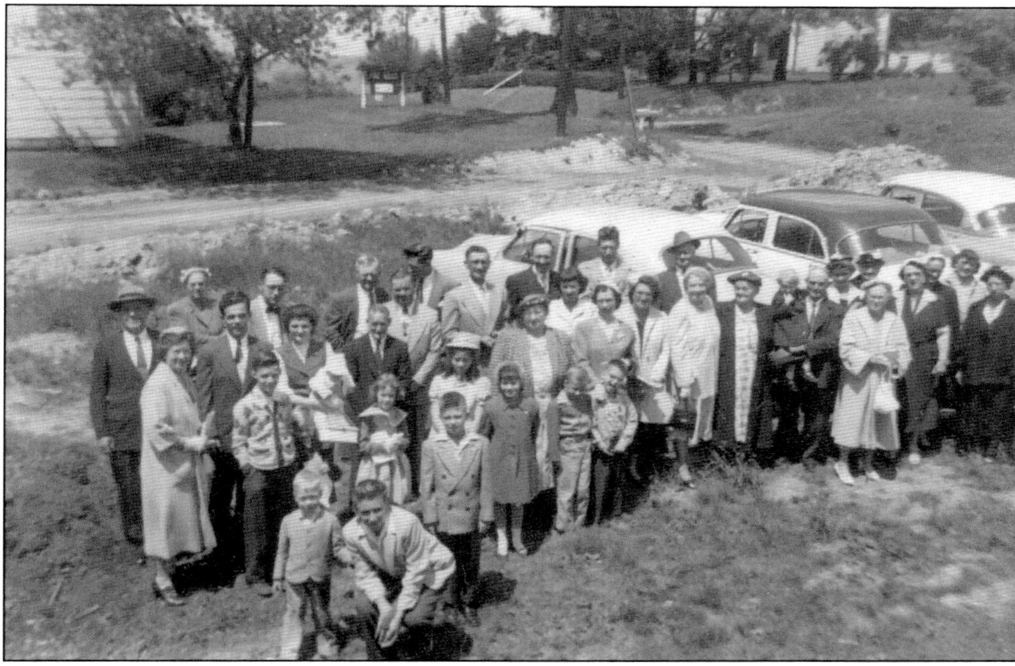

The congregation at Pine Creek Presbyterian Church is pictured here, perhaps at a gathering to witness the shift of the building. The intersection of Oak Knoll and Fox Chapel Roads is visible in the background. (Courtesy of Dorothy Preston Bauer via John F. Bauer III.)

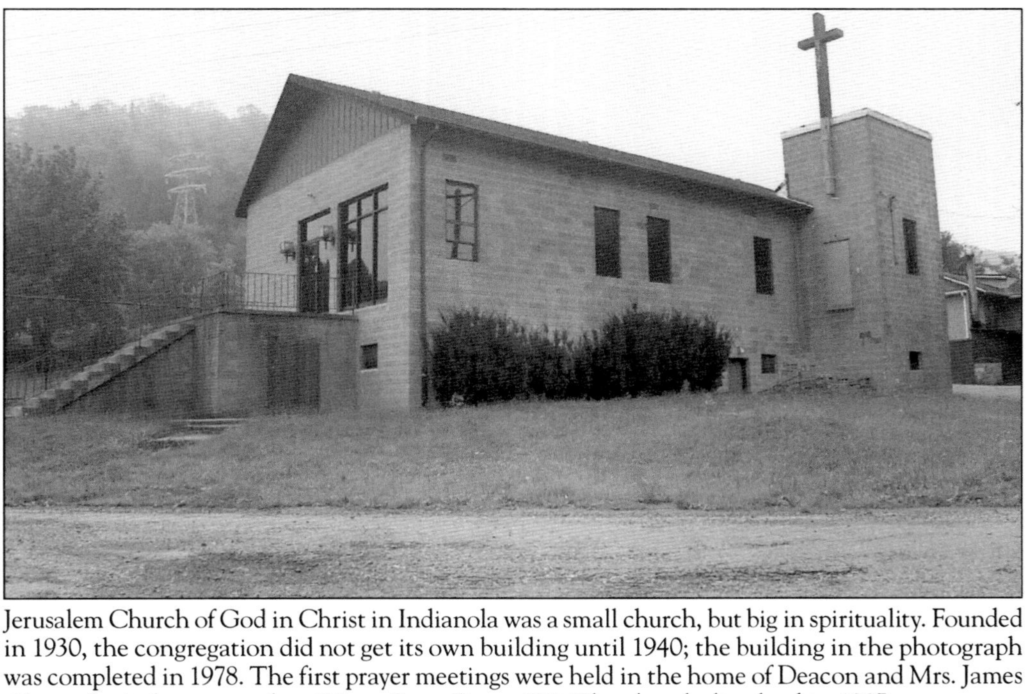

Jerusalem Church of God in Christ in Indianola was a small church, but big in spirituality. Founded in 1930, the congregation did not get its own building until 1940; the building in the photograph was completed in 1978. The first prayer meetings were held in the home of Deacon and Mrs. James Alexander in house number 199 on State Route 910. The church dissolved in 1987.

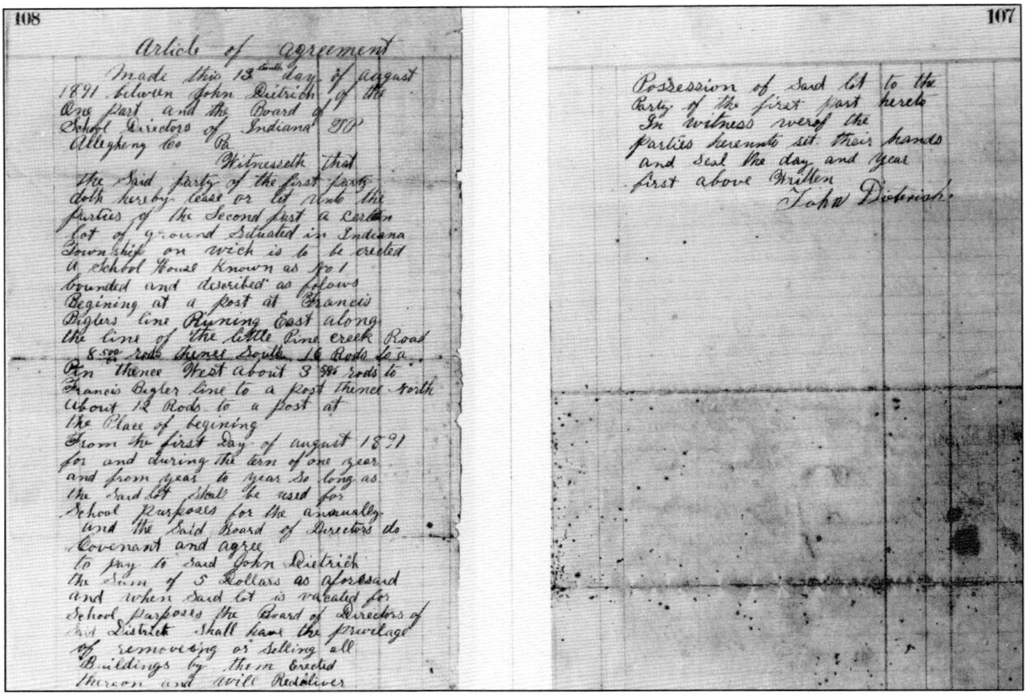

108

Article of agreement

Made this 13th day of august 1891 between John Dietrich of the One part and the Board of School Directors of Indiana TP Allegheny Co Pa

Witnesseth that the Said party of the first party doth hereby lease or let unto the parties of the Second part a certain lot of ground Situated in Indiana Township on wich is to be erected a School House Known as No 1 bounded and described as folows Begining at a post at Francis Biglers line Runing East along the line of the Little Pine creek Road 8 500 rods thence South 12 Rods to a Pin thence West about 3 [illegible] rods to Francis Bigler line to a post thence North about 12 Rods to a post at the Place of begining From the first day of august 1891 for and during the term of one year and from year to year So long as the Said lot Shall be used for School Purposes for the annually and the Said Board of Directors do Covenant and agree to pay to Said John Dietrich the Sum of 5 Dollars as aforesaid and when Said lot is vacated for School purposes the Board of Directors of Said District Shall have the privilage of removeing or Selling all Buildings by them Erected thereon and will Redeliver

107

Possession of Said lot to the Party of the first part hereto In witness wereof the Parties hereunto set their hands and Seal the day and year first above Written

John Dietrich

Pearl Dietrich Sallade recalled in a 1994 interview that this was the lease between her grandfather, John H. Dietrich, and the Indiana Township School Board for the ground on which Sunnyside School was located. Sallade's father, F.W. Dietrich, later owned the property. This lease was for the school that was built to replace the one that had burned.

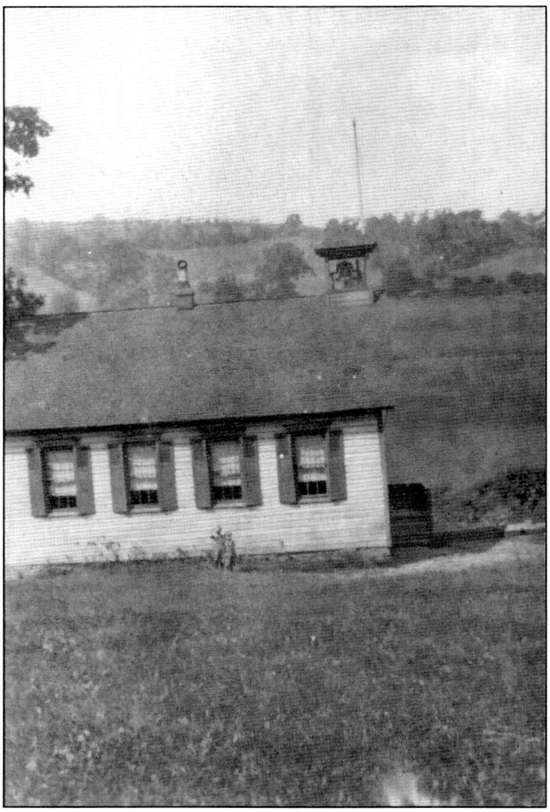

This is Sunnyside School—or, as it was originally called, School House No. 1. The original schoolhouse burned down, and a replica of the first one was built on the same site. In 1891, the schoolhouse was located on Saxonburg Boulevard below Harts Run Road. West Deer Township's Oak Valley Grange later bought this one-room building and moved the entire structure to the corner of Saxonburg Boulevard and Bairdford Road.

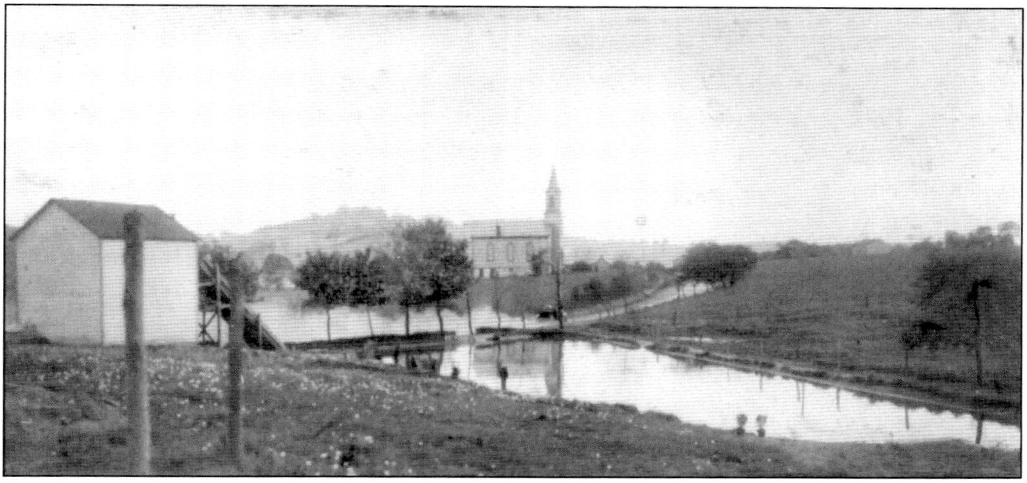

A vehicle motors down Saxonburg Boulevard towards Route 8 in the center of this photograph. Trinity United Church of Christ is in the background, and Shopene's icehouse pond is in the foreground. In the winter months, ice was cut from the pond and stored in the icehouse for use at Michael Shopene's hotel, the 12-Mile House.

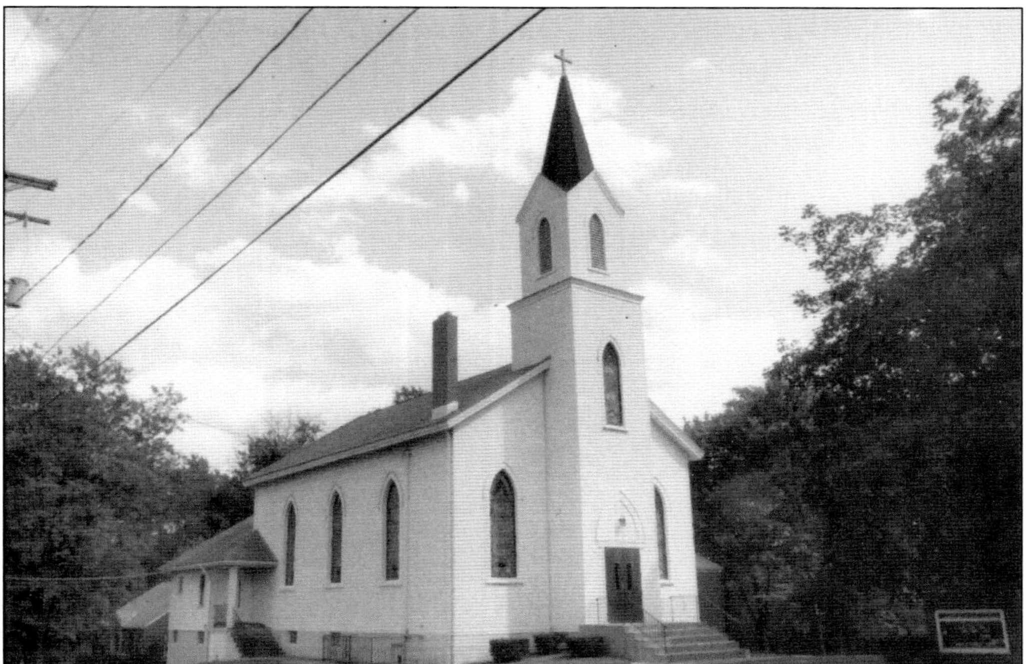

Trinity United Church of Christ, on Saxonburg Boulevard in Dorseyville, is possibly the second-oldest church in Indiana Township (the oldest is Pine Creek Presbyterian, which opened in 1815). Although no physical records mention this church's existence prior to 1851, Elizabeth Donhorst Wachter, born in 1830, often told her children and grandchildren about attending church and school in the little log structure.

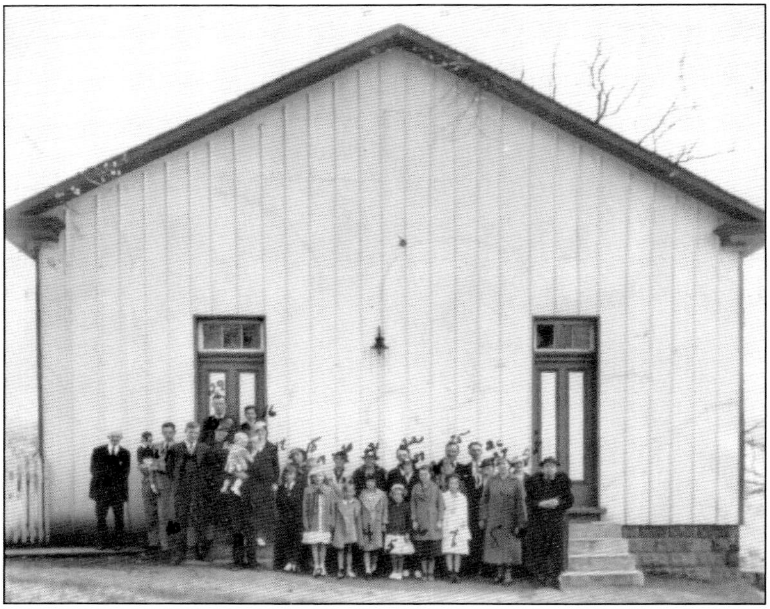

In 1863, the people of Rural Ridge started to hold prayer meetings at the Shadyside School. The crowds grew to such numbers that the schoolhouse could not accommodate them any longer. Daniel Walter drove a team of four horses up the riverbank to the main road with the logs to build the church in 1869, and thus Walter Chapel United Methodist Church was born.

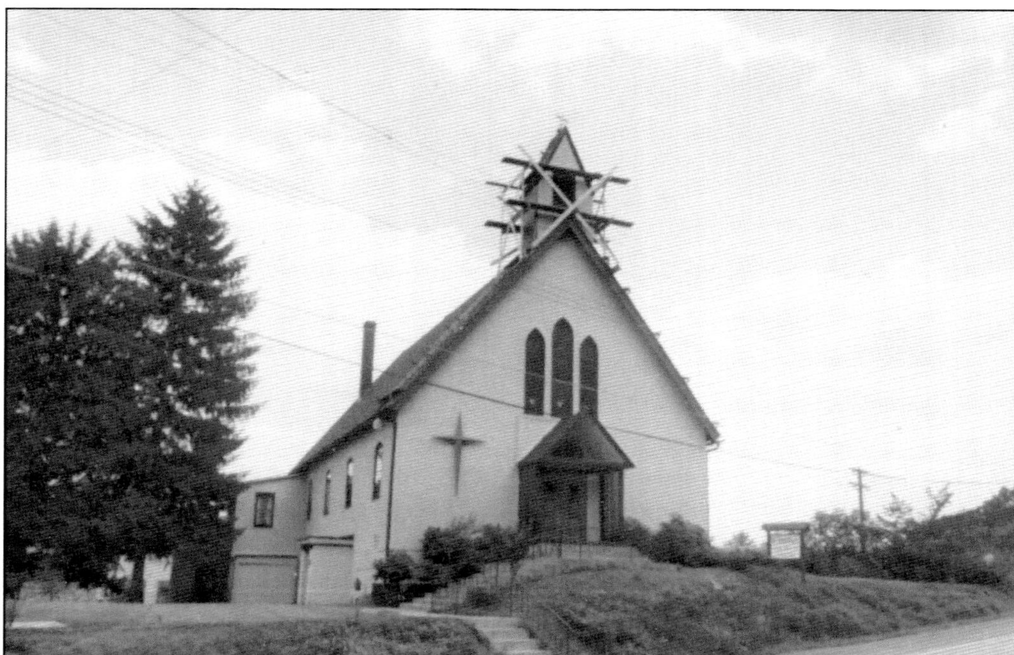

St. Timothy's Church was founded in Indianola in 1918, but the building itself was not constructed until 1920. Prior to 1920, services were held in a beanery. Fr. Clement Pfeiffer was the first pastor of the congregation in 1919 and wanted to name the building after the first director of the Confraternity of Christian Doctrine, Fr. Timothy O'Shea—hence the name St. Timothy's.

Six

Entertainment and Social Organizations

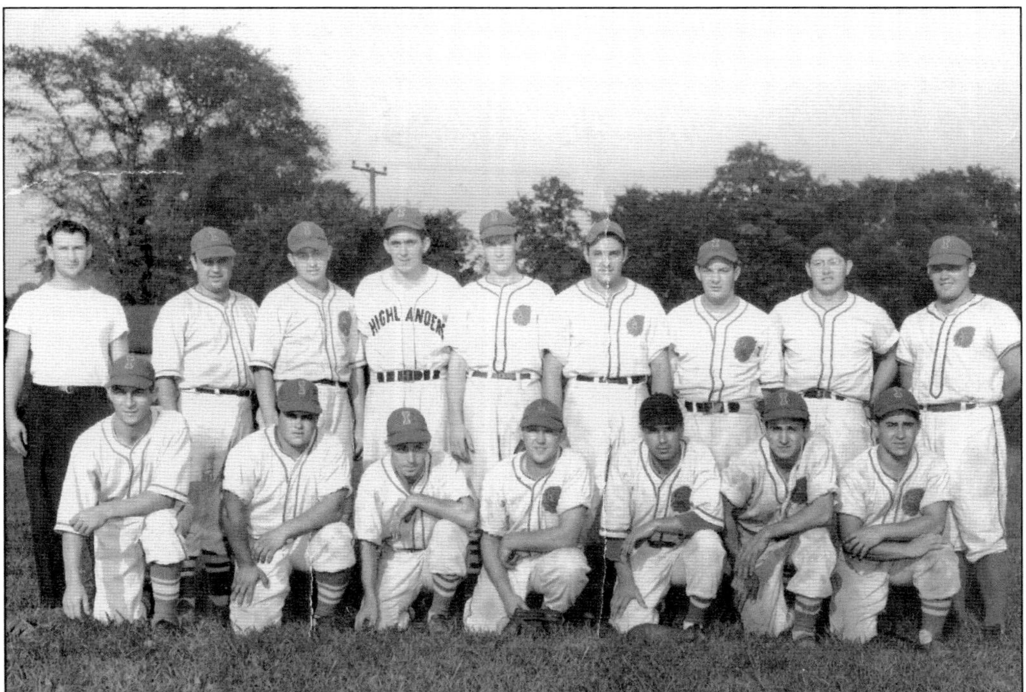

The Highlanders pose for a photograph on an unknown date. The "I" on the baseball players' hats stands for "Indianola." Baseball was an important and popular pastime for those living in Indianola and other mining communities; organized teams from each community competed against each other on the baseball diamond.

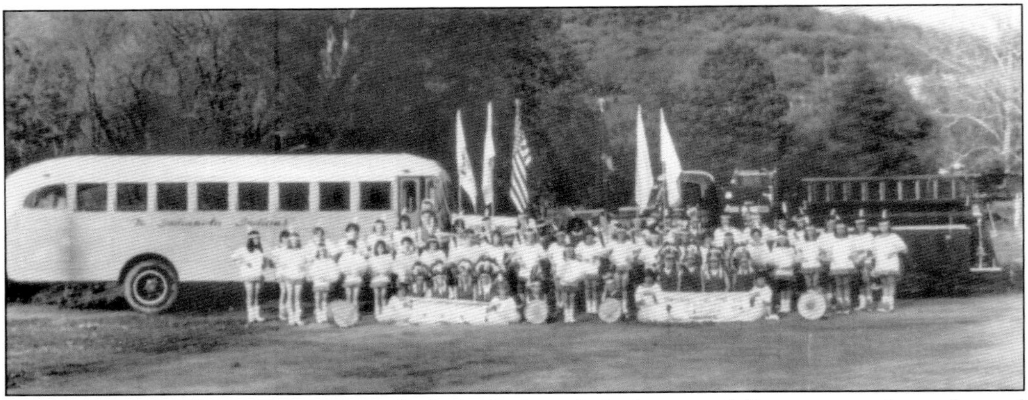

This group of girls and boys was called the Indianola Indians and Papooses and was formed around 1966, but dissolved around 1971. The banners in front of the group say they are marching for the volunteer fire department of Indianola in 1968. The Indians went to all of the parades and marched with the fire department. The Ladies Auxiliary organized the group. (Courtesy of the Papooses.)

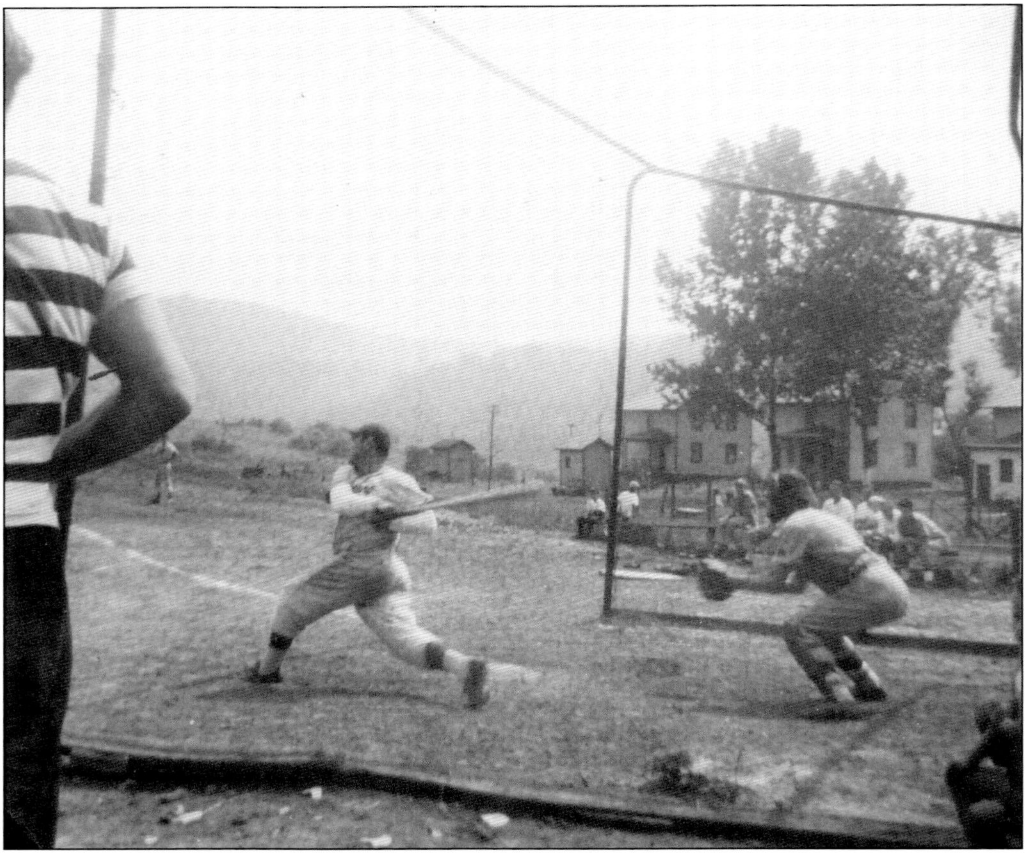

An action shot of a baseball team playing in the Rural Ridge schoolyard in the 1950s shows that with the decline of the mines and the shrinking of farms, Rural Ridge still had a fun social outlet. Group activities, such as baseball, kept spirits up and encouraged togetherness. (Courtesy of Mary Yelich.)

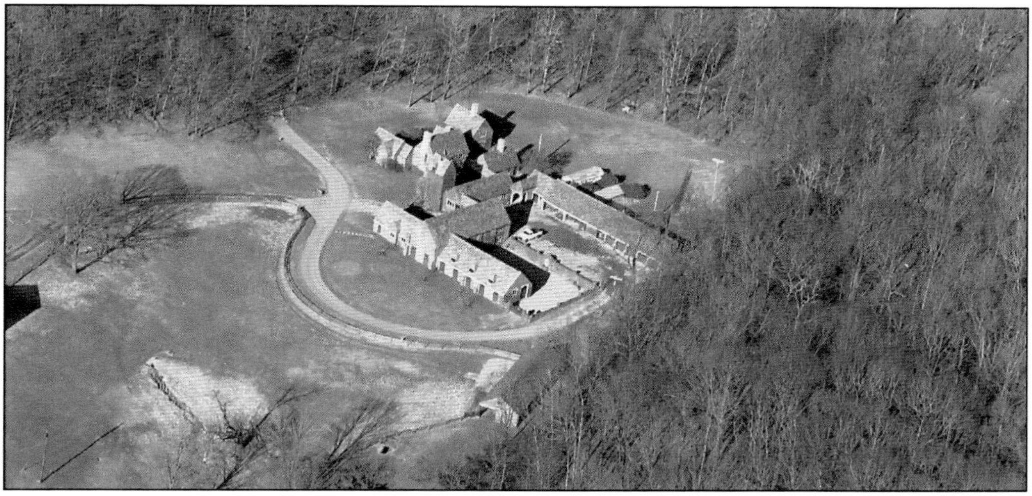

John and Mary Flinn Lawrence purchased this land in the late 1920s, and their mansion, Hartwood Acres (pictured), was built around 1927 by architect Alfred Hopkins. Hartwood was the site of many fox hunts and horse shows. Since 1976, Hartwood Acres Park has been open to the public for recreational use.

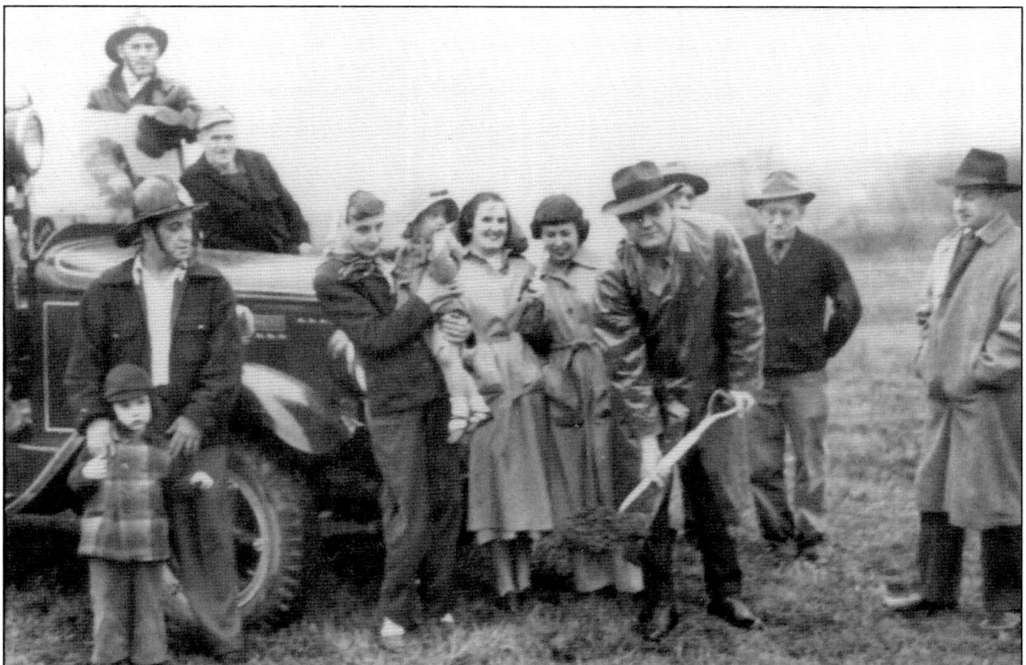

This April 13, 1951, image captures the ground-breaking ceremony for Dorseyville Volunteer Fire Department No. 1. Roy Miersch (left) and John Campbell are on the truck. In front of the truck are, from left to right, assistant chief Al Miller with his son Arthur, Theresa Lingusky (holding Jeanette Miller), Betty Miersch, Barbara Wunderlich, president Conrad Wunderlich (holding shovel), treasurer William Miersch (behind Conrad Wunderlich), Bill Critchlow, and secretary William Kirk. Dorseyville VFD No. 1 is located on the corner of Saxonburg Boulevard and Charles Street. Chief Willis Lingusky is not pictured.

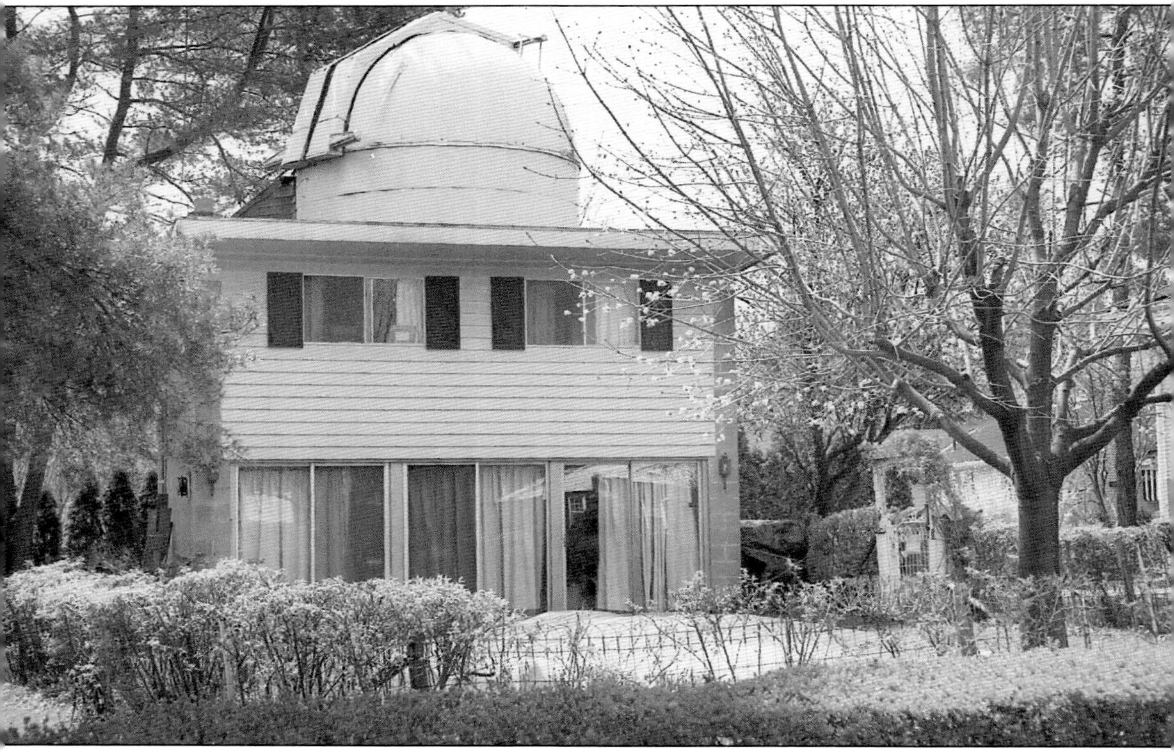

The "Dorseyville Observatory" was located at the corner of Saxonburg Boulevard and Weber Drive and contained a time capsule from 1968 compiled by Rody J. Clutter. He sealed the capsule, which contained items donated by his friends, relatives, and associates, into the concrete pier of his telescope. According to a letter written by Clutter, the time capsule was supposed to be opened sometime around 2075, but after this photograph was taken in 1991, the observatory fell into disrepair and was torn down in 2011. The Indiana Township Historic Commission is working with the current owners to try to retrieve the time capsule. Clutter began construction on this observatory in 1960, and it included features such as a 12-foot-diameter rotating dome, a combination swimming pool cabana and observatory, a 21-inch modified Cassegrain reflector, and a 560-cubic-inch time capsule.

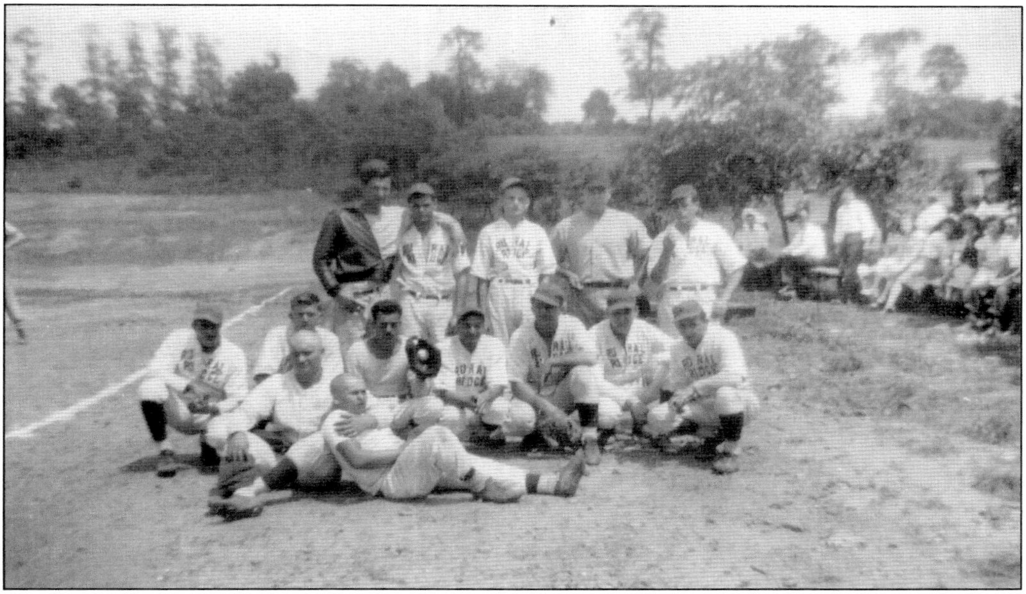

This is another photograph of the Rural Ridge baseball team, known as "The Ridgers," that was likely taken later than the previous Rural Ridge baseball team shot (on page 94). It was important for small communities like Rural Ridge to have activities or clubs like baseball or the volunteer fire department in order to create a sense of unity. (Courtesy of Mary Yelich.)

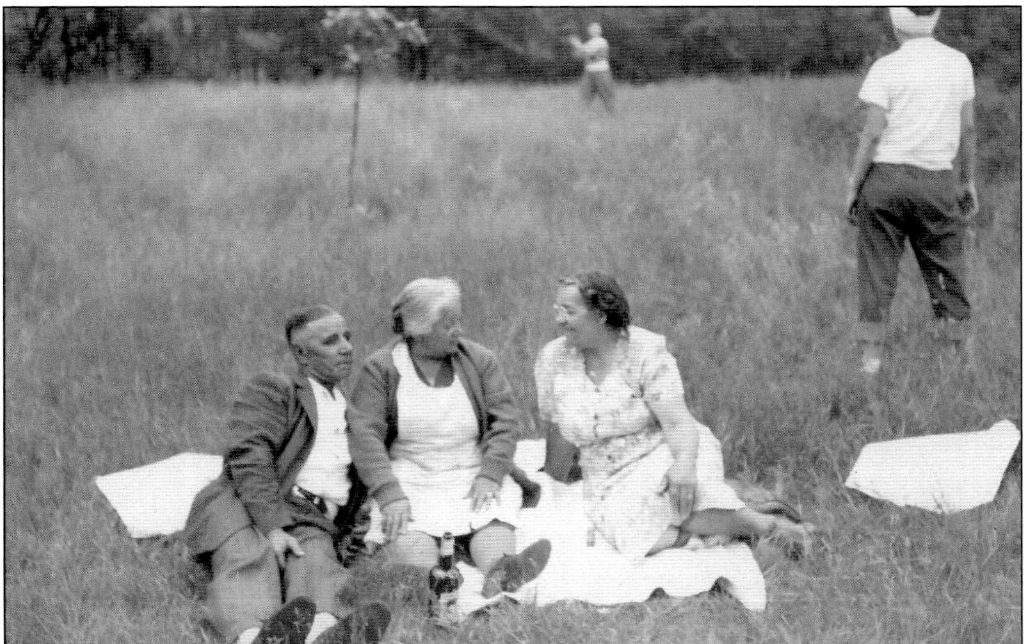

These picnickers—Paul Contento (left), Philomena Contento (center), and Stana Yelich—are probably at Ravera's on Voskamp Road in Rural Ridge. In the 1950s, Rural Ridge had many groves in which to gather. Note the bottle of liquor in the foreground and the boy at right playing baseball with a friend—he appears to have a bandaged head. (Courtesy of Mary Yelich.)

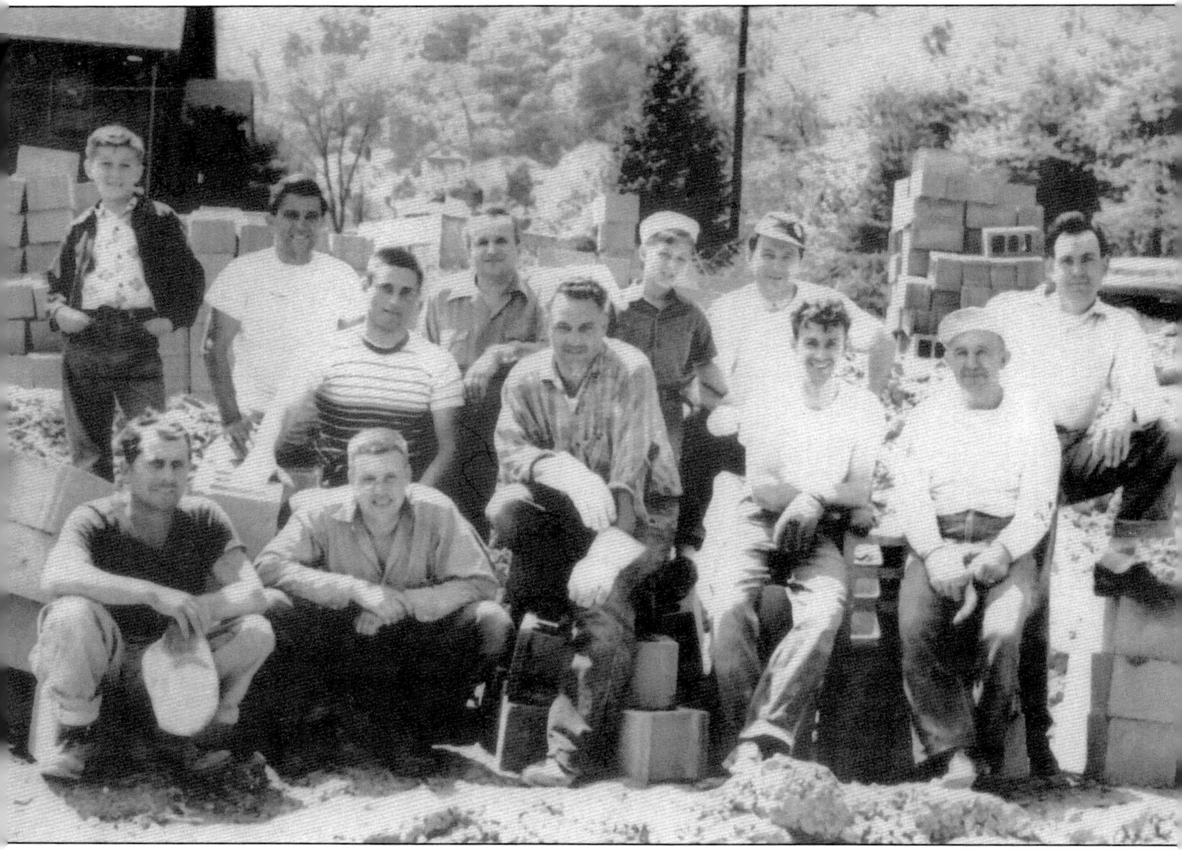

The Indianola Firehall opened in 1956. George Cingle was instrumental in obtaining the old Pittsburgh Pipe Line site for construction. Contractors Tony Ometz and Oscar Masci Sr. and volunteers Spitzie Pizzuto, Cingle, Augie Celo, Hartley Mumaw, and others donated their time and efforts to help with the construction. This photograph shows the men during construction. Part of St. Timothy's Church is visible in the upper left corner. Prior to the construction of the fire hall, there were fire sheds throughout the community that held fire hoses on large wheeled carts. If there was a fire, men employed by the mine would rush to the nearest fire shed, pull out the fire cart (which contained tools and hoses), run to the hydrant, and connect the hoses. The mine donated the hoses to the new fire company, but they were rotten and could not be used. The fire trucks were housed in the garages on the first floor, which also contained a kitchen where the fire company held spaghetti dinners to raise funds. (Courtesy of Jacque Rouggie.)

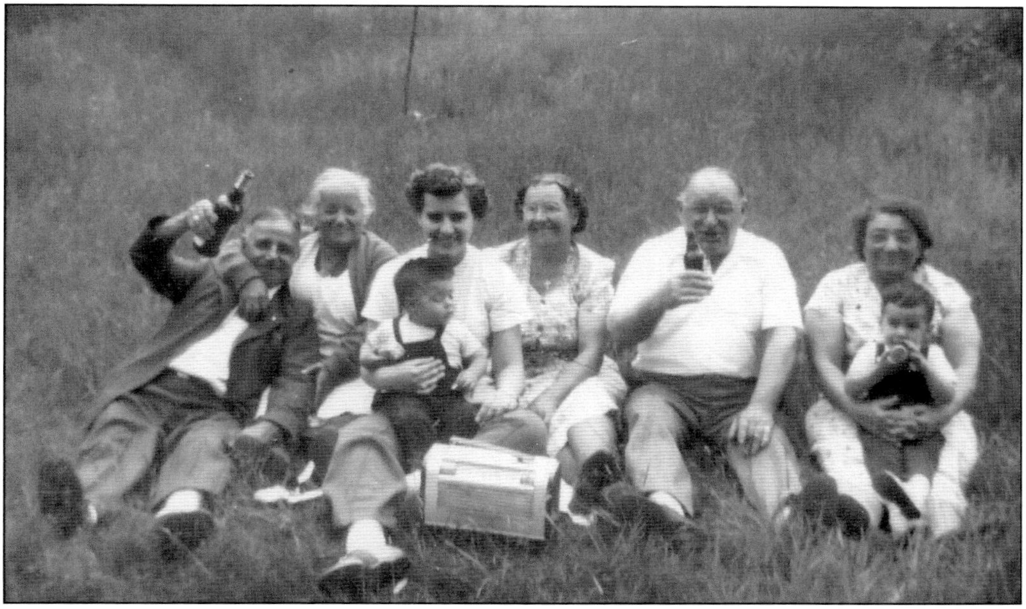

According to Rural Ridge's history book—compiled by Helen Rekasie—these picnickers were probably gathered in the 1950s at Ravera's, located on Voskamp Drive in Rural Ridge. Pictured here are, from left to right, Paul Contento, Philomena Contento, Mildred Yelich Susnjar (holding Billy Sabatini), Stana Yelich, Marko Pinazza, and Julia Sabatini Pinazza (holding Johnny Sabatini). (Courtesy of Mary Yelich.)

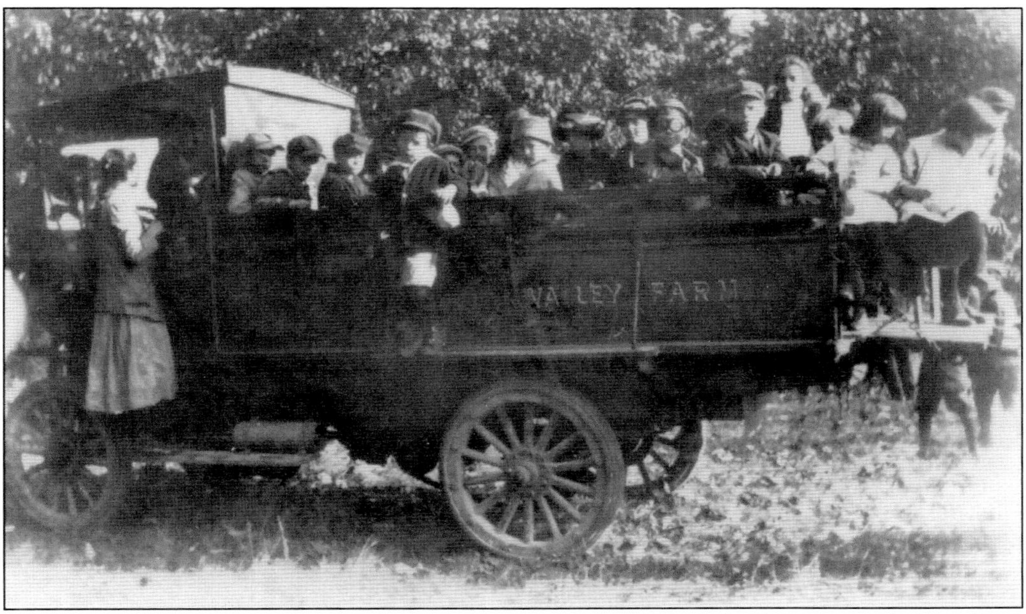

Pearl Dietrich Sallade furnished this photograph in 1988 and said, "this was my father's [F.W. Dietrich's] first farm truck, a 'Little Giant.' He built seats for it and hauled the schoolchildren to the Etna car line when our teacher took us on field trips to the Old Exposition and the H.J. Heinz plant in Pittsburgh. Before that, we walked the five miles to and from the end of the street car line in Etna."

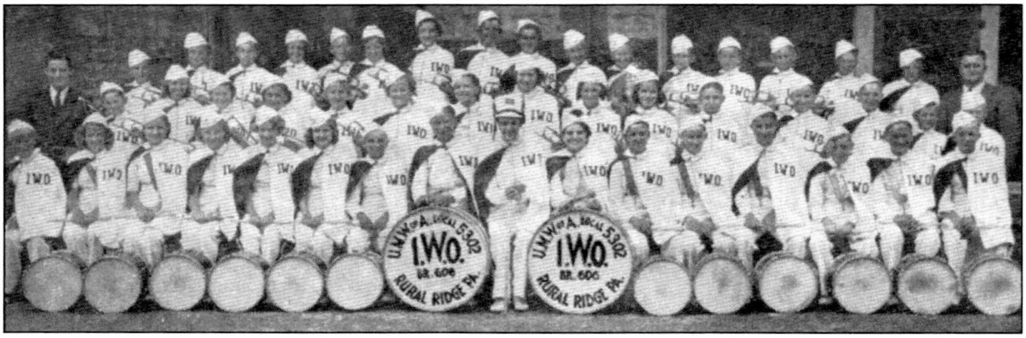

According to an untitled newsletter dating back to 1937, "the 47-piece Rural Ridge Band organized through the joint efforts of Mine Union locals and Branch 606." This group was the pride and joy of Rural Ridge. "It is the first Junior Corps to be jointly sponsored by an I.W.O. branch and a trade union." (Courtesy of Mary Yelich.)

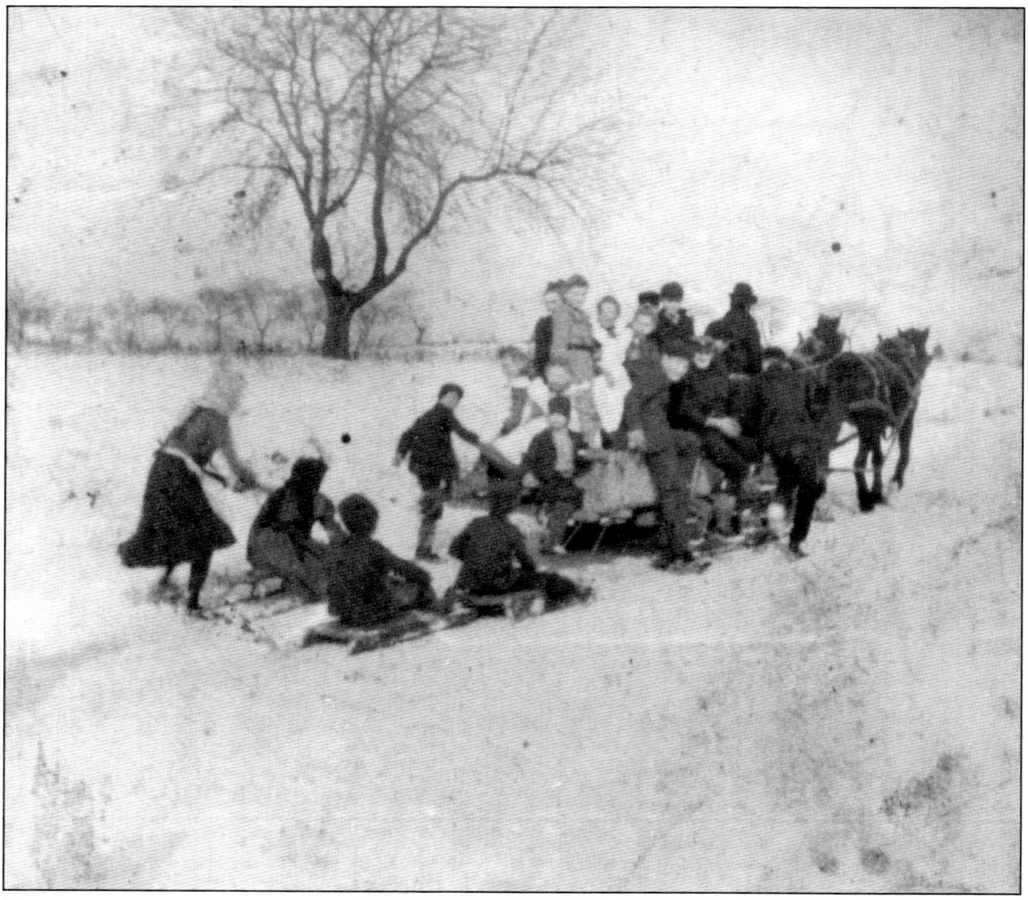

For wintertime entertainment, people would remove the wheels of hay wagons and replace them with runners, turning the wagons into sleighs. Children would tie their sleds to the back of the "sleigh" for a ride. According to Nancy Keck Meyers, this particular hay wagon was probably owned by John Keck.

The former estate of John and Mary Flinn Lawrence has been a training center for equestrian excellence for nearly 75 years. Hartwood brings polo back every year in order to remind people of the elegance the estate once possessed. Proceeds from this event go toward Family House, a "home away from home" for those needing treatments in Pittsburgh's hospitals. This photograph of a polo match at Hartwood Acres was taken from *In Touch Waterfront*.

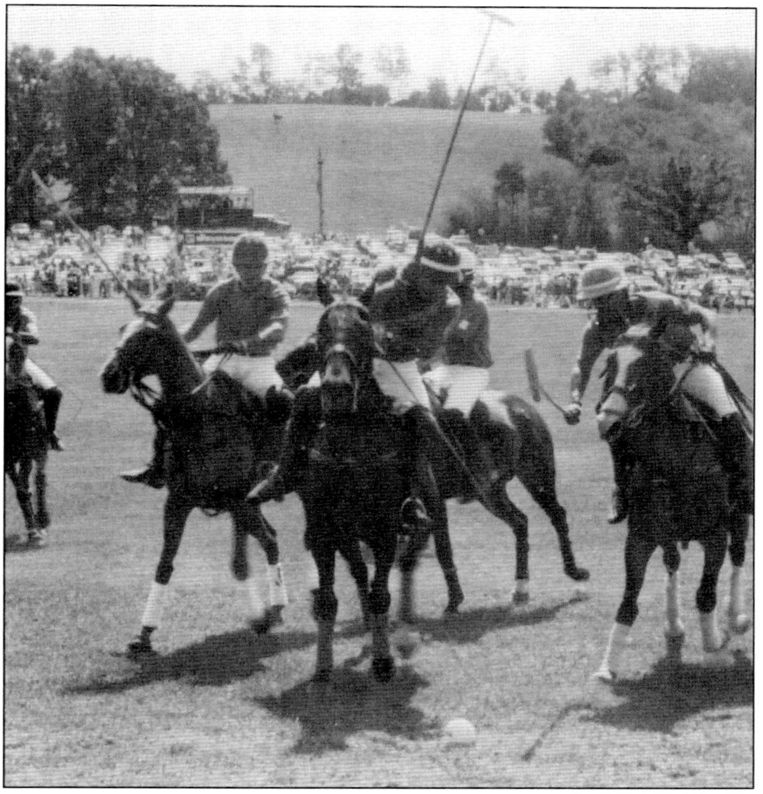

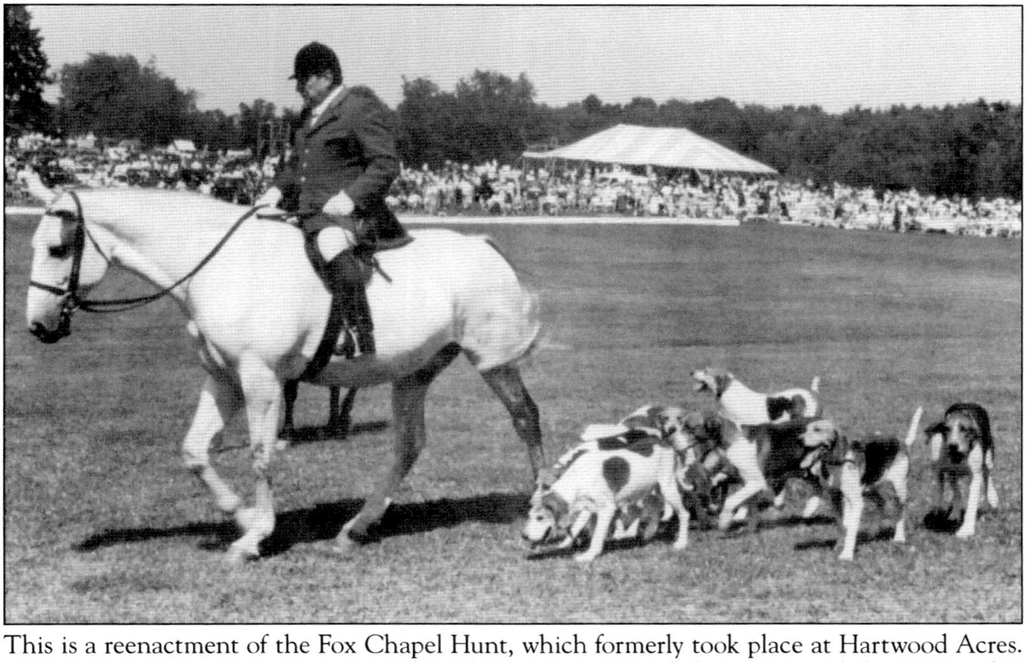

This is a reenactment of the Fox Chapel Hunt, which formerly took place at Hartwood Acres. Fox hunts were regular occurrences when the Lawrences resided at Hartwood. (Courtesy of *In Touch Waterfront*.)

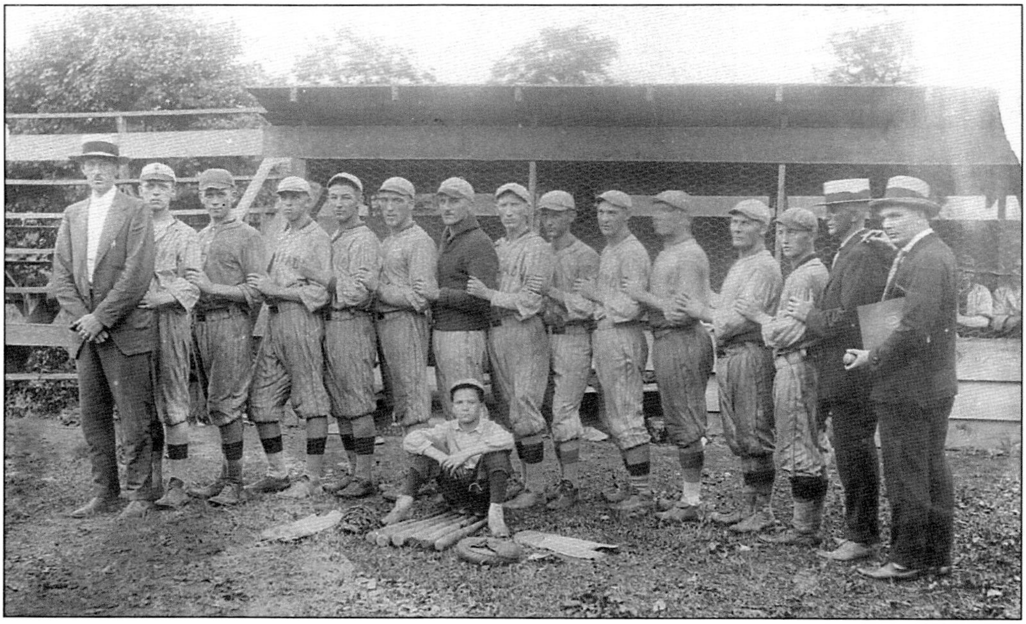

Raymond Bernabei, who was born in 1925 and moved to Indianola when he was two and a half, recalled that Indianola had three baseball teams in three different leagues at one time. The team pictured is from 1919—before Bernabei's time—but baseball has long been a favorite pastime for people living in Indianola. Three original wool uniforms worn by the Inland and Indianola baseball teams are on display at the township building. The uniforms are courtesy of Eileen DeRusha Shoemaker, whose mother, Edna, ran the boardinghouse above the mine.

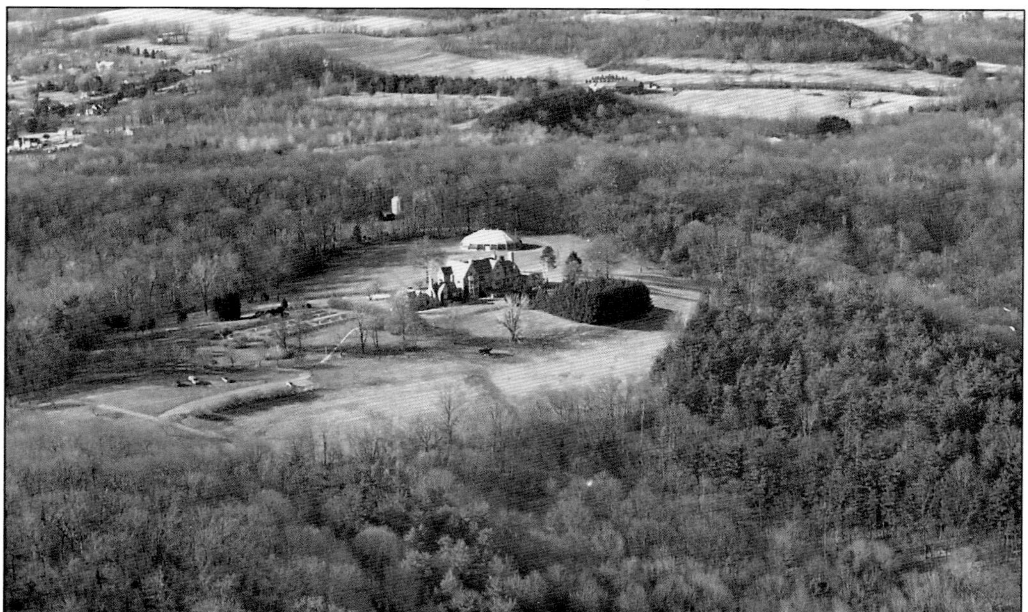

This aerial photograph of Hartwood Acres was taken in 1991. John and Mary Flinn Lawrence purchased this land in the late 1920s. The land had been a grant to the Hart family after the American Revolution. Professional theater is produced under the tent visible in the above photograph.

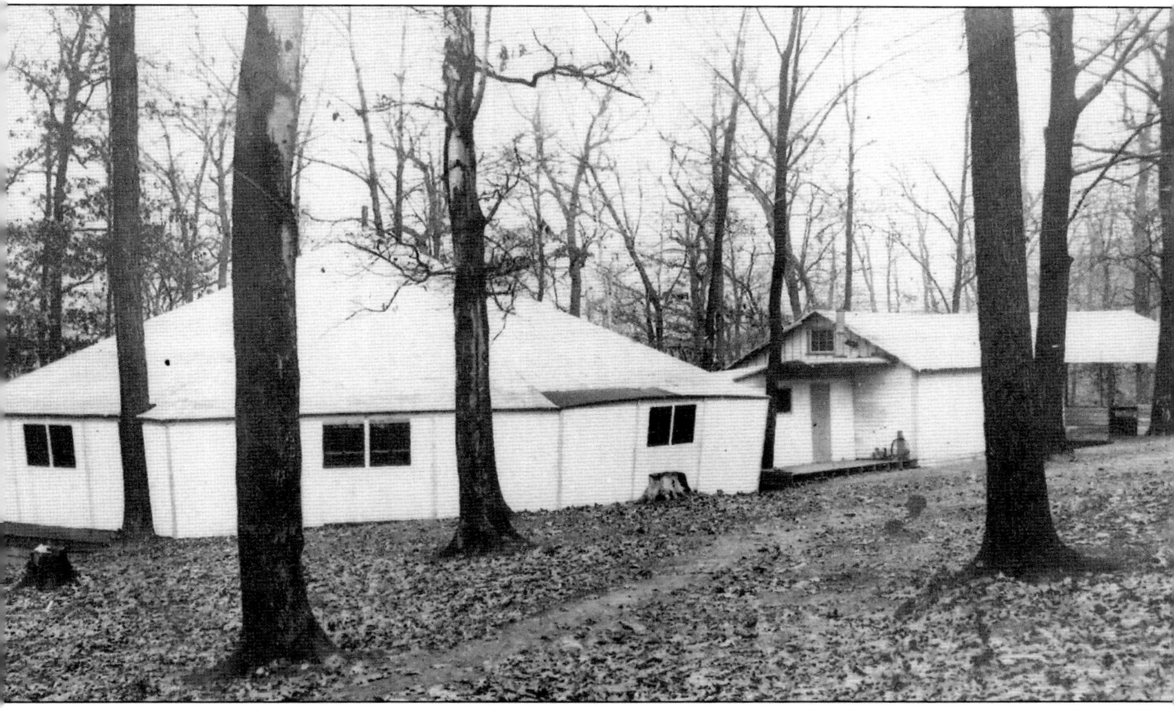

Thomas Umbrella Grove (or the Umbrella Grove) was located behind the Charles Thomas home on Church Lane. This was one of the most interesting and popular social gathering points within the township. The music and laughter from dances held every Saturday could be heard from quite a distance. Thomas built the grove in the form of a large umbrella, with a high support post in the center of the dance floor and ribs supporting the roof. The dance floor was in the form of a circle with open sides, and bench seats were placed around the perimeter. Refreshments and soft drinks were sold from an addition built at the entrance, which is visible at right in the photograph. (Courtesy of Roy Miersch.)

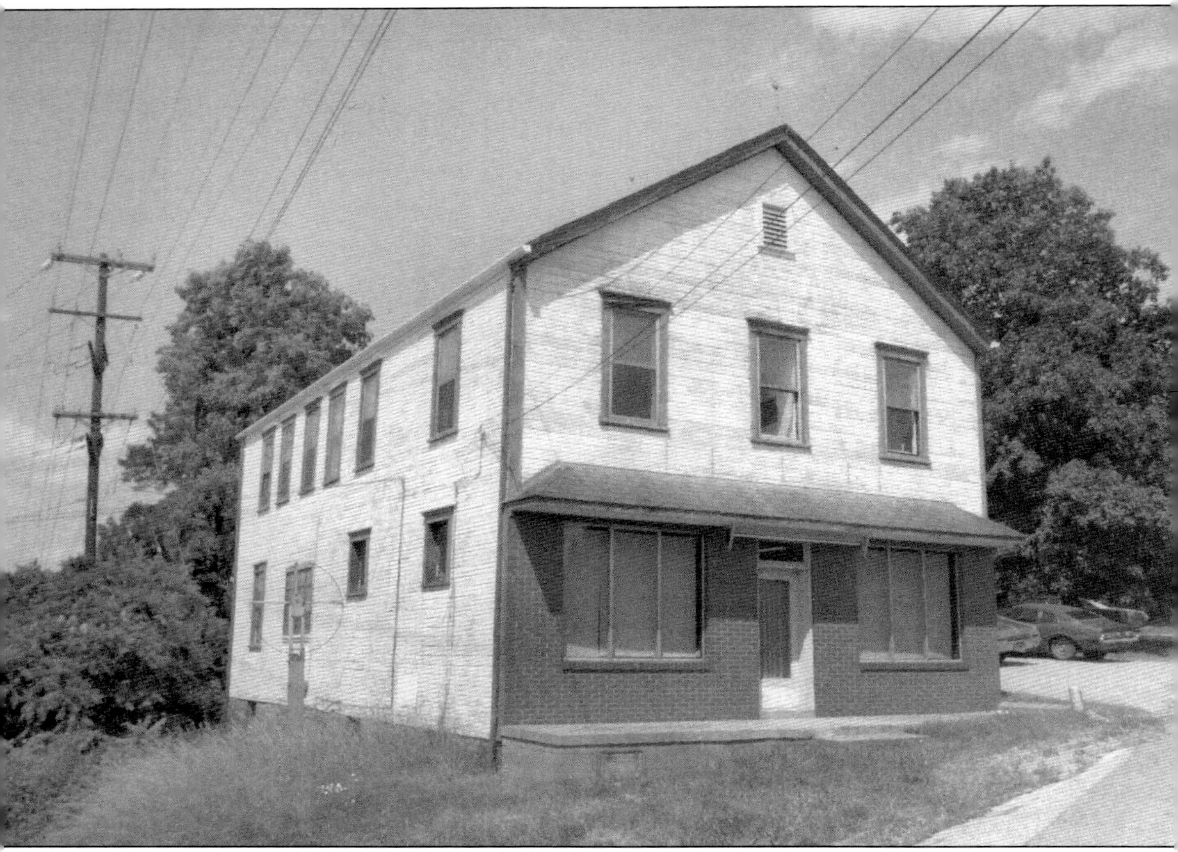

According to an interview conducted by Mary Pat Parsons, the Roehrs General Store was a gathering place for area men when there was not much work to do. They would play checkers, trade gossip, and have contests, such as a salt lifting, in which they would see who could most easily lift a 500-pound salt barrel from the floor to the counter. On Saturday nights, people from miles around would come by horse and buggy to the dance hall on the second floor of the building. A gentleman played the concertina to provide music. Many romances and marriages blossomed at the Saturday night dances. The Roehrs store was owned and operated by several generations of the Roehrs family and was situated at the corner of Saxonburg Boulevard (formerly Creek Road or KDKA Boulevard) and State Route 910, across the road from the Trinity United Church of Christ cemetery (Dorseyville Cemetery). The Roehrs sold food, clothing, shoes, lamp oil, farm tools, and other various items. The building still exists but is now a private residence.

Seven

Family Life in Rural America

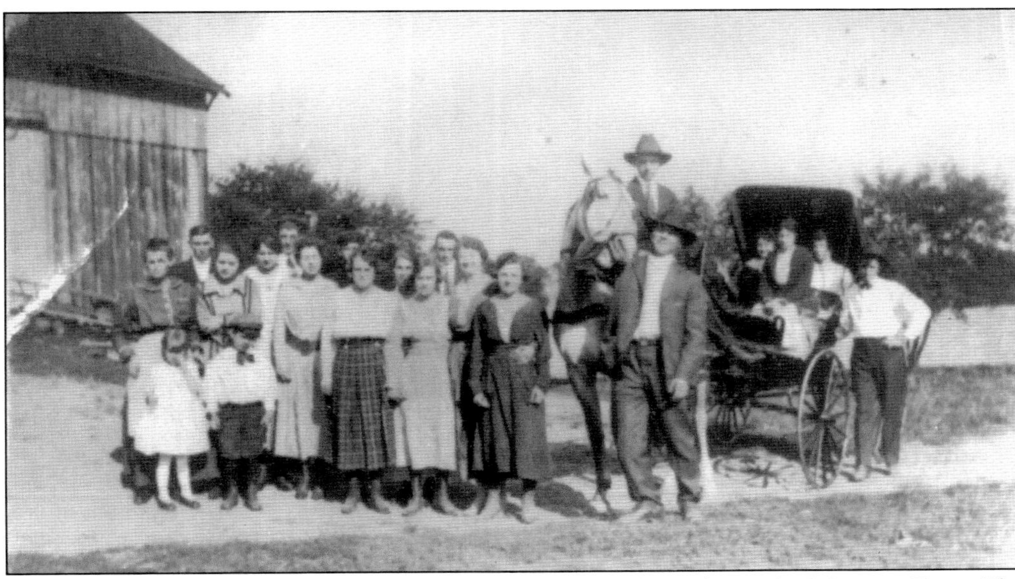

This 1920 photograph, "Having a crowd," captures a typical Sunday at the Pfirrman Farm. The Pfirrman farm is on Cedar Run Road. The horse's name was Russell, and the man on Russell's back is Richard Pfirrman. The two children in the lower left corner are Pearl and Wilbur Bliss, and the woman behind Pearl is Caroline Pfirrman. All of the other people are unidentified.

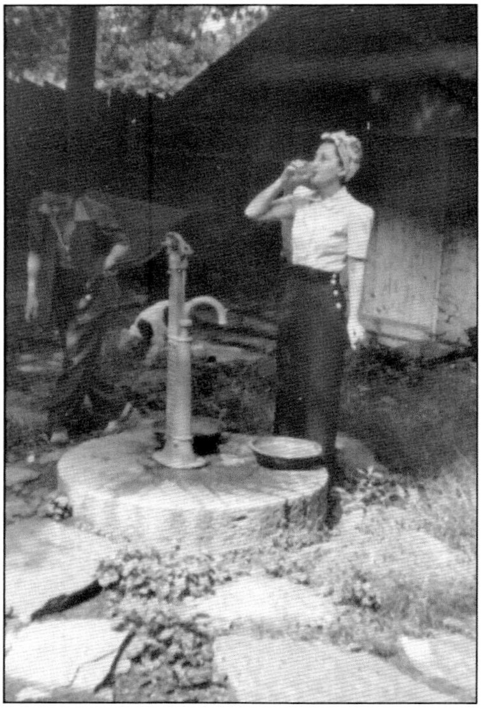

This c. 1943 image shows the old pump at the Emmerling House. These kinds of pumps were considered the first step to indoor plumbing, as one no longer needed a bucket, rope, and crank to retrieve water. Families were considered successful if they could install a battery-operated pump in order to draw water inside, allowing them to install indoor plumbing.

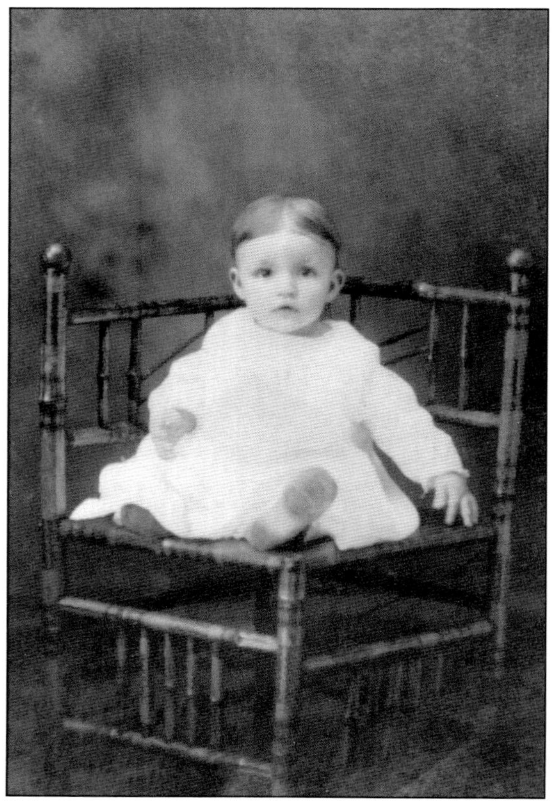

This undated image shows Sarah Baumgartel, daughter of Harry and Bertha Pfirrman Baumgartel. This image offers an example of how attire and props have changed in studio photographs of children.

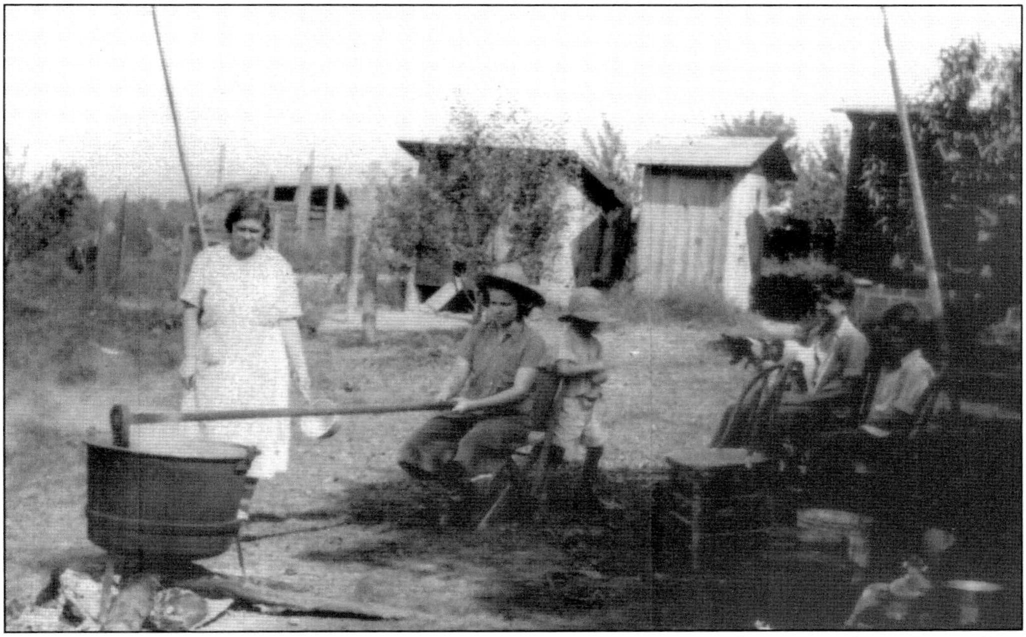

This image shows the process of making apple butter on the Giesy farm in Indiana Township. Families would often gather at each other's homes to help make apple butter. The stirrer is most likely sitting far away from the apple butter because of the heat. Note the number of outbuildings on the property. (Courtesy of Sara Giesy Scheerbaum Newcamp.)

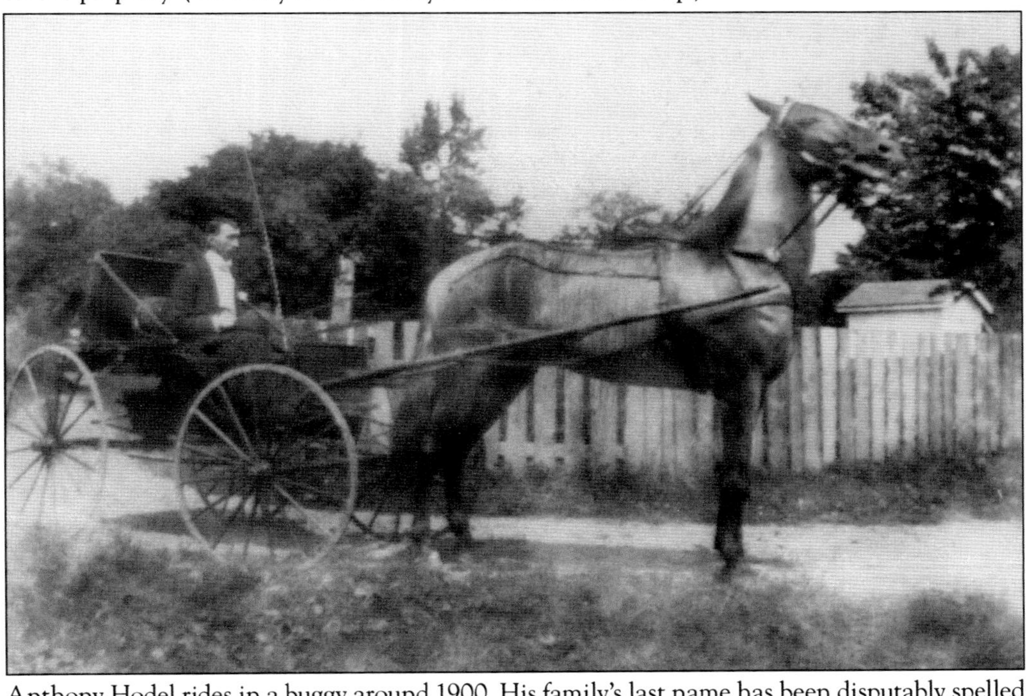

Anthony Hodel rides in a buggy around 1900. His family's last name has been disputably spelled differently—either Hodel, Hodil, or Huddle. The Hodils were one of the earliest families to settle in Indiana Township. This is a good example of how people traveled in the early 20th century.

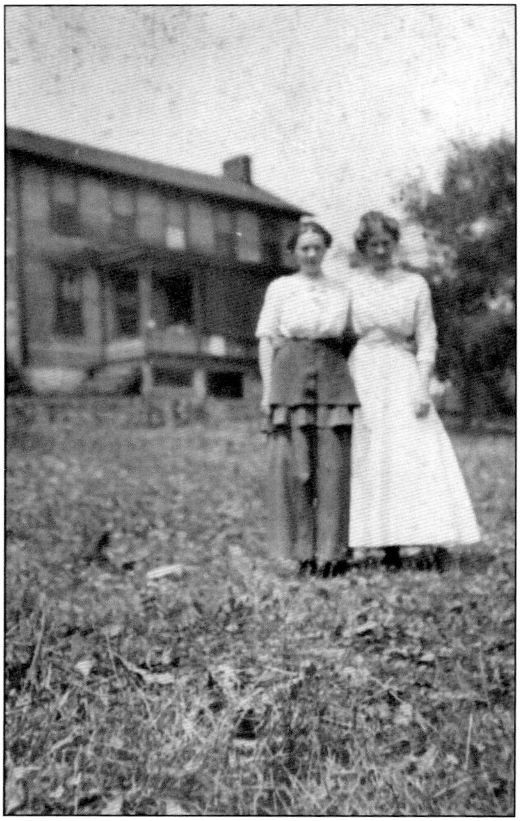

Lydia and Martha Foster are pictured in 1914 in front of their farmhouse. The Foster house was located on Fairview Road off Dorseyville Road. Patricia Hogsett White is a descendant of Mary Foster, one of Martha and Lydia's sisters. (Courtesy of Patricia Hogsett White.)

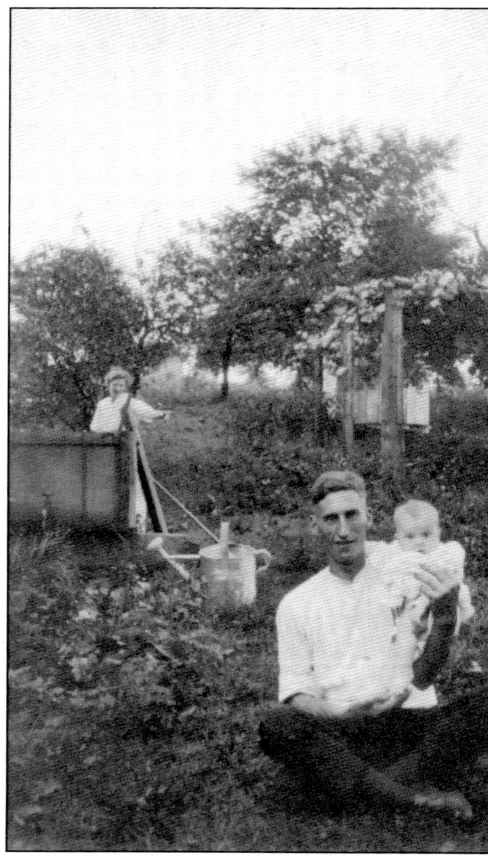

The man in this photograph is Jim Strohm, and the woman in the background might be his wife, Martha Foster Strohm. The only identification on the back of the photograph is "Jim Strohm." Martha Foster was one of four sisters who lived on the Foster farm on Fairview Road. The baby is unidentified. (Courtesy of Alice B. Foster.)

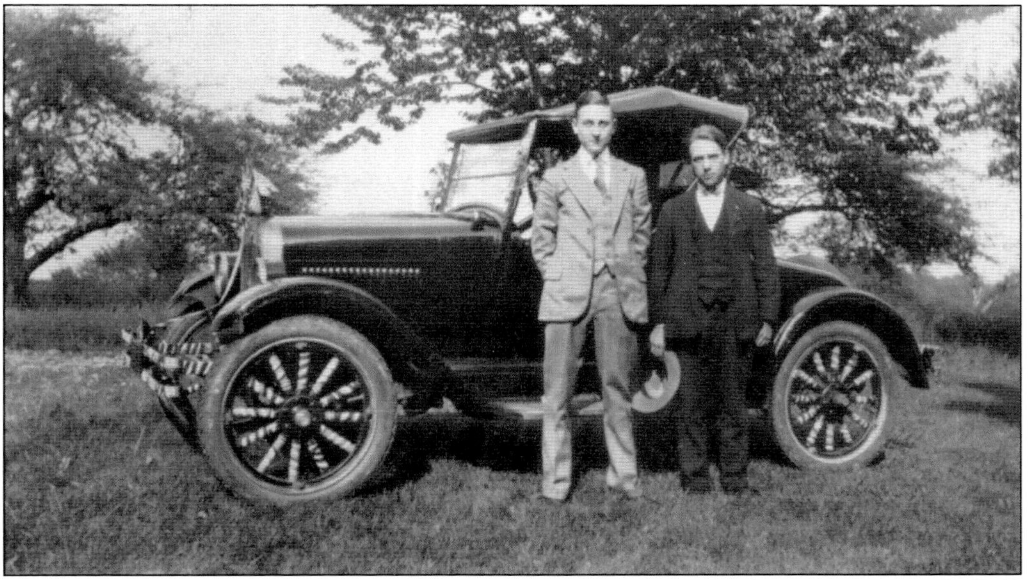

A 1923 Chevy Roadster was an impressive car to own, as shown by the faces of George Kelly (left) and George Geyer in this 1930s photograph.

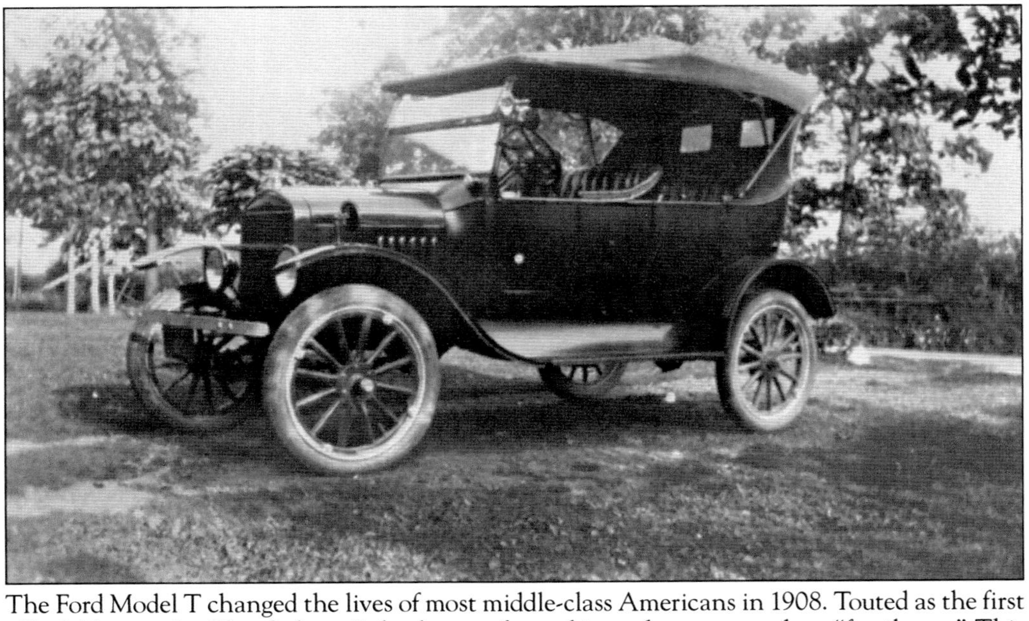

The Ford Model T changed the lives of most middle-class Americans in 1908. Touted as the first affordable car, the "family horse" slowly transformed into the more modern "family car." This model was produced from 1908 until 1927. Indiana Township roads needed an overhaul in order to accommodate the growing number of families who owned vehicles instead of horses.

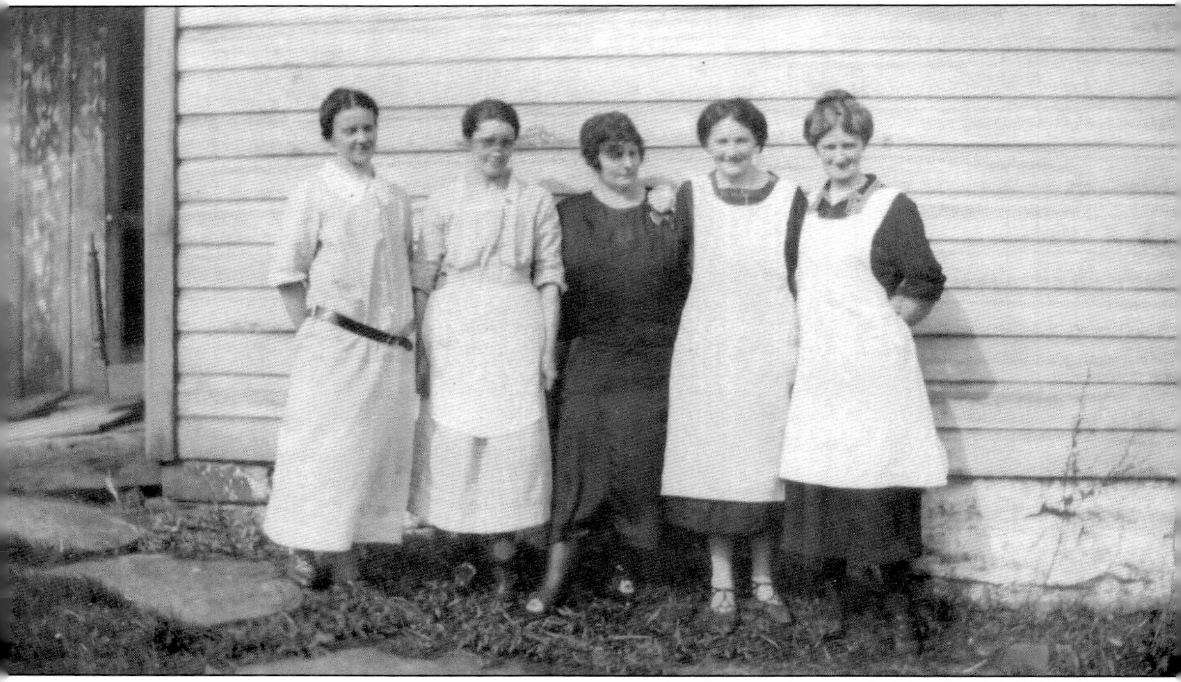

The Fosters had six children—four girls and two boys. Pictured beside the Foster house on Fairview Road are, from left to right, Mary, Margaret, Marie (possibly a family friend, Marie Miller from Millvale), Martha, and Lydia. Margaret, whose middle name was Caldwell (after her grandmother), married a neighbor, Lee Preston, in 1909. One of Margaret's daughters, Lauretta, remembers her mother talking about how Margaret and Lydia had to mow the hayfield by hand. (Courtesy of Alice B. Foster.)

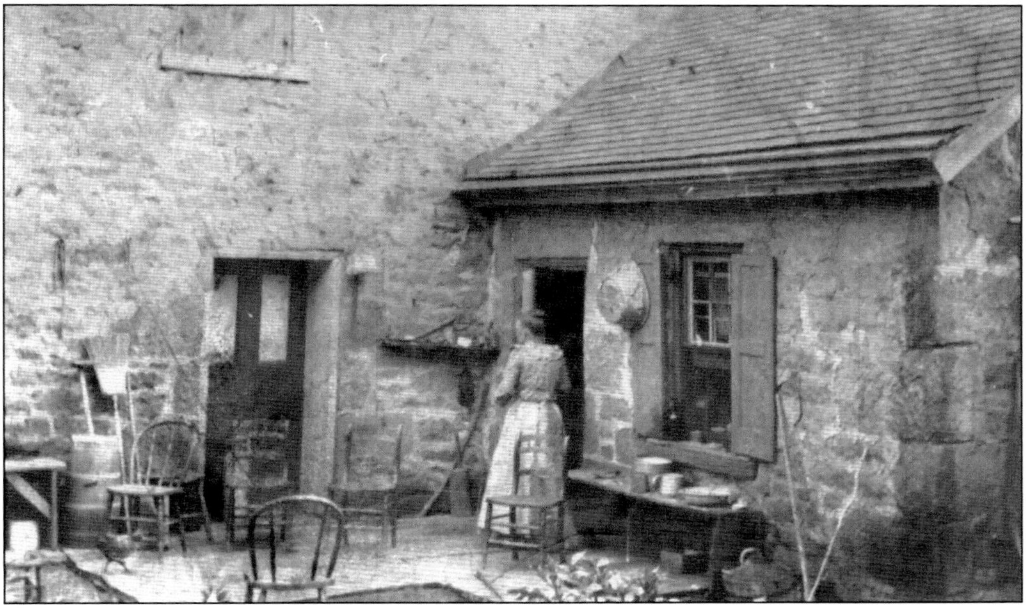

This two-story, old stone house was built by the Hazlett family and later owned by Robert Medill. Note the interesting items in the photograph, including a wooden upright butter churn, a wooden laundry basket, a wooden water bucket, a metal cow bell, a round basin on a wooden bench (used to do laundry outside), lye soap, a pottery cup, wheat straw brooms, a shoe last, a scythe, a handmade tool to close second-floor shutters, and bent wooden chairs.

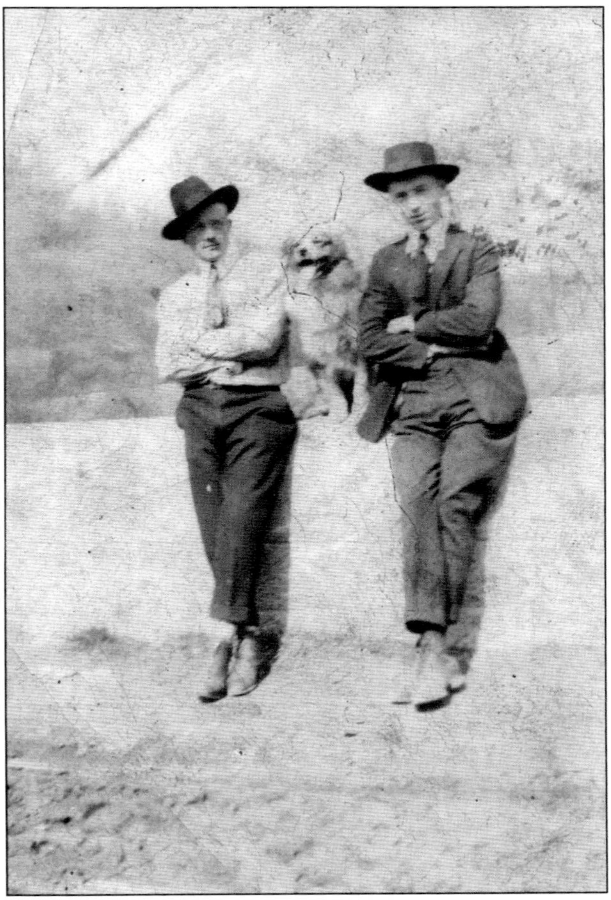

This photograph, which appears to be from the 1930s based on the attire and estimated age of the men, offers an example of how people dressed and posed for photographs in the early 20th century. Even today, dogs are an important part of group portraits. The back of the photograph reads: "Sam Foster, Dog, and Friend." "Sam Foster" is most likely Samuel James Silliman Foster, born in 1897, and not his grandfather Samuel James Foster, born in 1853. (Courtesy of Alice B. Foster.)

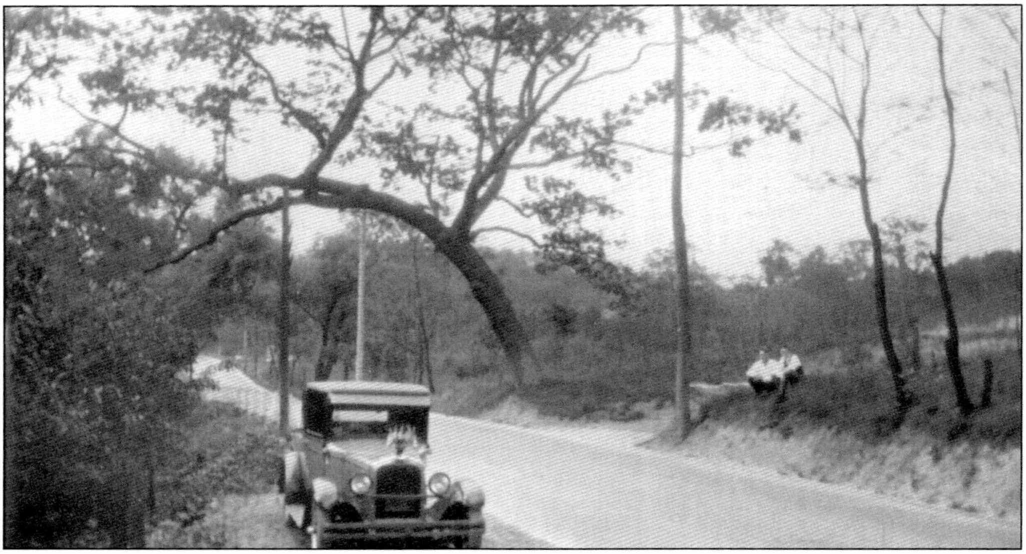

This photograph, "Bending Oak," was taken in the 1930s. Lee Schmidt and George Kelly are sitting on the hillside, with their 1923 Chevy Roadster on the other side of the road. The location of this "bending oak" could possibly be within the boundaries of present-day Fox Chapel, since there is a Bending Oak Road in that borough.

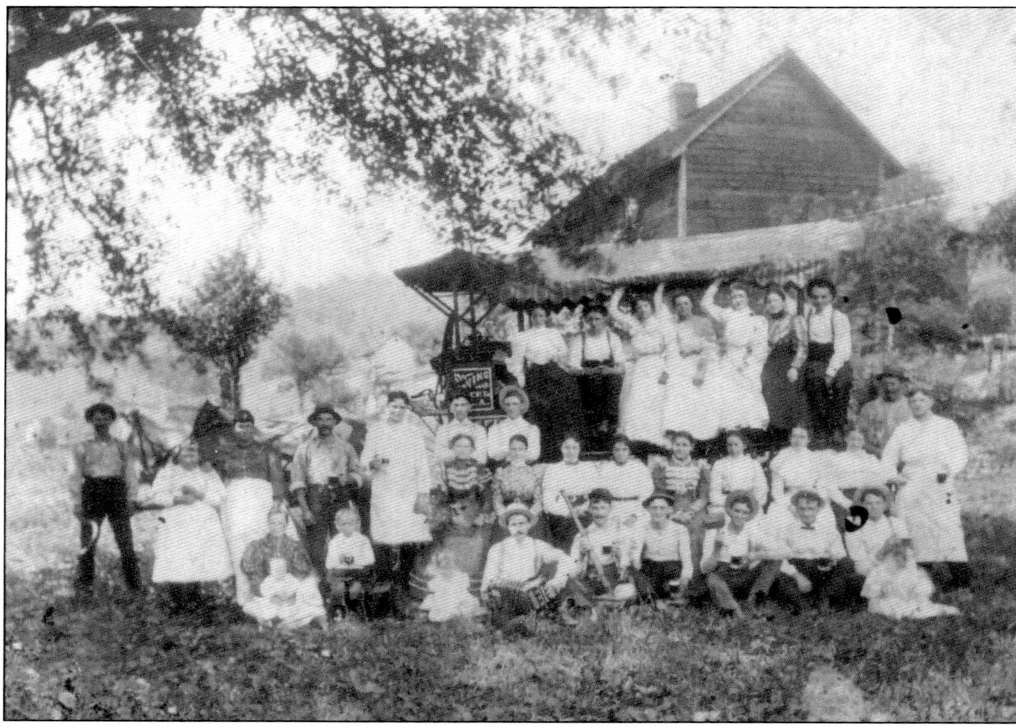

In earlier times, people were often surrounded and helped by friends and neighbors, as seen in the size of the gathering in this image captioned "moving day get-together" for John and Mary Bigler Claus. Portions of the original Bigler homestead still remain on Bigler Drive off Saxonburg Boulevard.

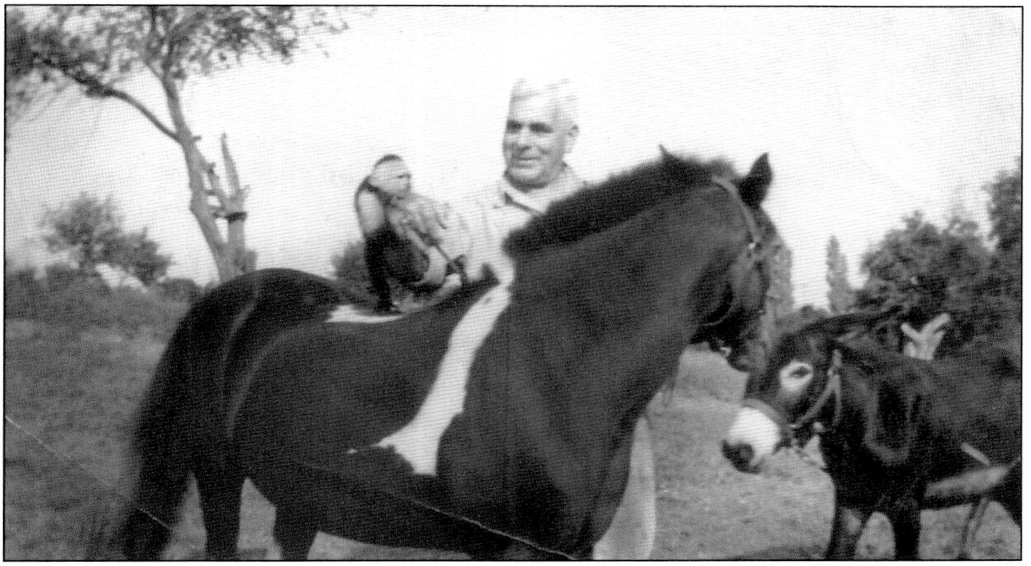

William C. Humes is pictured setting his pet monkey on top of his horse. Alfred "Hap" Humes, son of William, remembers this horse (and his pet donkey in the background). The Humes' property is part of the original acreage of Wunnahunny Farm, where, beginning in 1908, stage actress Fay Templeton lived for 22 years. (Courtesy of Alfred B. Humes.)

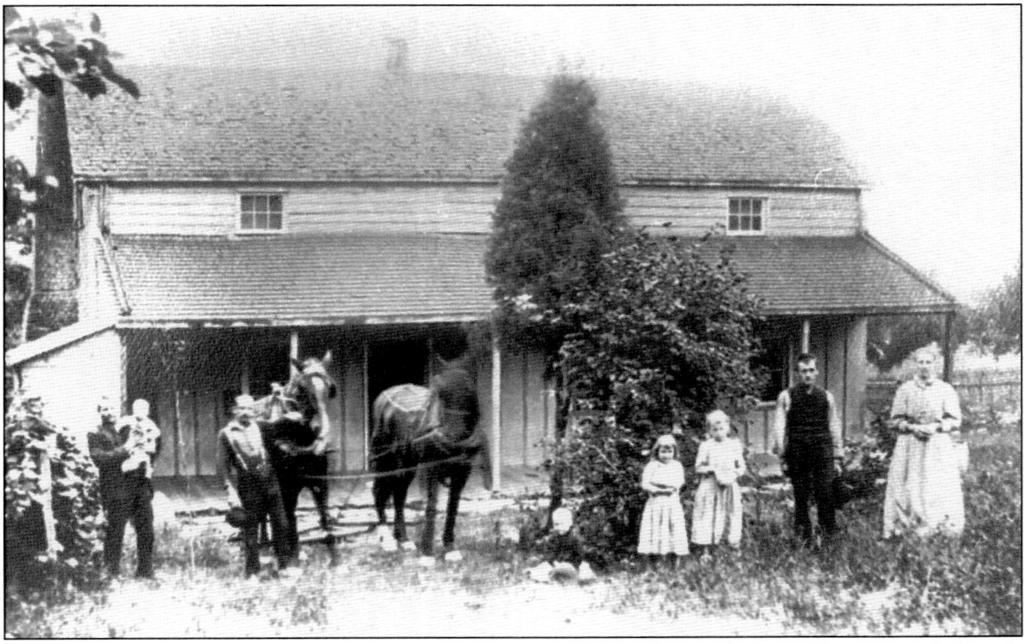

In this c. 1892 photograph, the Eggers family, headed by John and Anna Eggers, and friends stand in front of the family home on Cedar Run Road. The homestead later went by the name of Lodgegrass Farms. Pictured from left to right are John Eggers (holding Waldo Eggers), Charles Golla (hired hand), John Eggers (center, seated), Alice C. Eggers, Cora Eggers, Louis Prager (Anna's brother), and Anna Prager Eggers. (Courtesy of Virginia Black.)

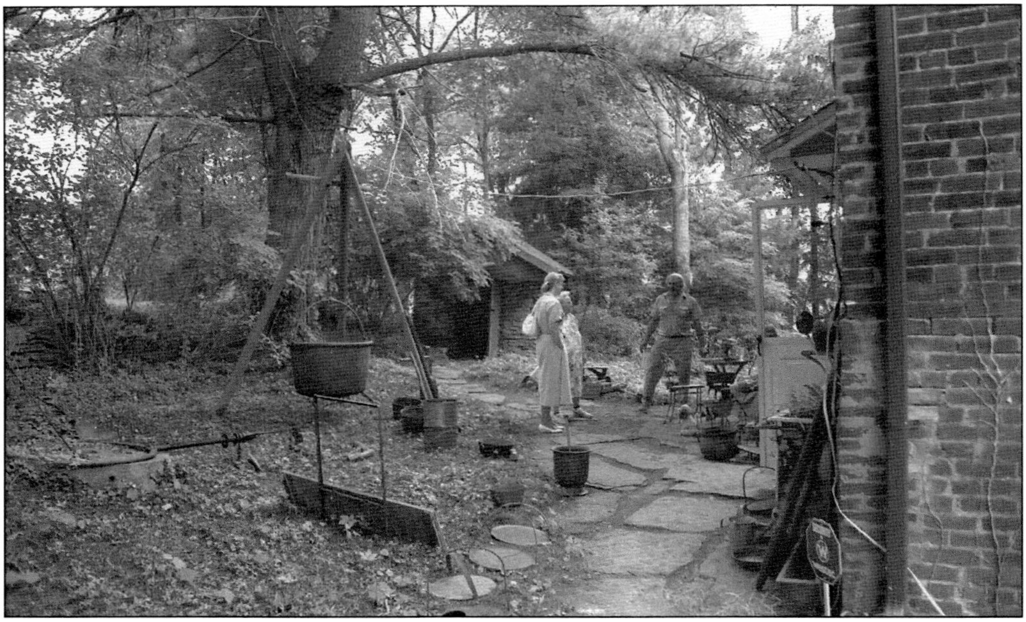

This photograph may have been taken at the Emmerling House, located in Emmerling Park off of State Route 910 and Cove Run Road, during the 1989 bus tour through Indiana Township that the historic commission organized for residents. In 1977, the Indian Hills Garden Club landscaped the entrance to the park and installed a plaque there honoring their founder, Adrienne Prosky. Facilities at the park include picnic shelters, baseball fields, a nature trail, a physical fitness trail, a handicapped bridge, and a water well drilled in 1973 by the Charles Thomas Well Drilling Co.

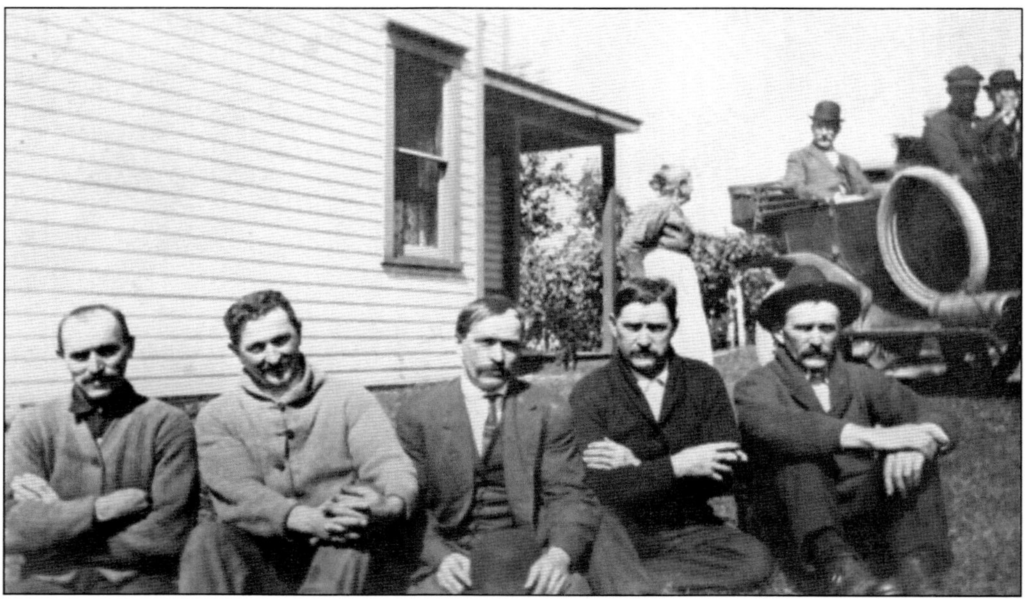

The Mink brothers (sitting on the ground) are, from left to right, Jacob, Peter, Edward, Henry, and William. Their mother, Elizabeth (Greenwald) Mink, talks to Squire Austin Stevens in the background. Peter, Jake, and Henry owned and operated a number of businesses on their property, including a sawmill and coal mine.

Eight

Farm Living

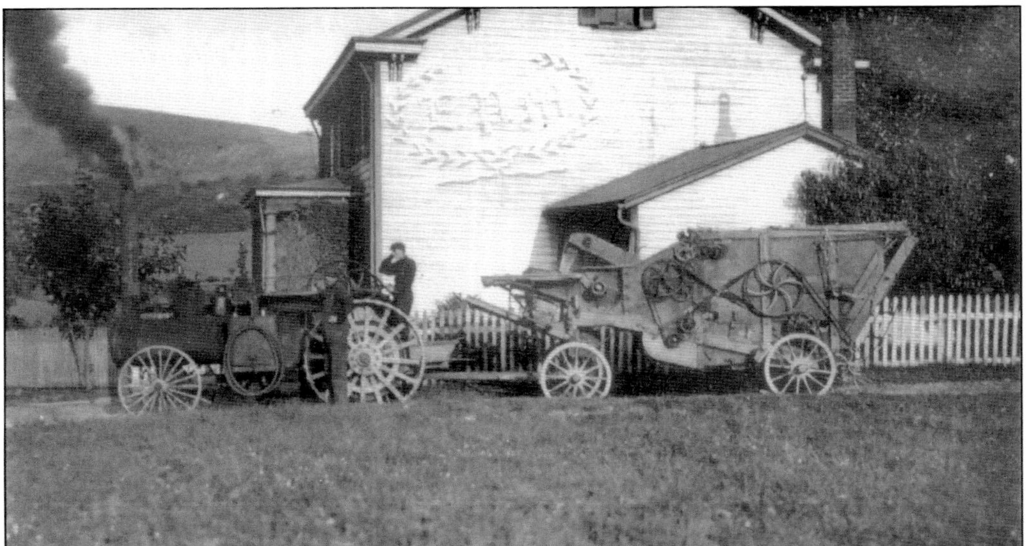

This steam engine thrasher was owned by Charlie Thomas of Church Lane. This photograph was taken at William F. Miersch's farm on Harts Run Road. Not many contraptions of this nature existed within the township limits, so Thomas visited many farms with his thrasher. A boiler ran the machine and was used in conjunction with a water wagon. (Photograph by Edwin Miersch.)

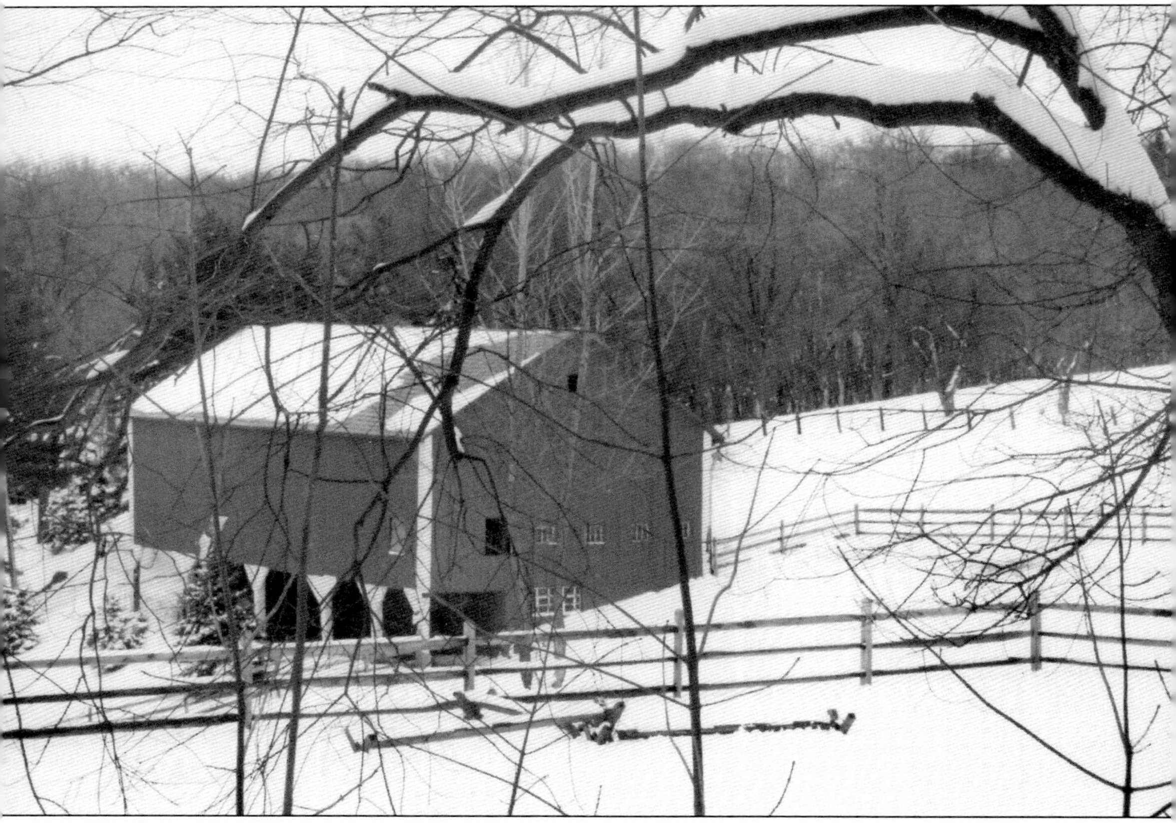

The barn pictured is on the property of Alfred B. Humes. Humes, who goes by "Hap," was the Fox Chapel fire chief for 35 years. Humes believes that the barn is at least 100 years old. The Humes farm is located on what was once known as Wunnahunny Farm, which originally spanned 63 acres and included a vast peach orchard. The orchard froze out in 1938, and dynamite was used to blast out the stumps. (Courtesy of Alfred B. Humes.)

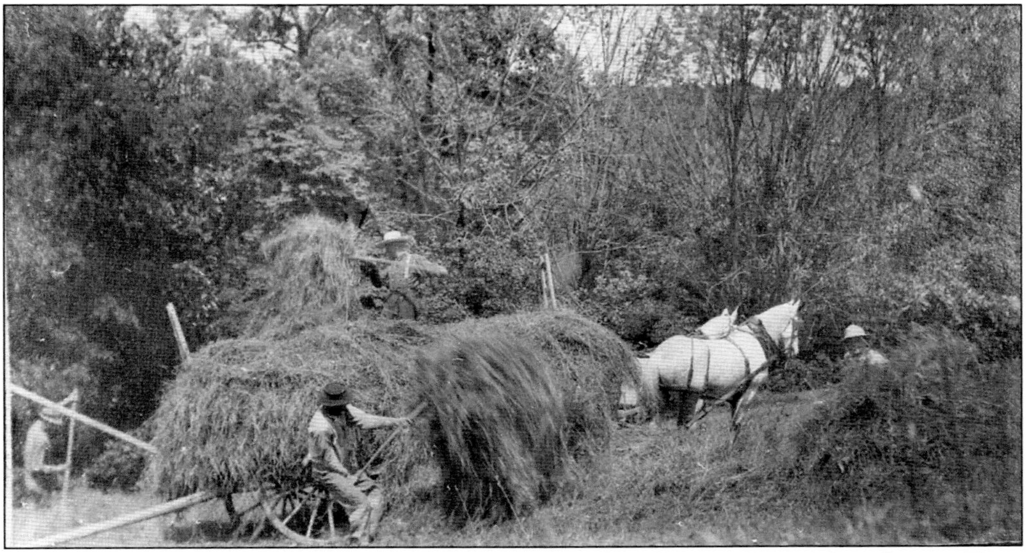

This July 1914 image shows the process of "haying" on the Pfirrman Farm. The Pfirrman Farm was located on Cedar Run Road, where the 175-acre BarGee Farms is now headquartered. BarGee Farms is touted as one of the best horse facilities in Western Pennsylvania. George and Barbara Bancroft bought the property from John and Caroline Pfirrman in 1938. Currently, Barbie Bancroft (great-great-granddaughter of George) is the president and CEO of BarGee Farms, and her sister, Kitty Bancroft, is the secretary and treasurer. (Courtesy of Wilbur Bliss.)

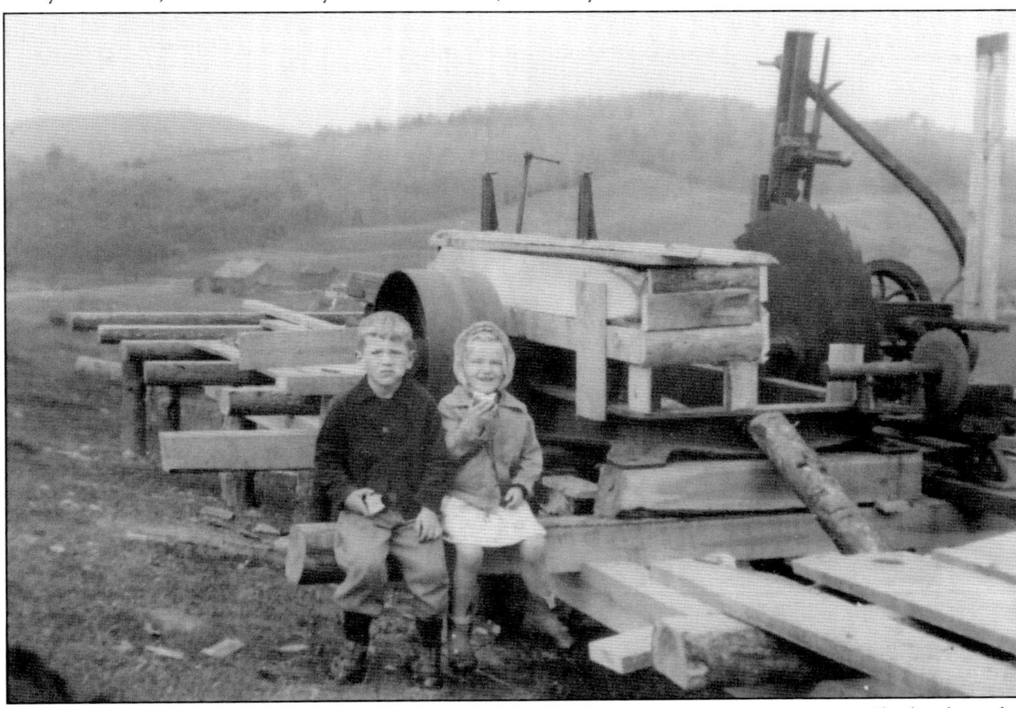

This photograph, which is also on the cover of this book (see the caption on page 2), displays the difficulty of building a sawmill in the middle of nowhere. Horses and manpower were all that were used in constructing the sawmill. (Courtesy of Dorothy Preston Bauer via John F Bauer III.)

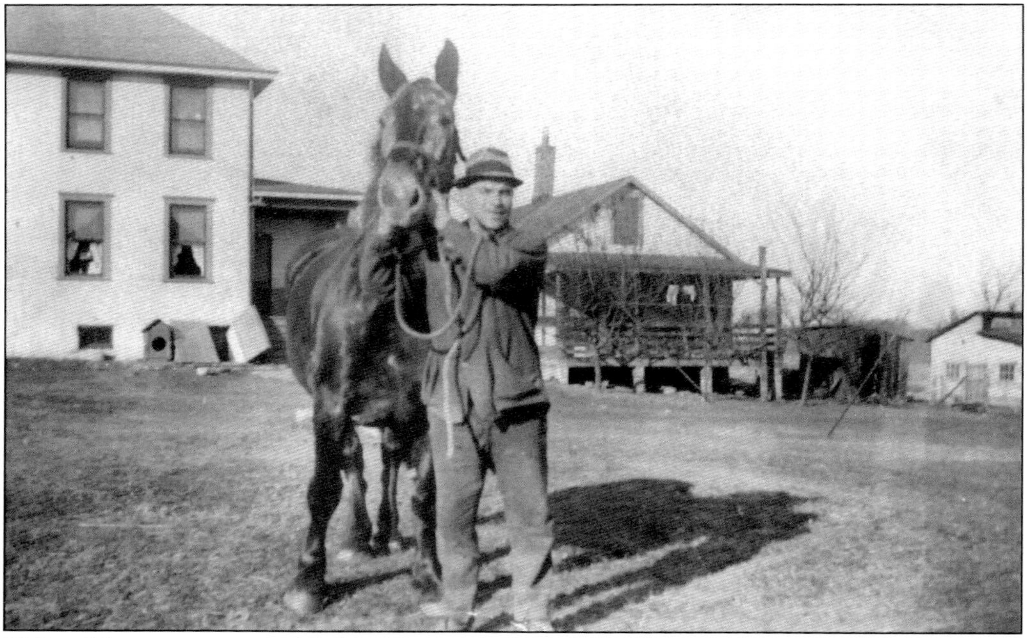

Wilber Pfirrman is pictured at his farm on Cedar Run Road. This photograph is undated, but it is probably from sometime before 1938, since that was when the Pfirrmans sold the farm and property to George and Barbara Bancroft, who started BarGee Farms. Note the old storm doors near the bottom of the building at left and the doghouse next to the storm doors.

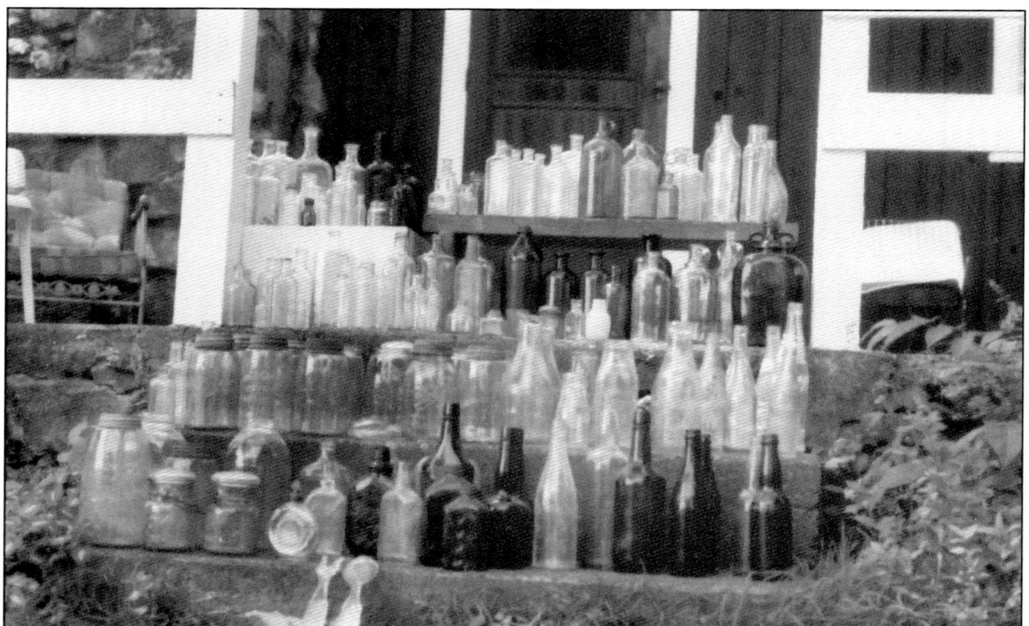

Theresa Smith Lingusky spent over 50 years collecting bottles on and around her farm. This photograph only shows about one-third of her collection. There is one unique bottle in her collection, probably the only one in existence—a bottle labeled, "Dividing Ridge Dairy Farm. Sharpsburg, PA. 1 Qt.," with a "W" on the bottom indicating that it came from Weber's Farm.

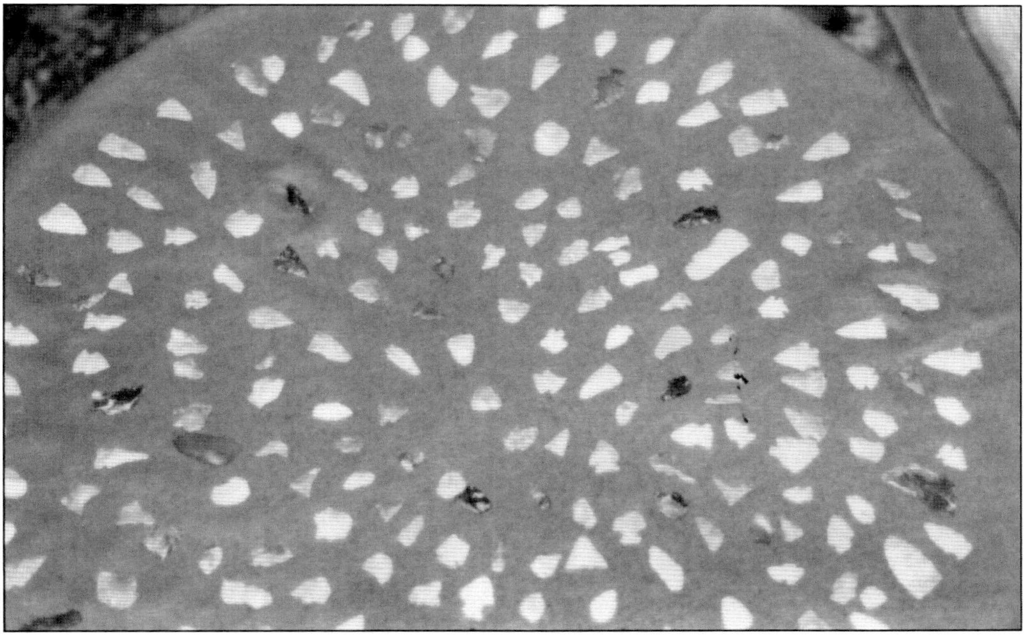

This Native American arrowhead and spearhead collection was also found on Theresa Smith Lingusky's property. From 1939 to 1993, Lingusky walked the fields collecting arrowheads that emerged after the soil was churned while plowing. The best time to collect arrowheads on a farm is following a rainfall after the plowing of the fields.

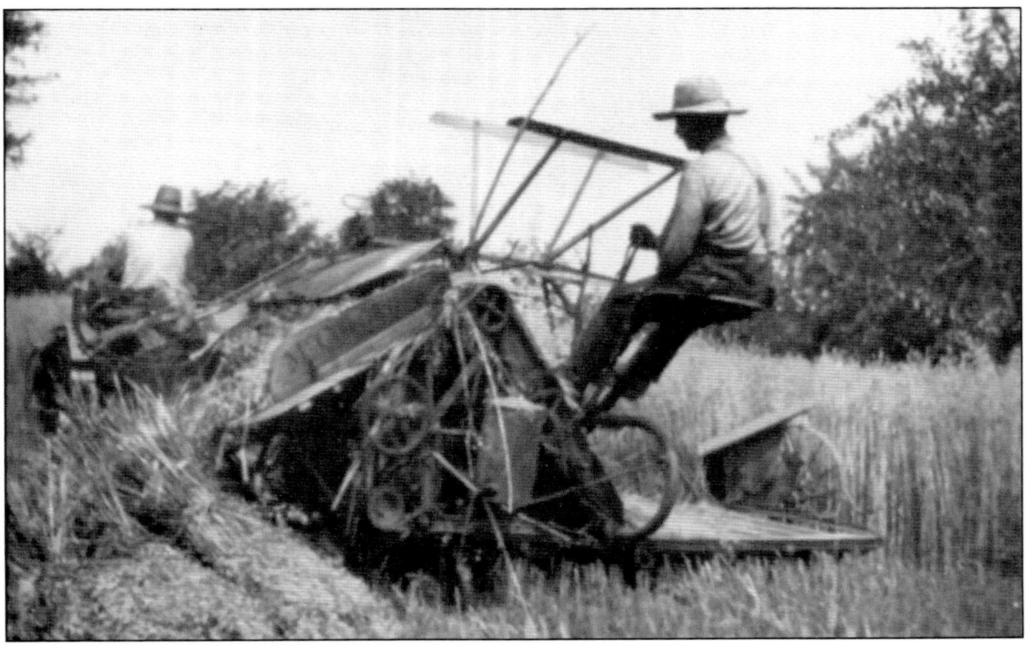

This machine uses the same process to comb wheat as the horse-drawn version, but using a tractor instead of a horse. The only downfall of using the tractor was that two men were needed to do this job instead of one man and his horse. Pictured here are John P. Prager (on the "comber" at right) and his son Homer.

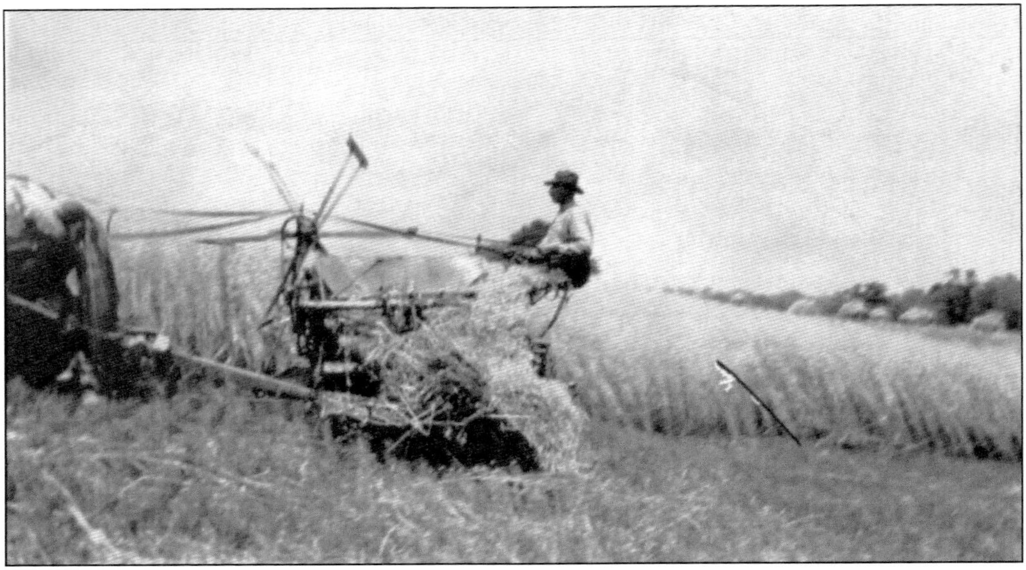

This machine cuts wheat or oats and ties it into bundles (shocks/shucks), then the bundles are set up to dry in groups of seven to twenty. This can also be done with a tractor, but using the tractor required two men instead of just one man and a horse. The dried bundles are then loaded onto a hay wagon and taken into the barn to be prepared for threshing, which separates the grain from the straw.

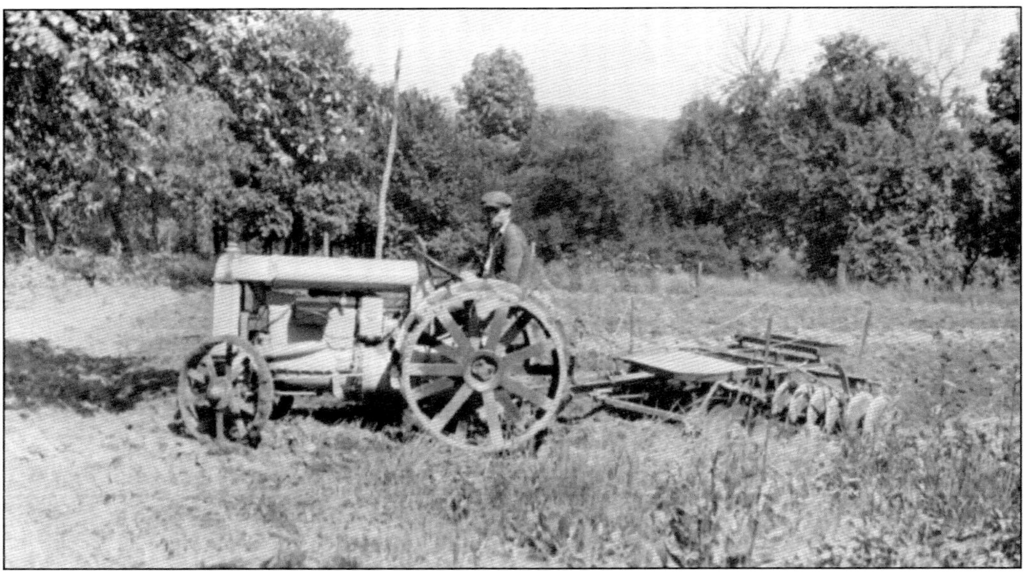

This photograph offers a look at the transition from horse-drawn plows to modern-day tractors. This is what "disking" with a steel-tired tractor (the wheels have no rubber) looked like in the 1930s. The man pictured may be a Mink family member working on Mink's farm—this photograph was in a pile of Mink photographs, but it contained no identifying information.

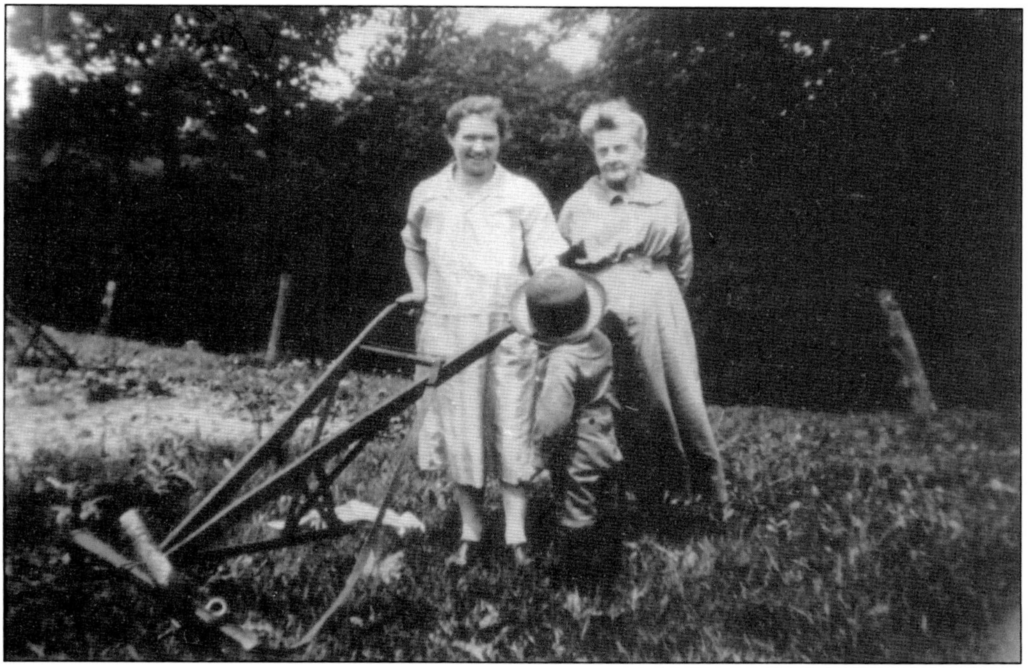

Pictured here are a Mrs. Shubert (left), Bob Preston (child), and Emma Florence (Alexander) Foster. These three are tilling the garden on Foster Farm in May 1926. Shubert's house burned down, so she came to live with the Fosters on Fairview Road. (Courtesy of Homer L. Hogsett via Patricia Hogsett White.)

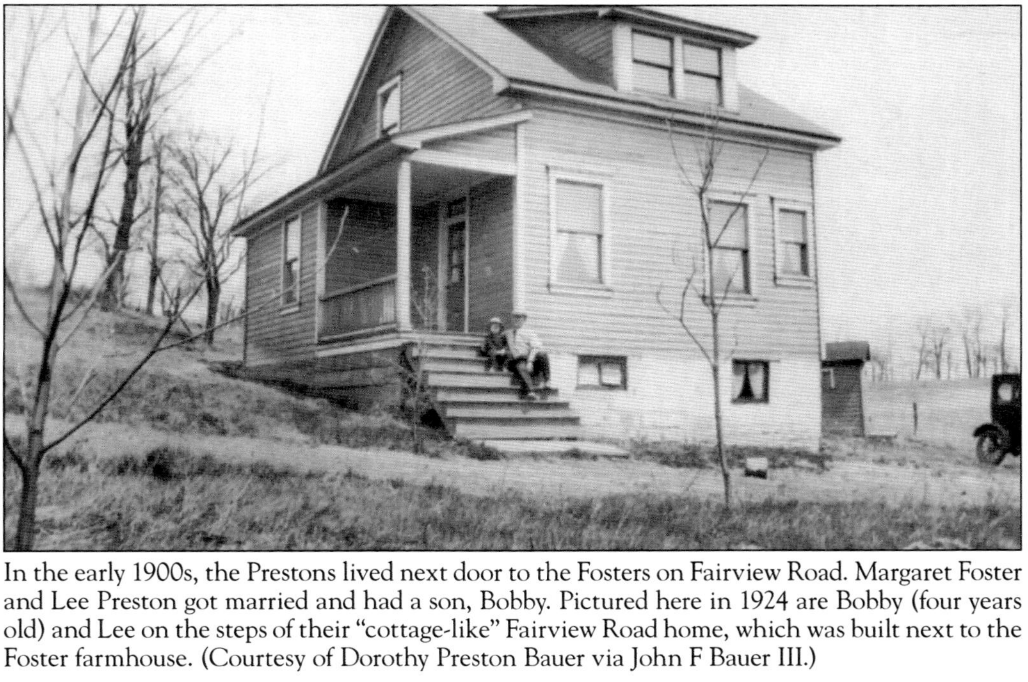

In the early 1900s, the Prestons lived next door to the Fosters on Fairview Road. Margaret Foster and Lee Preston got married and had a son, Bobby. Pictured here in 1924 are Bobby (four years old) and Lee on the steps of their "cottage-like" Fairview Road home, which was built next to the Foster farmhouse. (Courtesy of Dorothy Preston Bauer via John F Bauer III.)

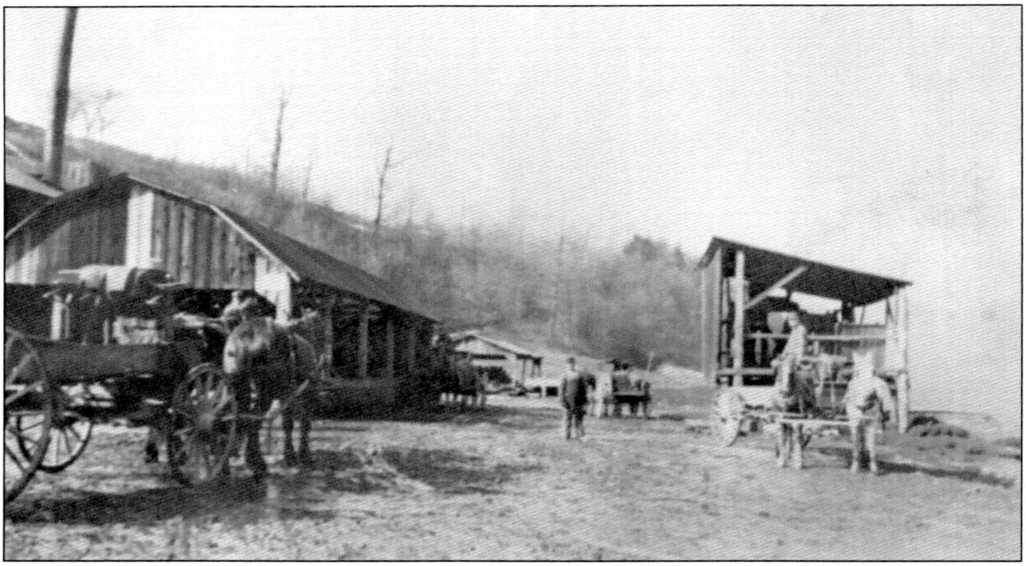

Mink brothers Pete, Jake, and Henry opened and operated a cider press and sawmill in 1910 on State Route 910. The cider press ceased operations in 1967, but the sawmill carried on until 1971. Some residents of Dorseyville still remember the Minks for their cider. Their homestead and business were located at the intersection of State Route 910 and the Pennsylvania Turnpike. The Mink barn is still standing, but now houses the Farm and Garden Center.

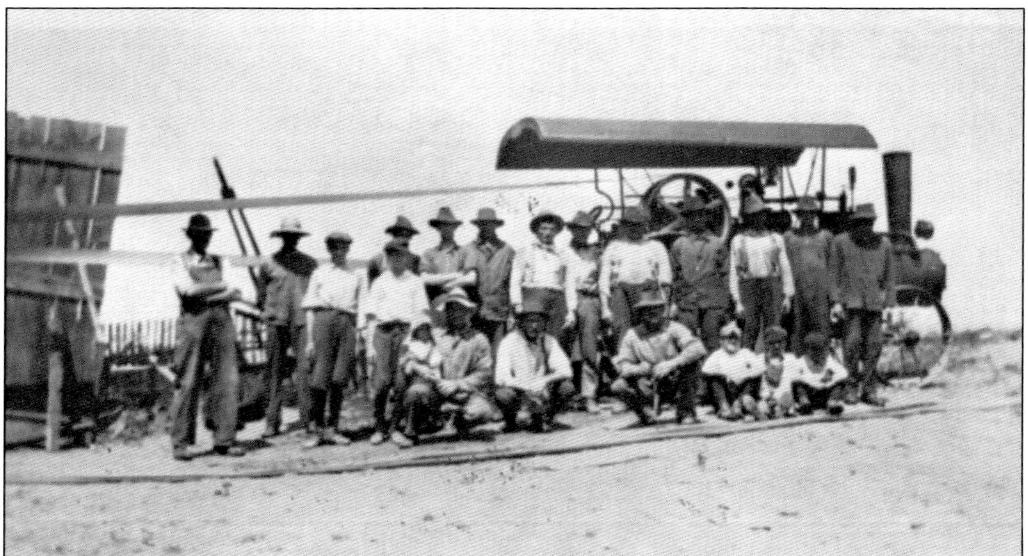

The Yost brothers were revolutionary by Indiana Township standards in owning a belt tractor to operate the threshing machine in the barn. Before the advent of the tractor to run the belt system for threshing, horses were used to separate the grain from the wheat. In this photograph, the large size of the belt connecting the tractor to the threshing machine is clearly visible.

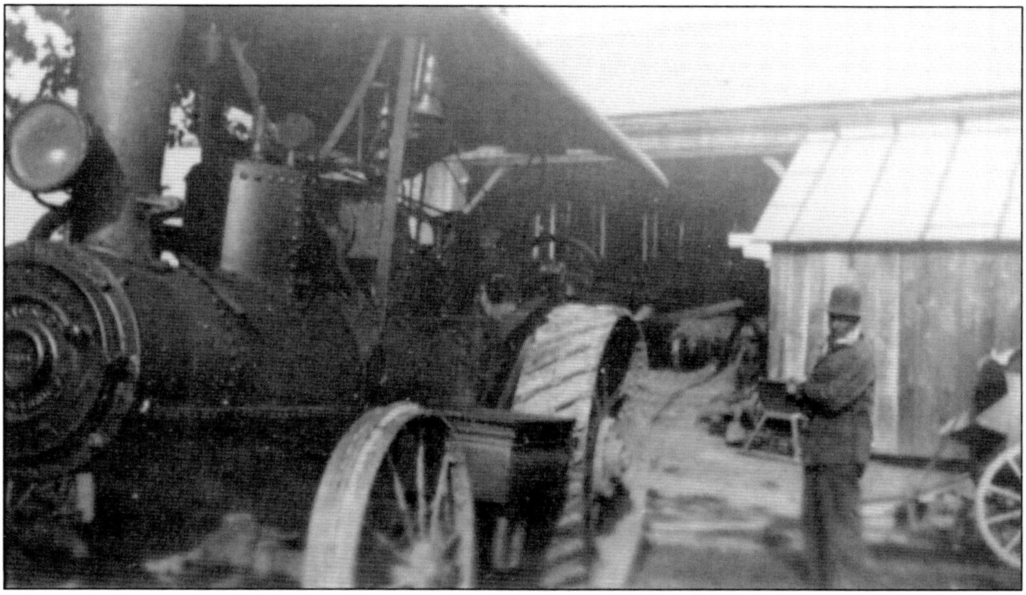

This is another glance at the Yost brothers' belt tractor. This photograph shows how far the tractor had to be parked from the barn while operating. Sparks from the firing engine of the tractor may have ignited the dried straw in the barn, so distance was maintained for safety reasons. Pulleys on both pieces of equipment (the belt tractor and the threshing machine, which was located in the barn) are connected by one large belt.

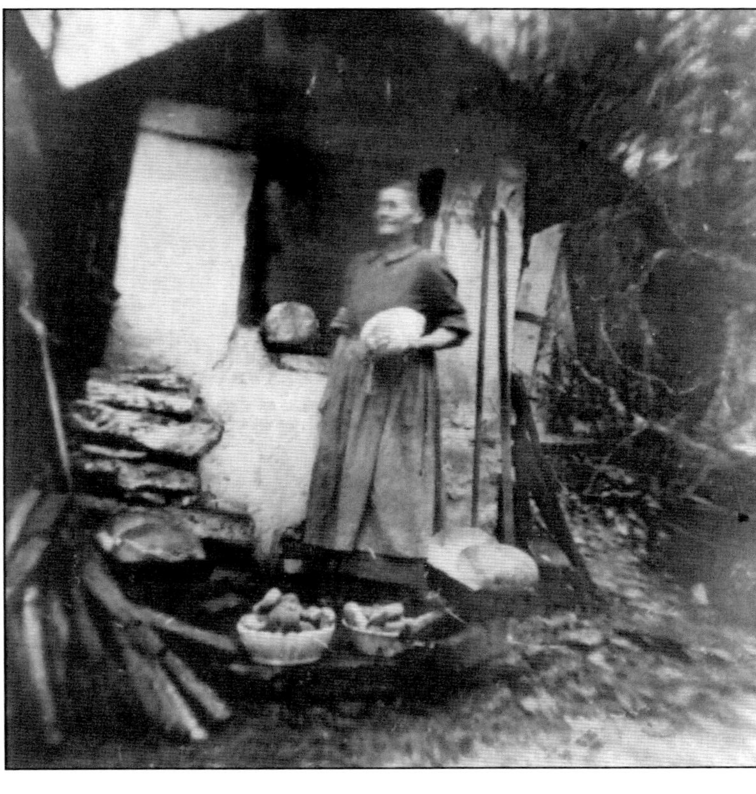

Pearl Dietrich Sallade recalls that this bake oven was located in the back of the old log house where John Dietrich lived before moving to Oil City. Here, Mary Frederick Dietrich, known to Sallade as Aunt Mary, is taking baked goods from the outdoor oven. The oven was used for many years after the new house was built. (Courtesy of Pearl Sallade.)

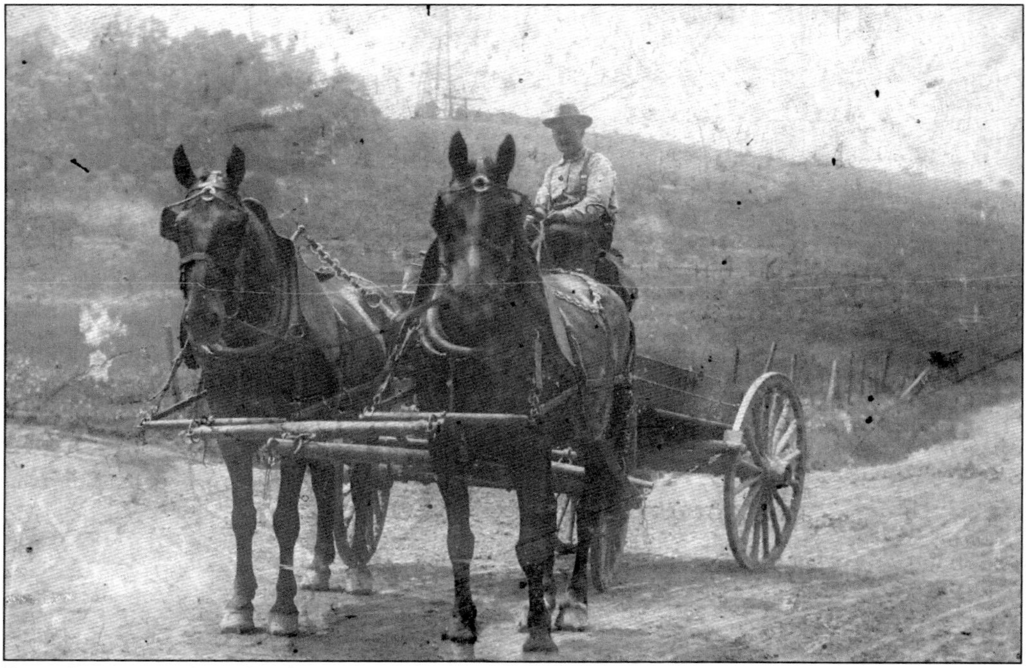

Dorothy M. Bartley Shockey-Sharp's grandfather Alfred G. Bartley is pictured with a team of horses. Alfred ran the livery stable in Indianola; the Bartleys also had oil wells in the area. (Courtesy of Karen Sue Haley.)

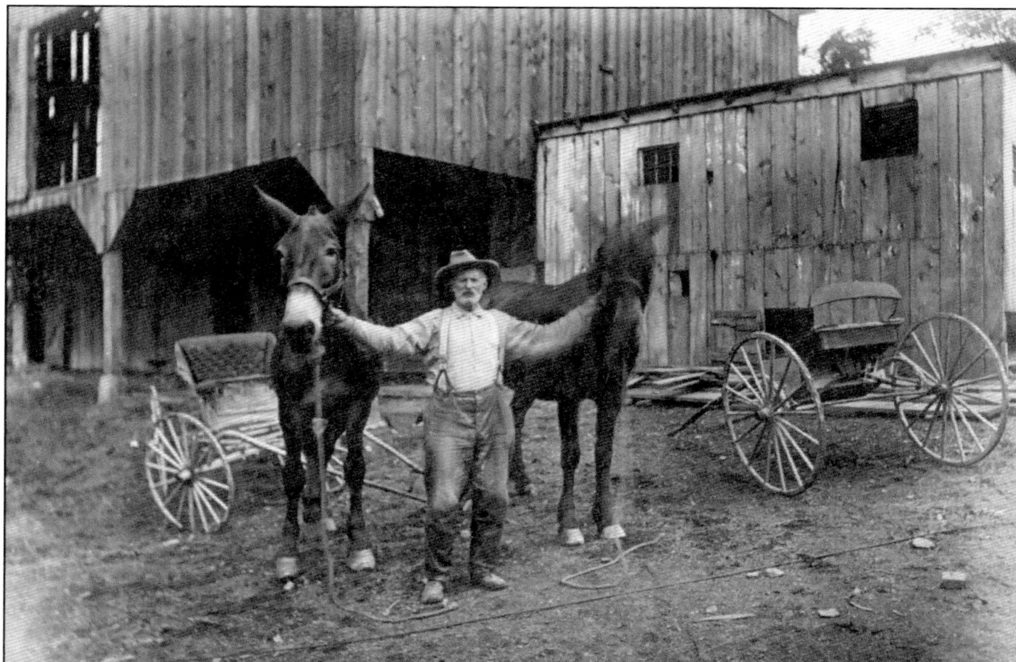

In this 1914 image, Alfred G. Bartley stands outside the livery stable he ran in Indianola. Note the horse-drawn rickshaws in the background. (Courtesy of Karen Sue Haley.)

BIBLIOGRAPHY

Indiana Township Historical Commission. *Indiana Township Preliminary History Book, 1988.* Pittsburgh: Indiana Township Historical Commission, 1988.

———. *Indiana Township History Book Volume II, 1994*. Pittsburgh: Indiana Township Historical Commission, 1994.

Rekasie, Helen Karan. *The Personal History of a Small Town: Rural Ridge Pennsylvania.* Pittsburgh: 1993.

White, Joseph B.C. "A Family Affair: Polo at Hartwood Scores Big for Charity." *In Touch Waterfront.* October 1988.

patheoldminer.rootsweb.ancestry.com/allindext.html

INDEX

About the Organization

Indiana Township Historic Commission was founded in 1986. The commission is responsible for planning and carrying out the Memorial Day activities of the township each year. The commission is also expected to keep the historical record of the township. Individual identification may be provided for photographs containing a large number of people. In most cases, the historic commission has these records on file in their safe and will be more than happy to share this information with anyone who asks. If anyone reading this book has any further information, or any corrections, regarding the photographs found within these pages, please contact any member of the commission. This can be done by calling the town hall at (412) 767-5333 or by contacting the commission via mail. Please send any corrections or further information to:

3710 Saxonburg Blvd.
Pittsburgh, PA 15238-1068
ATTN: Historic Commission

All of the captions for the photographs are accurate and true to the best of our knowledge. We credited people with photographs in cases in which had record of them on file. Much of the information for the captions was taken from the two previous history books compiled by the Indiana Township Historic Commission, along with the book *The Personal History of a Small Town*, by Helen Rekasie.

By no means is this an exhaustive collection of photographs available from the township. We have many more on file that were either not suitable for publication or did not fit the genre of Arcadia Publishing's Images of America series.

Consistent with our mission to preserve history on a local level, this book was printed in South Carolina on American-made paper and manufactured entirely in the United States. Products carrying the accredited Forest Stewardship Council (FSC) label are printed on 100 percent FSC-certified paper.

MADE IN THE USA